A Penguin Books Canada/McClelland and Stewart Book

Starting Out:
The Days of My Youth
1920–1947

Pierre Berton was born in 1920 and raised in the Yukon. He spent his early newspaper career in Vancouver, where at 21 he was the youngest city editor on any Canadian daily. He moved to Toronto in 1947 and at the age of 31 was named managing editor of *Maclean's* magazine. He was an associate editor and columnist at the *Toronto Star* from 1958 to 1962 and has written and hosted several national television programs. He is the author of thirty-six books and has received three Governor General's Awards for works of non-fiction including *Klondike*. He is a Companion of the Order of Canada and a member of the Canadian News Hall of Fame. Mr. Berton lives in Kleinburg, Ontario.

D1477508

Oh, talk not to me of a name great in story:
The days of our youth are the days of our glory;
And the myrtle and ivy of sweet two-and-twenty
Are worth all your laurels, though ever so plenty.

— *Lord Byron*

Pierre Berton

Starting Out:

The Days of My Youth

1920–1947

Penguin Books

PENGUIN BOOKS

Published by the Penguin Group

Penguin Books Canada Ltd, 10 Alcorn Avenue, Toronto,
Ontario, Canada M4V 3B2

Penguin Books Ltd, 27 Wrights Lane, London W8 5TZ,
England

Penguin Books USA Inc., 375 Hudson Street, New York,
New York 10014, U.S.A.

Penguin Books Australia Ltd, Ringwood, Victoria, Australia

Penguin Books (NZ) Ltd, 182-190 Wairau Road,
Auckland 10, New Zealand

Penguin Books Ltd, Registered Offices:
Harmondsworth, Middlesex, England

First published in Canada by McClelland and Stewart, 1987
Published in Penguin Books, 1993

1 3 5 7 9 10 8 6 4 2

Manufactured in Canada

Canadian Cataloguing in Publication Data

Berton, Pierre, 1920-
Starting out: the days of my youth, 1920 to 1947

Includes index.
ISBN 0-14-011760-I

1. Berton, Pierre, 1920-   2. Historians – Canada –
Biography.   3. Journalists – Canada – Biography.
I. Title

FC151.B47A3 1993   971'.0072   C92-095659-9
F1024.6.B47A3 1993

This book is for Lucy

Books by Pierre Berton

The Royal Family
The Mysterious North
Klondike
Just Add Water and Stir
Adventures of a Columnist
Fast, Fast, Fast Relief
The Big Sell
The Comfortable Pew
The Cool, Crazy, Committed World of the Sixties
The Smug Minority
The National Dream
The Last Spike
Drifting Home
Hollywood's Canada
My Country
The Dionne Years
The Wild Frontier
The Invasion of Canada
Flames Across the Border
Why We Act Like Canadians
The Promised Land
Vimy
Starting Out
The Arctic Grail
The Great Depression, 1929-1939
Niagara

PICTURE BOOKS
The New City (with Henri Rossier)
Remember Yesterday
The Great Railway
The Klondike Quest

ANTHOLOGIES
Great Canadians
Pierre and Janet Berton's Canadian Food Guide
Historic Headlines

FOR YOUNGER READERS
The Golden Trail
The Secret World of Og

FICTION
Masquerade (pseudonym Lisa Kroniuk)

Contents

Starting Out

Chapter One
On the Inside
1920-1931

1 "And now, ladies and gentlemen, without further introduction, the well-known personality, Mr. Pierre Berton."

The chairman resumes his seat as the Well-Known Personality rises slowly to his feet, takes a firm grip on his cheat cards, waits for the smattering of applause to die, and plunges into his address. As he starts his first joke, a vagrant little tableau pops into his head, provoked by that word "personality."

His mind goes back to Whitehorse (population three hundred), clinging to the banks of the Yukon River in the autumn of 1920. Down the snow-covered roadway, wearing a broad hat and a fall coat with a fur collar, comes the new mother, Laura Beatrice Berton, pushing a baby's sleigh. At the corner she encounters the formidable figure of Mrs. Arthur Coldrick, a woman of considerable heft with a florid face and a double chin — the same Mrs. Coldrick who, not two months before, had stood outside the hospital window and had been overheard discussing the expectant mother's funeral arrangements — a conversation that caused Laura Beatrice Berton to grit her teeth and swear that she would have her baby and live to raise it, in spite of the fact that she was well over forty and the last two kindergarten teachers before her had died in childbirth.

"Ah!" cries Mrs. Coldrick, gazing into the depths of the sleigh and fastening her gaze on the button-eyed infant whose birth had, against all odds, successfully confounded the doomsayers. "What a lovely child, Mrs. Berton! And

1

what are your plans for him? What do you intend him to become when he grows up?"

For that, Laura Beatrice Berton has a ready answer. "Why," says she, cheeks glowing, eyes alight with pride, "we're intending that he should become a Personality."

"A Well-Known Personality," the proud mother adds.

The Well-Known Personality, now well into his seventh decade, balding, white-haired, and as florid as the late Mrs. Coldrick, abandons the fantasy, finishes his speech, stares modestly into his coffee cup during the vote of thanks, and then prepares to make his escape.

A scrum of well-wishers bars the way.

"You're the second Personality I've met today," says one, mentioning the name of a hockey star of whom the Well-Known Personality has never heard.

A second suppliant grips his hand, stating that he wants to be able to tell his children that he has actually touched what he calls a Famous Celebrity. The Famous Celebrity is then requested to sign his name for somebody's child. "She'll just *kill* me if I don't get your autograph," the mother says cheerfully. The Well-Known Personality signs quickly to avoid matricide. Other voices are heard: "My father is your greatest fan. He's read *all* your books." . . . "My mother watches you on TV every single week." . . . "My grandmother would never miss your program."

The Well-Known Personality, promoted now to Famous Celebrity, takes it all with a grain of salt. He knows that no one — not even his wife — has read *all* his books; he himself cannot stand to read any of them again. He notes, a little ruefully, that nobody has admitted to having personally read anything at all by him or even to having seen a single one of his television programs. But he has long ago become hardened to second-hand praise.

Up comes the club president to rescue the Well-Known Personality from his bread and butter.

"It must be an awful responsibility being a Famous

Celebrity," says he. "You must get very tired of being forever in the public eye."

The Famous Celebrity nods wearily and mutters something about it coming with the territory. That, of course, is a lie. The Famous Celebrity has loved every minute of it: the chairman's effusive remarks, the audience's rapt attention, the fans and the suppliants — he's basked in it all. If he didn't like it he wouldn't do it. He has friends who are also Famous Celebrities and others who are Well-Known Personalities who profess to loathe the spotlight. He knows this is a pose. No one is forced to be a celebrity. People become famous because they want to be. Mostly, they've worked at it. They love the public glare, though it's fashionable to pretend it's irksome. There are disadvantages, certainly, but these are outweighed by the perks. Hotels send up baskets of fruit; snooty restaurants find you a good table; policemen occasionally ignore trifling traffic offences; big shots actually return your phone calls.

It's true that people stop you, a perfect stranger, in the street and insist on telling you their entire family history, the details of their work, or a chronicle of their illnesses, apparently in the belief that these are matters of intense interest. But, of course, you *aren't* a perfect stranger to them. You're the face in the living room with whom they've spent a weekly half hour. If you're any good at your craft, you're their friend, an ex-officio family member whom they feel they know more intimately than their own neighbours. So they take you by the arm and guide you into their lives as they would an old friend.

Anyone who knows me will admit that I am infuriatingly impatient, but I do my best to be patient with these strangers because I see something of my father in their faces. When we came out of the Yukon in 1931 my father couldn't resist talking to strangers about his life in the North. He'd talk to them in bus queues, in grocery stores, on streetcars.

"You think this is cold?" my father would say to anyone who happened by. "You want to see real cold, you've got to go to my part of the country." He'd wait for the respondent to ask what part of the country he came from, and if he wasn't asked, my father would tell him.

"Up in the Yukon we get it sixty below and lower every winter," my father would say, and then he'd launch into a long description of winter in the Yukon. Once, I remember, he walked into a florist shop that was displaying sweet peas.

"You want to see sweet peas, you've got to go to my part of the country," he said. "I bet you never saw seven sweet pea blossoms on a single stem, eh?"

Whereupon the florist said, curtly, "I've seen eight," and turned back to the customer he was serving. My father looked downcast and left the shop. "I don't believe that beggar," my father said shortly.

It strikes me now, after all these years, that to some people my father must have seemed a bit of a bore. And so when people come up and begin to talk of their part of the country, I think of my father and how astonished he would have been had he known the button-eyed baby in the sleigh would actually become a Famous Celebrity.

How he would have loved it! I can see him now, stopping strangers in the street and clerks behind counters to talk about his son, the Well-Known Personality. Come to think of it, he talked about me anyway, though he never lived to savour his boy's notoriety. He was uncommonly proud of both his children even though I don't think he expected too much from them.

My mother, on the other hand, was convinced from the beginning that I would become famous for *something*, in spite of overwhelming evidence to the contrary. I was scarcely out of my teens when she'd written a book about me entitled "It's a Boy!" Since I was totally unknown at the time and gave every indication of remaining so, she couldn't get a publisher. Years later, after much prodding from me, she was persuaded to leave the boy out of it and stick to other themes — the very theme, in fact, with which my father had been bending the ears of strangers: Life in the Far North. The book was called *I Married the Klondike*, and it gave her a measure of celebrity before her death. She revelled in it, for she loved giving speeches to women's clubs, being interviewed by the press, signing autographs, appearing on television, and acting like a character out of a northern epic, which, indeed, she was.

I was mildly surprised by this aspect of my mother's personality. "Your mother's a real character," people would say to me. I never thought of her as a character, only as a loving parent, a fairly strait-laced adult with conventional views, a one-time Regent of the Imperial Order of the Daughters of the Empire, a soloist on the Dawson stage, a member of the Anglican choir, a fine classical pianist and teacher (who was, alas, never able to teach me the scale of G). And then in her last years — I will not say her "declining" years, for these years were just the opposite — she emerged as both a character and a Personality.

She quickly cottoned on to the Celebrity Game. "I just loved your book," people would tell her, and my mother would modestly cast down her eyes. "Oh, well," she would murmur. "Oh, well, you know, it's just my little book." But, in fact, she was a proud and ambitious woman. It was only in my mid-thirties that I came to realize that my mother, so loving and so mild, had a considerable ego and that she had transmitted a good deal of it to me. It has become a dirty word, "ego"; as a boy I didn't think I had any, which means I had no confidence in myself. But it was there all the time, lurking in my genes. Without it I could not have become a writer.

I was, indeed, extremely fortunate in my choice of both parents and environment. When I was a boy growing up in Dawson City in the Yukon I didn't think my parents were at all remarkable. They were simply Mamma and Daddy. I

5

didn't even realize that they were older than most parents. A school friend once asked me how old they were, and I went home and asked. When I told him my father was twenty-four and my mother twenty-three, he laughed uproariously. I couldn't for the life of me understand why. But my father was forty-seven when I was born and my mother forty-two. My sister, Lucy, followed fifteen months later, after we moved from Whitehorse to Dawson.

My mother used to say to me regularly, "You're not the same as the other boys, you know." I never understood that, either, but I suppose it had to do with her age at my birth, though, oddly, she never made the same remark to Lucy. Girls got shorter shrift than boys in those days. My parents' ambitions were focused largely on me. It was assumed, of course, that Lucy would go to university, but I think it was also assumed that she would marry and, to use the phrase of the day, "settle down."

I sometimes used to puzzle over that phrase "you're not the same as other boys." I assumed then that she meant I was a frail and sickly child. I wasn't actually, but it may be that *she* thought so. Both my parents were fiercely protective of me, perhaps because I had nearly died of pneumonia at the age of two. They talked constantly about that terrible fortnight when I lay in a delirium in the hospital under the hill; obviously it was for them a searing experience. My mother had suffered one miscarriage and had then boldly gone ahead with two more pregnancies against all advice. Miraculously, my parents had acquired a family when they were both into middle age. (Lucy's arrival on the scene when my mother was in her forty-fourth year was almost certainly a welcome accident.) They had no intention of losing either of us.

Whenever I caught the slightest sniffle, let alone the flu, they pulled me out of school for days, even weeks, bundled me up fiercely, and put me on a special diet. "You owe your good health to us," my mother used to say in her later years. No doubt she was right. Apart from that bout of pneumonia I didn't have to be admitted to hospital for another half century. But was that all she meant when she said "you're not like other boys"? I think perhaps there was more to it. I think she harboured a mystic belief that she and I had both been spared for a reason. Many years later when I was in my late teens or early twenties I found that she had squirreled away all my early writings — letters, documents, scribblings, drawings, school essays. When I asked her about it, she simply said, "Someday you're going to be famous and somebody will need all this." I wish now that I'd taken more account of that.

I have written a good deal about my father in my book *Drifting Home.* He was one of those eternally curious men who seek knowledge purely for the love of it and gain great joy from transmitting it to others. His father had died of a heart attack when he was in infancy, and he, Frank Berton, and his brother, Jack, were brought up in Saint John by my paternal grandmother, whom I never knew. Somehow she was able to put him through the University of New Brunswick from which he graduated as a civil engineer, a profession he never actually practised.

I believe my father's university fees were paid for by the Masonic Lodge; thus it was for him a very real tragedy when the Masons in Dawson blackballed him. I'm not sure why; but there's no doubt that in the Klondike, which he loved, he was seen in some circles as a fish out of water, a bit of an eccentric, a man who didn't quite fit in. For one thing, he was, in that Low Church town, a High Anglican who insisted on genuflecting before entering the pew and crossing himself, Anglo-Catholic tricks of the trade that were seen in some Masonic eyes a perilously close to popery. He never talked about his rejection by the lodge, and that suggests the depth of his disappointment, for he talked of almost everything else. It was my mother who told me the story. "Those Masons!" she'd say, shaking her head. "Those damn Masons. Poor Daddy."

He really ought to have been a university professor. He was perfectly cut out for it, a graduate engineer who had a variety of other skills. He spoke good French, not because of his heritage, which was Huguenot, but because he'd once lived for a year with a family in Quebec. He had, in fact, applied for a post at Queen's when the gold fever struck. He had reached the foot of the Chilkoot when a letter caught up to him saying he'd been accepted. By then it was too late. He simply had to see what lay on the other side of that wall of mountains, and so he climbed the pass, built a raft, and floated down the river to Dawson. He intended to stay two years. He remained for almost forty.

After he arrived in the Yukon he took a variety of jobs. He staked a claim on Quigley Gulch, built himself a cabin of green logs, prospected for gold, found only clay. He'd been apprenticed to a cabinet-maker and could do wonders with a plane and chisel. He was for a time principal of the Dawson school. He worked as a special constable for the North West Mounted Police and once told me how he'd cleaned the skull of a murdered man. He worked in the mining camps thawing frozen ground with steam points, a hard and hazardous business. He gave French lessons to young schoolteachers, one of whom was my mother.

I know nothing more about his life in those pre-marital years. Did he have girl friends, unhappy love affairs? Did scandal ever cross his path? Did he "go down the line" in the brothels of Lousetown with the other young bloods? How, actually, did he live in that decade before he met and married my mother?

Dawson in his day was a wild, wide-open town. My father was twenty-five and physically strong when he arrived. The place teemed with prostitutes, dancehall girls, gamblers, and rowdies. Was he one of the gang? Perhaps; probably not.

Once he told me of the time he'd got drunk in Dawson back in "the early days," as everyone called them. It was hard for me, a small boy, to imagine my father inebriated, staggering down Dance Hall Row, a figure of fun like Walter King, the town drunk. My father made fun of it, too; it was obvious from the context of the story that it was the one and only occasion that he'd come under the influence. It had made such an impression on him that it must have been a solitary experience.

In spite of his garrulousness with strangers on the Outside, he was basically a shy man, quite incapable of making a speech in public — a bookworm who, in my memory, read *Beowulf* in the original Old English and Homer in Greek, played chess, toyed with algebra problems as a diversion, read his way twice through all the plays of Shakespeare and all the books of the Bible, collected wildflowers, and who in his later years took up dentistry, astronomy, and weaving. A jack of all trades and master of most — not quite right, perhaps, for the Masonic Lodge.

My mother's story is still in print, and so it's not necessary to go into the details of what once appeared to me to be a very ordinary life and now, in retrospect, seems quite remarkable. It was, after all, a considerable step for the cloistered daughter of an intellectual family to sever all her roots and head for a wilderness mining camp more than four thousand miles to the northwest.

Her contemporaries thought her mad. Actually, she was an innocent, as most women were in those days. Moreover she was crowding thirty and had no prospects. She may not have admitted to herself that she was looking for a husband — well-bred young women did not do that in her day — but surely it was in her subconscious. At any rate, she met my father and hit the jackpot. They were married in 1912.

What a strange alliance it was, on the face of it! My father was an arch-Conservative, who worked for the party as a scrutineer during election time and expected to get a patronage job in the civil service when and if the government changed (as it did and as he did). Now he was faced with asking the most notorious Marxist in the country for his daughter's hand in marriage. Phillips Thompson, who had worked for most major publications in Toronto, was one of the best-known journalists of his day. He had already sent his future son-in-law a copy of his most radical work, *The Politics of Labor*, a polemic that was surely anathema to him or any Tory. Decades later, going through my mother's effects, I came upon the letter my father had written, asking for her hand in marriage. I marvelled at the finesse with which he navigated that slippery tightrope.

"... I have also to thank you, Sir, for the honour you have done me in sending me ... a copy of your book, 'The Politics of Labour', which I have been reading with a great deal of interest and pleasure. I must compliment you on its clearness of argument and vigour of style. I was particularly struck by the admirable manner in which you discriminate between the different senses in which certain terms are often employed, as, for instance, the word 'Capital.' It is the confusion of ideas caused by the use of the same word to represent two or more distinct ideas that so often carried an argument from correct premises to a false conclusion. As John Locke says in his 'Essay on the Human Understanding...'"

My father mislaid the book, or loaned it out, or perhaps discarded it. More than forty years later, Colin Low of the National Film Board, wandering up Sourdough Gulch where my mother and father had spent their honeymoon, came upon a crumbling cabin and there discovered my grandfather's book, signed and dedicated to his future son-in-law. Low, at the time, was filming a documentary to be called *City of Gold*, for which I subsequently wrote and read the narration. Thus does history sometimes come full circle.

My parents were deeply in love. They would have to have been to head out to Sourdough Gulch without a penny and live in a tent with no prospects of work when the mining season ended. They remained deeply in love for the rest of their lives. I have fond memories of my mother seated on my father's knee, her arms around his neck, kissing him gently and even cooing into his ear. Sometimes when we camped out on one of the islands in the river they'd leave Lucy and me in the tent and vanish for several hours, to return flushed and cheerful, my mother humming under her breath, my father with his arm around her waist. In these days I simply thought they'd gone for a walk. I was ten years old by then, but that was an innocent age. When I was younger, my parents thought nothing of wandering about the house nude, but until I was twelve I received no instruction in sexual matters. When I was first told, at the age of seven, how babies were conceived, I simply did not believe it. The information was faulty, anyway.

"It takes three days to make a baby," Howard Elliott told me knowingly.

"Where do they keep it when it's being made?" Ewart Ford asked him.

"I think in the clothes closet," said Howard vaguely.

"But how do they *make* it?" somebody asked.

"It's the piss, washing together," said Axel Nordling.

Thus were sown the first seeds of scepticism. The adult world, I soon discovered, was involved in a series of scandalous coverups. First Santa Claus and the Tooth Fairy; now the stork.

I suppose I must have been five or older when I first heard the dreadful word "fuck." I had no idea what it meant and did not know it was a dirty word. I decided to ask my mother about it.

"Not now," she said hastily, trying her best to preserve the stork theory. "I'll tell you later."

Later came during a formal dinner party. By "formal" I mean white tie and tails for the men, long dresses and pearls for the women. That's how people dressed for parties in Dawson in the twenties. We children were always allowed a place at the table during my parents' dinner parties; no locking us in the bedroom for them. Democracy, alas, was done in when I piped up: "Mamma, you promised to tell me what 'fuck' meant." Even today I can remember the dreadful silence that descended for one long moment on that glittering assembly and then the sudden buzz of cover-up conversation that followed. My mother simply pretended that she hadn't heard me. Nor did she ever explain the meaning of the taboo word, which eventually was defined for me at school by my peers. On the other hand, she never uttered so much as a syllable about my outburst, the enormity of which is difficult to understand in these days when all taboos have been shattered.

But then, she came from a remarkable and tolerant family. Her elder sister, my Aunt Florrie, was a painter who had once lived and studied on the Left Bank. Her younger sister, Maude, was an Anglican deaconess. Neither had ever married. Her half-brother, my Uncle Phil, was a newspaperman like his father.

If my grandfather and uncle helped provide me with a writer's genes, my mother provided me with a writer's environment, for she was always typing away on an old Remington in the kitchen or on our dining-room table. She did "write-ups" of local events, which I delivered by bicycle to the *Dawson News*. There, Harold Malstrom, editor-cum-printer-cum-office-boy, set them on the same linotype that had once sliced off two of his fingers.

She wrote also for the *Family Herald and Weekly Star*, for the old *Saturday Night*, and for other publications, which rejected her material as often as they printed it. She was not a professional writer; she had the amateur's enthusiasms, phobias, and naïveté. But her material was compelling because it dealt with life in the North.

Yet most of the time my mother was working on a novel, not about the fabled Klondike, but about a family farm in southern Ontario and a young nobleman who marries the farmer's daughter. It was intended, I believe, to be a trilogy — my mother was nothing if not ambitious — and it never occurred to any of us that the novel was unpublishable. We lived with it day in and day out for a decade. I can remember lying awake at nights listening to my parents discussing the book in the tiny living room — my mother reading passages of it aloud to my father, who sometimes helped by pecking out the words on that ancient typewriter.

We were all convinced, as novices are, that the novel would become a best seller and we would all be filthy rich. What would we do, we asked ourselves, with all that money? My sister and I decided we would spend most of it on rides in the amusement parks, which we had read about in the comic strips but had never actually seen.

I am reminded of my mother and her novel regularly because no week goes by when I do not receive a letter from some hopeful author in a small town announcing that he or she is writing a novel. If I will only collaborate, the author claims, we will both become wealthy beyond our wildest dreams. And then I think again of my mother, scribbling away furiously in the heart of the glamorous Klondike, writing about a farm in Ontario. In the end I was able to do for her what I have not done for hundreds of other eager young writers — help her construct a book about a far more exciting subject, her own life.

2 It was not easy to convince my mother that her own life was exotic. Although she had written and published short pieces about the Yukon, these were mainly social notes or articles about the wildlife. The great drama of the gold rush seemed to her and, indeed, to most people who lived in Dawson to be rather commonplace. My father sometimes mentioned his experiences on the Stikine Trail in 1898, where he had been driven back by impassable swamps, or on the slippery incline of the Chilkoot, but he

didn't make a big thing of it. Years later when I decided to write a history of the great stampede my mother was incredulous. "Why would you write about *that*?" she asked me. "Everybody knows about that."

To her, the gold rush wasn't history; it was something that had happened during her lifetime, and to people she knew. When I grew up in Dawson in the twenties, the gold rush was only a quarter of a century behind us — no farther into the past than the sixties are today.

At school we learned the names and pedigrees of all the English monarchs, but we learned nothing of the history of our own community. Yet history surrounded us. Our own house was on Harper Street, named for the first white man in the Yukon. Next to it was Hanson Street, named for a famous trader. Joe Ladue's sawmill still stood down by the riverbank, but nobody told us who Ladue was — that it was he who sent Robert Henderson off to supply the tip that caused the great stampede; that it was he who brought his sawmill to Dawson and helped lay out the town. One of my closest friends was Chester Henderson, but I did not know that he was the grandson of that same Robert who is now credited as co-discoverer of the Klondike's gold, his name immortalized today on a bronze plaque on Bonanza Creek.

It took me many years to realize that the town where I was raised was unique — perhaps the strangest and most romantic community in all of Canada — and that this environment must have had some kind of influence on me. Certainly the time would come when it would provide me with almost endless raw material for my writing, as it is doing even as I type these words.

To me, Dawson did not seem to differ greatly from the other small towns sprinkled over North America that formed the background of so many of the books I was reading. I could relate easily to Tom Sawyer because we too had a great river running past the community and an island not too far away, very like the one where Tom and Huck

14

Finn had camped. When I read Booth Tarkington's *Penrod and Sam* it did not seem to me that their community with its tree-shaded streets, big verandahs, sand lot, and ice cream parlour was very different from my own. I accepted Dawson City as the norm, as other boys do in other small towns. But of course there was nothing normal about it. It affected me more than I knew.

It occurs to me that there are few people living today who enjoyed the kind of childhood I had. For I was raised, in the 1920s, in the most unusual ghost town in Canada. When my parents arrived back in Dawson in 1921, after the war and a brief hiatus in Whitehorse, the town was a shell. It had once enjoyed a settled population of some twenty thousand and a floating population of ten thousand more. But in my day, twelve hundred of us, and sometimes fewer, rattled around in a community of empty buildings.

Empty it certainly was, and sometimes lonely, but there was a richness of texture there not to be found in the average Canadian small town of the period. When I rode my CCM bicycle along its wooden sidewalks it was as if I was pedalling through some deserted Hollywood set. Here were streetscape after streetscape of vacant emporiums, saloons, dancehalls, theatres, brothels, hotels, and boarding houses all padlocked and boarded up. They may have been old and decaying, these two-storey frame structures — slanting every which way like drunken old men, because of the unstable permafrost — but they had *style.* For all of my childhood I was surrounded by the faded elegance of Victorian frontier architecture: false fronts, fretted porticos and pediments, elaborate bay windows and cornices, pillars and dormers and neo-classical façades, all created from dressed lumber or stamped out of metal to counterfeit the architectural glories of the European past.

And the interiors! Squinting between the boards that protected the windows, I could distinguish, in the gloom, an unholy tangle of bric-à-brac and old junk, heaped

15

together and left to tarnish, decay, and rot because it was too expensive to take it back Outside. Here were brass spittoons, seltzer bottles, carved walking sticks, embroidered pillows, framed portraits, and glass decanters, piled up on top of Morris chairs, overstuffed sofas, gaming tables, fancy pianos and organs, all stacked against mountains of picks, shovels, gold pans, and bits of mining machinery.

I took it all for granted, of course. Wasn't every town like this? Only in later years, looking back on this great, crowded attic of a community, did I realize the uncommon nature of my background.

In all my boyhood years in Dawson I never heard of a building boom or a housing shortage. There were already too many buildings; no new ones were needed. I can't recall any construction in the town itself except for the extra room my father built on our house about 1926. The process by which other communities grew and flourished was reversed in that strange community, where buildings were torn down, burned down, or allowed to fall down. We lived with the ghosts of the past, not the promise of the future.

Dawson was a junkyard, crammed with the artifacts of history, but I didn't know that. To me most of these were gigantic toys, expressly designed for my pleasure. Behind the school were two enormous Keystone drills, discarded long ago by the mining companies, over which we boys crawled and clambered. Close by were a couple of monstrous boilers in which more than one of us could hide. I remember spending most of a summer's afternoon concealed in one of those boilers. It was my own sanctum, a magic retreat that rendered me invisible to the world.

Dawson harboured such delights at almost every corner. Bits and pieces of mining machinery lay strewn everywhere — hidden among the willows and alders of the vacant lots, strung out along the high bank of the Yukon not far from Dance Hall Row, or half submerged in the gravels of the shallow Klondike. Here were mysterious knobs and wheels, levers, gears, and gauges that moved and jiggled and delighted a small boy's imagination.

I didn't have an electric train; I had something far better. I had only to cross the bridge across the Klondike River to come upon a real train complete with locomotive and passenger cars, sitting on its tracks in the scrub bush. The Klondike Mines Railway, which once served as a link between Dawson and the miners working on upper Bonanza Creek, had long since been abandoned. But the train was still there and so were the rails. One day when I was about nine, a group of us boys, following the old track along Bonanza, came upon a handcar in perfect working order. We couldn't believe our eyes! Here, waiting for us in the wilderness, was a marvellous device that we could actually operate. Off we clattered along the rusty right of way at a spanking pace, each fighting for his chance to pump the handles.

When we got tired of playing trainman and conductor we could always play at being steamboat men. Few of us had ever seen an actual working locomotive, but we were all familiar with the stern-wheelers that plied the upper and lower river. Six of these sat abandoned in an old shipyard a few miles downstream. We'd take the ferry across the Yukon and then make our way through the woods until we saw the silhouettes of the smokestacks and the old pilot-houses rising above the birches. Our excitement grew as we reached the base of the first trio of ships — the ones that were in the best condition. Off we'd go in a rush to climb aboard the *Julia B.* or the *Schwatka* or the *Lightning,* each of us racing up the stairs to try to be the first on the upper deck so he could be captain. And so we frolicked away the summer afternoons, clambering down into the engine room, pretending to be passengers and crew, taking our turn in the pilothouse working the big wheel high above the surrounding forest and shouting "Full speed ahead!" Those days are long gone. All too soon the old boats crumbled away, the sternwheels rotted, the superstructures collapsed under the weight of the winter snows until only the hulls were left, warped and splintered, soon to be hidden in a tangle of alders. No more can Dawson's children play steamboat captain or railway engineer.

As a child, I lived surrounded by decay. Every season at least one building burned down. The hockey rink, the library, the theatre all went, for these were frame buildings overheated by wood furnaces and red-hot stoves. My parents lived with a dread of fire. I could not understand why they refused to allow me to go to the movies unaccompanied. But when the movie house burned down I knew why. Nothing was safe. The Eagle Hall — my father's lodge — was consumed. To my mother's horror the only thing saved was my father's photograph; she had never liked it. Apparently herculean efforts had been made to salvage this one framed portrait, which showed my father staring blankly ahead with glazed eyes, like a stuffed eagle.

"Why in hell would they bother with that?" I remember my mother asking, using an expletive rare to her. "Wasn't there something better they could have chosen? Now I am supposed to congratulate the heroes who saved that dreadful portrait from the fate it deserved."

3 If history shaped us, geography and climate shackled us. Permafrost, of which we knew almost nothing, was our enemy. My father was forever jacking up or propping up our house as the ground melted around the foundations. The derelict buildings were ignored, so that the town looked warped, each structure adopting its own cockeyed position, like dying trees tottering in a swamp.

For nine months of the year we might as well have been living on the moon. From early October until mid-June there was no way out of Dawson unless you were prepared to sit up for five days in an open sleigh drawn by a tractor.

Nobody wanted to go Outside in the winter except in a dire emergency, although my mother had done it years before.

In the winter we went to school in the dark and came home in the dark. For six weeks we didn't see the sun. My mother fed Lucy and me lashings of Scott's Emulsion, which had a cod liver oil base and, I suppose, was a kind of Vitamin D supplement, though I never heard the word "vitamin" in those days. At any rate we didn't suffer from the lack of sunlight, which seemed quite normal to us.

Indeed, sunshine in December would have seemed as unreal as darkness in July. It never occurred to me that there might be some other community where dusk fell early in the summer evening. All the same, none of us like being sent off to bed at nine o'clock with the sun still brilliant in the sky. My mother would pull down the blinds to try to darken our bedroom, but nothing was really dark in Dawson in that brief six-week period when the sun set for less than two hours.

In those bright evenings, it was difficult to know what time it was. Sometimes my father would forget and we'd get an extra hour of play, only to complain bitterly when bedtime finally came. Once, at Wolf Cub camp, we eight-year-olds all rose in the brightness of what we thought was late morning. It was actually 2 a.m.; but only the Cub Master had a watch, and he slept until seven. By suppertime we could hardly keep our eyes open.

But children accept their environment, however bizarre. I thought no more of the northern lights, sweeping across the sky in green curtains and coloured bands, than I did of the clouds themselves; indeed, I thought they *were* clouds, suitably tinted each winter like the flowers of spring. I thought men drank only coffee and women drank tea because that was the way it was in my family. I thought people who put sugar in coffee were odd, because my father didn't use it; sugar was for tea, the way my mother drank it. I thought high schools were so named because they were always on the top floor of the school, as ours was. I thought women went to church in the morning and men in the evening because that was the division my parents had worked out; it didn't occur to me that this was simply a convenient baby-sitting arrangement. And it was the same with the change of seasons in the Yukon: winter days were pitch dark; summer nights were dazzling bright. That's the way the world worked.

August, in my boyhood, was an autumn month, and even today I have difficulty thinking of it as summer. The first frost occurred around the twentieth. Winter began about six weeks later. Snow and twilight are inseparable in my memory, for they came together. There was something quite wonderful about being able to play in the white fields, making snowshoe trails in the lavender dusk, or to skim, belly buster, on a fast sled down the Church Street hill in the gathering dusk, with only the wan street lamps for guidance. And all this before supper!

In the dead of winter, when the thermometer dropped and the smoke rose in tall pillars against the frost-blue sky, an eerie hush fell over the town. There was no breeze; the trees stood motionless; no creature called. The horses were stabled, the automobiles locked away, the townspeople, snug in their frame homes, protected from the cold by double walls filled with sawdust. Only we children, apparently impervious to the elements, ventured out.

We felt the cold, of course — our feet were *always* cold — but that was the way of things. Sometimes my friend Alex McCarter, the postmaster's son, and I would hike up the hill behind our bungalow, wading hip deep in the dry snow to stand in the blue twilight among the skeletal birches and the spectral aspens, enveloped in a cocoon of silence and by the lifeless world that pressed in on us. We would talk rarely, and then in whispers, for the sound of our own voices was jarring. Occasionally a tree would crack like a pistol shot in the frost. (At night our houses did the same thing.)

The tiniest sound can travel long distances on a cold day. Sometimes we would hear somebody's cough half a mile or so away, proof that there actually was a community only a few hundred feet below us. Then the silence would close in again. I have not known such moments since my childhood in the Yukon.

In the endless night of winter, another eerie sound swept across the town — the cries of the husky dogs howling at the moon. Huskies cannot bark; they can only whine or howl. When the moon rose they howled incessantly. The howl became a living sound, a wave moving slowly across the community and on down the river like a soul in torment. Usually it began with a single dog in the south end of town making his lonely supplication to the night. A neighbouring dog would pick up the chant, and another and another — our own two dogs included — until the dogs at the north end were all howling, followed by the dogs at Moosehide, the Indian village around the river's bend, and other dogs in trappers' cabins far down the river, until at last the first dog ceased his cries. Then the howl would finally fade and vanish into the distance, only to return again, like a wandering spirit. Sometimes it was joined by the howl of the wolf pack somewhere back in the hills, so that the howl, filtered through the black spruce, moved out of our pinpoint of civilization and was lost and swallowed by the endless forests that stretched north almost to the Arctic's rim.

I cannot remember that our school ever closed, even when the thermometer dropped below minus 60°F. Sandwiches froze as hard as cement in our pockets; licorice sticks turned brittle in our mitts; our eyelids froze together, and we quickly learned never to touch metal with our bare hands. One day some of us persuaded Alex McCarter's little sister, Helen, to lick a doorknob, with devastating results.

Yet even to us children, the Yukon winters became monotonous. I longed for the sun; and when it returned in late January, I longed for the spring. It burst upon us in April, a short, sudden, magical season accompanied by the sweet sound of rushing water. To this day I cannot hear the gurgle of a stream or the babble of a cataract without my mind returning to those spring days in Dawson when the purple pasque-flowers poked up above the melting snows and the mosses squinched under our feet like sodden sponges. Dozens of freshets tumbled down from the hills above, over the rocks, through the newly awakened trees, and under the sedges, filling the six-foot ditches that were supposed to drain that swampy townsite, and spilling over into a network of shallow ponds and small lakes.

For us boys, it was a watery paradise, a natural amusement park in which we could splash, tumble, and push each other to our own delight and our mothers' despair. To the adults, it was a pain in the neck. One day when I was about five I looked out from our front porch and saw a lake surrounding the Administration Building where my father worked. The river had overflowed its banks, as it often did, and flooded half the town. For Dawson was built on a flood plain surrounded by hills riddled with springs.

"Why on earth would they ever build a town here?" a newcomer once asked my father, who explained, reasonably, that this was where the gold was found. Bonanza and Eldorado, the richest creeks of all, were only a jump or so away from the town. All summer long, night and day, we could hear the whine and the screech of the great gold dredges tearing these once verdant valleys to pieces in their search for treasure.

Like the howls of the huskies, the grinding and shrieking of these great floating machines was an unforgettable sound. It terrified me as a small child, for I believed the dredges were alive — monsters chewing away at the valley, whining in the distance like lost souls, and probably coming for me in the night.

In summer there were other sounds. We were never free from the roar of the shallow Klondike as it swept over the sandbars at its mouth and hurled itself into the hissing Yukon. Like the distant wail of the dredge, it was part of the seasonal background, and when it vanished with freeze-up, the silence of winter was intensified by its absence.

The most cheerful sound of all was the sonorous whistle of the steamboat, signalling its arrival as it puffed round the Yukon's bend. Lucy and I would rush down to the dock to watch each stern-wheeler nose in — the *Casca* or the *Whitehorse* from the upper river, the *Yukon* from the lower, and sometimes the *Nasutlin,* the *Aksala,* or the big freighter *Klondike.* We'd hang around Front Street hoping one of the tourists would give us two bits so we could buy two cones or a sundae at the B & F store up the street. When my parents learned that we were actually accepting money from strangers, they were appalled. We were told, in no uncertain terms, that this was something you just didn't do. But all the others did it.

The tourists lived aboard the steamboats and wandered all over town during their brief stay. You could tell they were tourists because they never said hello when they passed you by. My friend Billy Lowe, who was a fount of information about the Outside, told me that people there actually went by you on the street without a greeting. I found that hard to believe. In Dawson, everybody said hello to everybody else, even tourists.

Chappie Chapman took the tourists in his big orange bus around town and out to the creeks to see the sights. There, nestled in the woods, was a small cabin with a pair of caribou antlers over the door — part of the landscape as far as we children were concerned. But the tourists piled out of the bus to crowd into the cabin, for this was the former home of Robert Service, the bard of the Yukon, now retained as an attraction for visitors by the Imperial Order of the Daughters of the Empire. Here the poet had written

23

Ballads of a Cheechako, Rhymes of a Rolling Stone, and his novel, *The Trail of '98,* before departing forever for sunnier climes.

Lucy and I would stand in the ditch beside the road, gawking at the tourists. It never occurred to either of us to enter the cabin ourselves. We knew who Service was, of course. Volumes of his poems, bound in fringed caribou hide with real nuggets on the front, lay on our hall table. My mother had known and dated him. But to us it was just another cabin; we'd been in dozens; we saw nothing special about this one. Thirty years went by before I saw the interior of Dawson's most important shrine.

As the tourists boarded the bus again, Chappie would call their attention to our own house and garden, "a fine example of Dawson horticulture," which it certainly was. My father had planted canary vine to cover the outer walls in summer. In his garden he'd grown delphinium, monkshood, Arctic and Shirley poppies, and sweet peas, Schizanthus hung in baskets from the verandahs and fat pansies lined the garden walks. The tourists oo-ed and ah-ed at the profusion of colour — fancy a tropical jungle here in the heart of the frozen North! I was less enchanted, for it was I who had to do the weeding, and the weeds grew just as swiftly as the flowers in those sunlit summer nights.

To us, the tourists were a foreign species, rather like visitors from some obscure planet. No doubt they saw us, too, as a strange and perhaps barbaric breed. To his dying day, my father would remember and recount a remark he overheard one of them make. "These *aliens,*" the tourist remarked, indicating a group of locals, "these aliens seem quite respectable."

What were they doing here? I wondered. *Why had they come? What were they peering at so intently? What was it about Dawson that had caused them to travel four or five thousand miles to spend a day and a half in our community?* Some years were to pass before I understood their curiosity.

4 When I returned to Dawson after a long absence and visited our old house, I couldn't believe how small it was. The rooms in which I was raised seemed to be the size of closets; the little hallway that had once seemed so spacious was almost claustrophobic; the screened porch on which I used to sleep in the bright summer nights was cramped and tiny.

The house was even smaller in my pre-school days. We all slept in the one bedroom, my parents in a double bed, Lucy and I in cribs on either side. In those days I used to make up stories and tell them to my sister as we lay there, or to my mother when I climbed into her bed of a Saturday morning. I cannot remember these tales very well; they were all fantasies about small animals who owned motor cars or flew about in airplanes. Later, my father built a kitchen on the north end of the house and the stories stopped. The old kitchen was given to Lucy, my father's old den became my bedroom, and our parents at last had some privacy.

We had no bathroom. The waterwagon came around every second or third day, and two men stamped into the kitchen carrying four-gallon wire-handled gasoline tins, crusted with icicles in the winter. A cistern in the corner held our water supply. As small children we were bathed in porcelain basins on the kitchen table. Later we enjoyed a Saturday-night bath, as our parents did, in a galvanized iron tub. To reach the one-holer in the cellar, you pulled up a trapdoor in the kitchen floor, climbed down a ladder, and tried to get a few moments of privacy next to the furnace. The scavenger, whose name was Charlie McFarland, came around twice a week.

We lived on Eighth Avenue at the corner of Harper, on the very edge of Dawson's neat checkerboard of streets. Later I learned there had once been a Ninth and a Tenth Avenue, but these had long since vanished into the encroaching thicket. Thus our bungalow nestled on the rim of the wilderness, which stretched back into the beyond — hill after hill after hill, empty of humankind — the domain of the lynx, the bears, and the wolves. On a winter's night when we heard the cries of the wolf pack in the far hills mingling with the howls of our own huskies, I could feel the shivers up my spine. For the wolves both fascinated and terrified me. I had by then a well-developed imagination, stimulated by the dark presence of the wilderness, by the books I devoured in the local library, and by the cowboy movies I was sometimes allowed to see, starring Tom Mix, Hoot Gibson, or Ken Maynard. I no longer made up stories for my sister or my mother; I made them up for myself. I saw myself in a white ten-gallon stetson, mounted on a pure white horse, riding at the head of a posse of vigilantes, saving the entire Dawson community from some dreadful fate — but from what? I could never fantasize a catastrophe suitable to that peaceful community. Besides, the town was patrolled by the Mounted Police, and all of *them* rode horses.

My father encouraged me in this make-believe. When the Douglas Fairbanks movie *The Iron Mask* finally reached Dawson, he made me a wooden sabre with a coffee tin for a hand guard and a shield fashioned from a tin plate. Every kid in town wanted to be d'Artagnan that month.

I had read all of Andrew Lang's collections of European fairy stories, full of giants and dwarfs, gnomes and elves, but none of these supernatural figures seemed to fit into the folklore of the Canadian North. Helen McCarter, my best friend's sister, once insisted that she had seen two giants on Eighth Avenue, but I didn't believe her. She was, after all, only four. I was more taken with the Walker of the Snows, the Silent Hunter who leaves no footprints behind and whose chill breath freezes the unwary traveller. *That* certainly fitted the environment.

But it was the thought of the wolves that unnerved me. The Walker of the Snows was a ghost; the wolves were real. In the library I had come across some illustrated Russian tales. The picture of a family in a troika racing madly across the frozen wastes and tossing out their children to appease the pursuing pack stayed with me. And there were other stories — Canadian ones — of wolves surrounding a lone trapper, crouching in an ever-diminishing circle, waiting for the campfire to die. These were nightmares to which I could easily relate. The forest was only a few yards from our front door. I was convinced there were wolves there, lurking in the underbrush, waiting for a chance to pounce.

And yet, in all my years in the Yukon, I never saw a wolf. I saw moose, caribou, brown bears, lynx, coyotes, and all manner of wildlife from Arctic hares to porcupine, but never a wolf. It was this invisibility that haunted me: the unseen was the unknown. The wolf was like a spectre, uncanny and mysterious, a distant wail in the night, a footprint in the sand. I saw such a footprint once on the beach of a small island in the Yukon River. My father called me over. "Here's something to see," he said, pointing at a gigantic imprint, complete with claws. "It's a wolf," he said, "and quite fresh." I shivered, knowing that somewhere beyond the tangle of scrub brush the enemy lurked.

I was tormented by another fear. I was terrified that one or other of my parents would die before I grew up. My father was a powerful man, bursting with energy; to me he was immortal. But what if my mother died?

One scene stands out in my mind from those days: Lucy and I, my mother, and our two dogs, Grey Cloud and Spark (named by me for Barney Google's comic-strip horse, Spark Plug), hiking across the Yukon River one day in the early spring. The weather was glorious — crisp, with just a touch of frost. The river, as always in winter, was rumpled; great blocks of ice had ground together and frozen into position. Through this labyrinth we picked our way, my mother in her parka and breeches just ahead, gambolling with the dogs. I don't know why such a gloomy thought should have struck me just at that moment; no doubt it came as a contrast to the sunlight dazzling on the snow and the exuberance of the scene — the dogs leaping almost into her arms and then bounding down again, dashing about in mad circles, she laughing and calling to them and ruffling their fur as they rushed about. I thought: *Oh, please God, don't let her die! She mustn't die! I couldn't bear it if she died. Please wait until I'm old enough to cope with it.* Perhaps my prayers were answered, for she outlived my father by twenty-two years, dying peacefully at the age of eighty-nine, not knowing by then exactly who or where she was, as much a release for her as for her family.

I prayed a great deal in those days. The church placed a considerable emphasis on prayer. As a small child, I had prayed once for two automobiles — a big one for me and a smaller one for my sister — the kind that I had read about in a book called *Uncle Wiggly and Jacko and Jumpo Kinkytail.* I was shocked and disillusioned when I opened our front door the following morning to discover that the little road in front of our house was empty. Was God, then, in the same category as the Stork and Santa Claus? I asked my mother about it one evening as she tucked me into bed and was shocked when she looked at me pensively and said, "You know, it's quite possible that there *is* no God." At that dreadful revelation I burst into tears.

The more I think about my mother the more I realize that she was not quite what she appeared to be. On the surface she was the very personification of a proper Dawson matron. She was certainly a pillar of the church. She sang in the choir, attended communion regularly, helped out at the church bazaars, teas, and Sunday School picnics. Yet I think she secretly remained a sceptic. Her father, who had been born a Quaker, had refused to enter any church during his lifetime, and she was, in many ways, her father's daughter.

She sang hymns constantly around the house, for she had a fine voice; but I don't think she took them seriously. The one hymn she sang more than any other was "Work for the night is coming (when man works no more.)" "That dreadful hymn," she called it. "Imagine having to drudge away for the rest of your life."

She also sang Victorian music-hall songs with gloomy titles: "She Laid a Wreath of Roses on His Cold and Chilly Brow," or "Softly She Turned from the Grave and Cried, " or "But, Oh, I Am So Hungry, Sir, a Penny Please for Bread." But there was nothing gloomy about the way she sang them, and it came to me that in her quiet way she was really spoofing the genre.

Although she was a faithful member of the Imperial Order of the Daughters of the Empire, I'm not sure she took their Imperialism very seriously. She had a delightful sense of the ridiculous, which came to the fore in later life. In my father's time, she deferred to his ideas, but I had more than one hint that she felt the ladies of the IODE, with their long white dresses and their forest of Union Jacks, were faintly comical. She kept her own political views hidden. On the face of it she was, in that highly political town, a Conservative, and therefore one of the anointed. After all, my father had got his job for service to the party. *Her* father, on the other hand, was a Marxian socialist of long standing. I once asked her to explain communism to me, and she gave me a simplistic answer. "The government owns everything," she told me. "They come around to your door with groceries. They'll say: 'Here's some bread! Here's some milk! Here are some vegetables!'..."

The significant thing, of course, was that she never suggested, as many mothers might have, that communism was wicked.

There were no Marxists in Dawson, naturally, and no one who would own up to being a socialist. I suspect that my mother secretly voted for the Liberals, if only because her best friend's husband, W.E. Thompson, was the local candidate. If she did, she never told my father; nor did he, always a gentleman, ever ask.

The idea that my father might someday die, as I have said, never crossed my mind. He had one close call that made very little impression on me, possibly because it occurred on the same day I received the greatest gift any boy can have: a Daisy air rifle (or "BB gun" as we called it).

"Go down to Mrs. Thompson's," my mother told me. "She's found an old air rifle in her shed and she says you can have it."

Unbelievable! It was as if a genie had emerged from a beer bottle (the only kind I knew) and offered me my heart's desire. I dimly remember that my father was down with a painful case of sciatica and that the doctor was on his way, but that was of small moment to me. I rushed out of the house and down the street to W.E. Thompson's home across from the school and received from his wife's hands the magnificent gift.

I caressed it, stroking the wooden stock, holding it against my shoulder, and sighting down the barrel the way Hoot Gibson did in the movies. I ambled around the town, trying to look casual, holding the rifle in the crook of my arm, as I'd seen my father do with his real rifle. It may not have been the only BB gun in town, but it was one of a very few. Carrying it, I had acquired instant status.

The day moved on. Twilight fell. I walked back along Fifth Avenue and sauntered across the park, aiming my rifle at various objects, which might have been Comanches or Sioux. A friend ran toward me shouting. I can't remember who it was; I can only remember the air rifle.

"Your father's real sick. You better get home. Your mother's lookin' for you."

"I've got an air rifle," I said. "Want to try it out?"

"You *got* to get home. Your father's turned blue."

I shrugged and headed home, wondering what the fuss was about. My mother met me at the door, looking exhausted and distraught. I showed her the air rifle, but she didn't even notice it.

"Your father's in a bad way," she said. "God knows what would have happened if I hadn't been here."

"Daddy turned blue," said Lucy. "And he shivered like he was ice cold."

"That damned doctor," said my mother. "He gave him an overdose of something in a needle. God knows what it was."

"Mrs. Thompson says I can keep the air rifle," I said. "It's mine."

"The worst is over," my mother said. "I piled the blankets on him. He's got some of his colour back, and he's stopped shaking. I stuffed the bed with hot water bottles. Thank God I was here. Oh, that damned doctor!"

What was it? An overdose of morphine, I think. I never found out. The doctor was a quack who left town shortly afterward and in later years got into trouble as a kitchen-table abortionist. As for my own attitude, it wasn't really the air rifle that caused me to take my father's close call so casually. It was simply that I didn't believe he was vulnerable. As far as I was concerned, he was indestructible.

I think my parents paid more attention to their children than most, perhaps because they continued to be astonished that they *had* any. I really don't think they wanted me to grow up. I wore a long, pageboy haircut and velvet shorts until I was six years old, scarcely appropriate for a small boy in a mining camp. More than anything else I wanted to wear long pants, like most of my contemporaries, but these were denied me until I was twelve. I was often called a sissy and beaten up by older and larger boys. I accepted this as part of my lot in life and don't recall that I attempted to fight back, perhaps because I lived in deathly fear of getting punched in the nose.

My parents clearly wanted me to be an achiever. My father was anxious for me to get good marks at school for intellectual reasons rather than practical ones. Material success meant very little to him. He liked his job as Mining

Recorder for the Klondike district, and he was good at it. As a civil engineer he was able, often in his spare time, to draw careful maps of the surveyed claims along the gold creeks, some of which are still in use. But he didn't give a hoot about money and he didn't care about advancement. He was interested in the pursuit of knowledge for its own sake. He would rather read the *Scientific American* (his favourite magazine) than the latest novel from the newly formed Book of the Month Club. He would rather spend his time gazing at the constellation of Orion than at Tom Mix in *Hello, Cheyenne,* unless there was an animated cartoon playing. The magic of Felix the Cat captured his scientific imagination.

It's odd the things you remember from childhood. Trivial incidents, quickly forgotten by adults, stay in your mind; major catastrophes grow foggy. One of the sweetest memories I have is of one summer's evening — I was eight, perhaps nine, years old — when, after supper, my father casually suggested that he and I go for a stroll.

Off we went down the hill and across the little park to Fifth Avenue with its raised board sidewalk — deep ditches on either flank — and its row of old-fashioned telephone poles. I can still hear the sound of the wind in the wires, for each pole had ten crosspieces supporting a veritable spiderweb of wire — one for each telephone in town (or so I believed), and all humming like stringed instruments.

More than any other street, Fifth Avenue returns periodically in my dreams, for it was the link between the Administration Building where my father worked and the school. We passed one of the Mounted Police cottages, occupied by Sergeant Cronkhite, a legendary figure whom we boys worshipped because, it was said, he had the strength of ten and was able to wrestle demented prospectors into strait-jackets after a winter bout of cabin fever. A few doors away on a side street stood a handsome Georgian frame house, the residence of the Anglican bishop, Isaac O. Stringer, a deceptively mild man who was best known for staving off starvation by eating his boots on the Rat River divide. *Did he boil them or roast them?* we wondered. *Did he have salt and pepper? Did he pick them up in his hands or use a proper knife and fork?* Chaplin's *Gold Rush* had not yet reached us or we might have had the answers.

Next we wandered past a long line of greenhouses run by Mr. Paddock, who supplied the town with its spring lettuce and tomatoes — crops too tender to survive without protection. It was widely whispered, at least among us children, that Mr. Paddock fertilized his fledgling plants with his own manure. (Certainly my mother washed them carefully before putting them on the table.) Just beyond the greenhouses we passed Mrs. Boyce's bakery shop, where you could buy gigantic doughnuts, covered with granulated sugar, freshly baked and so soft that when you sank your teeth into them they deflated like small balloons.

The school lay ahead, a handsome Edwardian frame building with a cupola on top, built in the same architectural style as the post office, the Mounted Police headquarters, and the Administration Building. Just beyond, at the corner of Fifth Avenue and Queen Street, was another Edwardian structure, built originally by the Dawson Amateur Athletic Association to house both a skating rink and a theatre, which served as dance pavilion, concert hall, and movie house. As we approached I could see a knot of people standing outside and a poster advertising a Tom Mix movie, *Yaqui Gold*.

We stood for a moment, looking across the street at the crowd.

"Let's amble over and have a look," said my father, poker-faced.

Over we went to stare at the poster showing the cowboy star in his white ten-gallon hat, brandishing six-guns.

"Two tickets, Fred," I heard my father saying. "One adult, one for the boy here."

At first I couldn't believe what I'd heard. We went to very few movies in Dawson; like the comic strips, they weren't considered a good influence on small children. Now, here was my father actually gesturing me in. Suddenly, it dawned on me that he had planned it all along as a surprise, timing our walk carefully so that we would arrive at the show just before it began.

"Got any cartoons around, Fred?" my father asked.

"Why, I believe I've got a couple," said Fred Elliott. "I'll put them both on first if you like, Frank."

I have forgotten many childhood incidents and have had to be reminded of others, but everything about that evening comes back sharply, from Oswald the Rabbit in *Mississippi Mud* and *Panicky Pancakes* to the last scene in the movie where Tom Mix rides off alone into the sunset, astride his horse, Tony, leaving the girl to another man. *Make them . . . happy,* the subtitle read. But more than anything else I remember the pains my father had taken to make *me* happy and the realization, which swept over me like a warm bath, that he really cared.

The toys he gave me or made for me were intellectual. He bought me a microscope to show me what hair looked like when magnified. He bought me a toy steam engine to demonstrate James Watt's principle. He built a miniature catapult for Lucy and me to explain medieval warfare. He interpreted the Fourth Dimension so that I could understand it, took me into the woods to study wildflowers — shooting star, arnica, twinflower, Indian pipe — and pointed out the stars in the heavens so that today I can still identify the major constellations. From the age of five, I struggled to learn French from him. I was unable to master it any more than I was able to master carpentry, although he, a former cabinet-maker's apprentice, did his best. I had no mechanical ability.

My mother pushed me in other directions. She insisted that I take part in the school plays, coaching me in my lines, making me say them over and over again until I got them right. She urged me to volunteer to do recitations at the school concerts. The lines "An' the gobble-uns 'll git you/Ef you don't watch out" are the ones I remember best because they came from the poem "Little Orphan Annie," the precursor of the popular comic strip. Night after night she went over it with me, explaining how I should stand in character, with my thumbs in my pockets and a cap pulled low over one eye. In my earliest stage appearance — I couldn't have been more than seven — I committed a terrible *faux pas* by actually waving to my parents in the audience, a practice they quickly squelched.

I was also encouraged to take part in the essay contests sponsored by the IODE. One essay I wrote in Grade 6 dealt with the discovery of gold in the Klondike, a sensible project in light of its neglect in the official curriculum. I can remember sitting up late into the night, struggling with my prose, my mother sitting across from me at the table in our tiny dining room as I crossed out and rewrote sentences. I actually got one of the IODE prizes, but not for that particular essay. We couldn't know that one day, to my mother's astonishment and even bafflement, I would write about the same events in greater detail and with greater success.

It would be pleasant to put down at this point that this early excursion into history had a seminal effect on me — that it gave me a sense of the past, a burning desire to become a writer, thus setting me on a long career. It's not true. For me the whole enterprise was an extracurricular chore, which kept me up late at night and intruded upon my spare time. I found it heavy going and so, apparently, did the judges. But I didn't hold any of this against my mother. The main thing was that, like my father, she *cared*.

I do not recall that Lucy was pushed in the same way. It is true that she was sent off to Mrs. Humby's dancing class, and I still have photographs of her — a round-faced little girl with dark bangs and enormous eyes, solemn and black

— in one dressed as a fairy complete with gossamer wings and in the other costumed as a Dutch maid with her partner, Edgar Hunter, a Mountie's son. But my mother didn't force her to take the music lessons that I grew to loathe.

"Some day you'll thank me for these," my mother would say as she attempted to teach me the key of G. "You'll be the life of the party." Lucy was spared all of this. Later on in my army days, I *did* become the life of the party — dancing the night away while some other poor devil was shackled to the piano, unable even to spend time with his girl friend.

Lucy's marks at school weren't questioned in the way mine were. If I got 90 per cent my father would ask why I hadn't got 95. If I stood second, he wanted to know why I hadn't stood first. Worse, when Lucy misbehaved, I was blamed.

"You're the oldest," my mother would say. "You're responsible. You should have stopped her."

When I tried to stop her, of course, she howled, and when she howled I got blamed. There were times when I could have strangled my kid sister. No doubt there were times, too, when she could have strangled me.

"What a chauvinist you were then," she said to me not long ago. "Remember the Be-a-Boy Club? You started it just so I couldn't join."

I formed the Be-a-Boy Club when I was about six years old, and though it was true that Lucy was excluded from full membership, she was certainly allowed an associate membership because there were no other Be-a-Boys, and I was lonely. As an associate she was permitted to engage in daredevil feats, just like a boy, and climb with me up the galvanized iron roof of Mr. Corps's cabin across the lane. Teetering on this dizzy pinnacle we pulled our toques over our faces and slithered down the steep sides to bury ourselves in the mountains of snow that had been shovelled from the peak.

It is these moments with Lucy that I remember best.

Somewhere I have a photograph taken by my father (and, of course, printed and developed by him, for he was an enthusiastic amateur photographer) showing the two of us, a pair of chubby moppets, muffled to our ears, covered in snow, laughing and squealing into the camera.

My friends at school were a mixed lot — the sons and daughters of tradesmen, Mounted Police officers, civil servants, mining company officials, and, of course, trappers and woodsmen. These last were mixed-bloods — we called them half-breeds — who lived at St. Paul's Anglican Hostel during the winter and returned to the bush with their Indian mothers and white fathers in the summer. There were no Indians at our school; they went to their own school and their own church at Moosehide, the little native village around the bluff, downstream from Dawson. There were a good many French-Canadian kids in town, too, whom we knew well enough to call by their first names but rarely so intimately that we were invited to their homes. For these were Roman Catholics who went to the separate school and because of that were considered separate from the rest of us. Only once in all my years at Dawson was I invited to a Catholic home — to a little girl's birthday party. I felt a little strange, as though I were entering a forbidden room or trespassing on private property.

As in most small towns, Dawson's population was stratified. I'm not sure my father was aware of that; he lifted his hat to Maggie Cobb, the black washerwoman, and always called her Miss Cobb (never Maggie) when he passed her on the street. He switched easily to French with Father Rivet, the Roman Catholic priest. He was at home with all the strange men who lived in old log cabins in the hills and along the creeks and who often came to him for advice. As an amateur dentist in the winter — the real dentists only practised during the warm months — he filled the teeth of everybody from George Jeckell, the gold commissioner, who was his boss, to the Indians from Moosehide, chatting easily to all. But my mother knew who was who. Mrs. George Black, the wife of the local member, was the doyenne of society. Along with the police commissioner, the gold commissioner, the mining company heads, and the bishop, she was upper class. We were in the middle, above the tradesmen and the labourers, the Low Church people, and most of the "foreigners" — that is, those members of the ethnic population who still had an accent and worked at menial tasks. English public school graduates were accepted, of course, no matter what they did.

We had, as I have said, a town drunk — Walter King. I would pass him as he waddled down Fifth Avenue in his broad-brimmed hat and his shapeless clothing, his face and his nose bright red, a glint in his eye and a smile on his lips, carrying something in a brown paper bag — a messenger boy who was paid in booze rather than dollars. I was afraid to greet him, for I had a terror of drunks; but it occurs to me now that he may have been the happiest man in Dawson. There were several other odd characters: "Slivers," another black woman with an angular yellow face, who lived in Lousetown but strode through Dawson in her masculine whipcord breeches as if she owned the city; "Jerusalem Joe," a voluble prospector from, I think, the Levant, who entertained us boys with stories of his adventures; "Dummy West" and his wife, who weren't at all stupid but who spoke in sign language, being deaf mutes; a mysterious Oriental, half Chinese, who seemed to have sprung up from another world and was the source of great curiosity among us boys; a Japanese shopkeeper who ran an Asian gift shop; and a Japanese gardener who was said to have had an affair with his female employer, one of the leading members of Dawson's high society.

It was hard to keep a secret in that isolated community where everybody not only knew everybody else but also everybody's business. Even small boys heard things or put two and two together — if not then, eventually. In the Arctic

Brotherhood Hall, where many of the big dances were held, there was always a dumpy little woman with a hooked nose, her chalk-white face half concealed by a light veil, who sat alone in one of the boxes. Who was she? Why did no one ever sit with her? My parents evaded my questions. There she sat, looking down impassively on the whirling dancers, never leaving her box or speaking to a living soul. It took me a long time to figure out that she had once been a leading light in Dawson's *demi-monde* during the early days and was, no doubt, reliving vicariously those great moments when, rouged and lipsticked, in a similar box she had drunk champagne at thirty dollars a pint, paid for by one of the Kings of Eldorado.

5 We made our own fun in Dawson; everybody did. There was neither television nor radio, of course, and, for most of the decade, only one movie house, which played silent pictures as late as 1931. The town thrived on ritual; it was the glue that held the community together. This seasonal parade of special days had a powerful effect on me. They were like anchors in the confusing stream of time, something to look forward to and also to look back upon. Today, in my own family, we cheerfully celebrate every birthday and anniversary as well as most feast days. It's a legacy from my years in the North.

In Dawson there were special ceremonies tied to climate, geography, and history. When the ice broke in the Yukon River early in May we celebrated, gambling on the exact moment of the breakup. Everybody — shops, schools, families, our own included — ran an ice pool. We celebrated again in June when the first steamboat arrived, bearing a cornucopia of fresh fruit: oranges, grapes, bananas, things we hadn't seen since the previous October. On the day of the summer solstice there was another celebration: the entire adult town climbed to the top of the Midnight Dome above Dawson to view the Midnight Sun, which, of course, never appeared since we were well south of the Arctic Circle. It didn't matter; by midnight everybody was too drunk to care.

The next great event came on August 17, the anniversary of the discovery of gold in the Klondike by George Carmack and Robert Henderson, whose grandson, my friend Chester, was always chosen to play Santa Claus in the Christmas pageant. For me, Discovery Day was another magic milepost. I looked forward to it for weeks — to the parade and its floats, to the races in the park, to the free strawberry pop, all you could drink from Mr. Schwartz's pop factory — and to the big dance that night to which every child was invited.

Our main autumn ritual was played out in a lower key. Once again, we gathered on the dock to say goodbye to the last boat of the year. That phrase, "the Last Boat," still rings down the corridors of my memory. There was a finality to it, for we all knew that when the Last Boat raised its gangplank we were entombed for nine more months, sentenced to live on potatoes, turnips, and carrots from the root cellar, and spinach and peas from the mason jars put up for the winter. It's a standing joke in my family today that I love canned spinach and canned peas. It's true. They take me back to my boyhood days in a town cut off from the world and more than a little behind the times, when the movies were silent and people were still singing "Ta-ra-ra boom-der-é"; when couples danced the minuet and took their partners for the supper waltz; when the minstrel show and the shivaree were acceptable diversions; when our entertainments were live and only the vegetables were canned.

After the last boat moved slowly out into the black river, with the first snowflakes already in the sky, those who were left were caught up in the social whirl of winter. No fortnight passed, it seemed, that I wasn't enlisted to crank the ice cream freezer to help prepare the pineapple sherbet my mother liked to serve at bridge parties, socials, and formal dinners. All winter long we went to concerts, masked balls, minstrel shows, musicales, and even the occasional amateur play. My father worked for weeks, as everybody did, preparing a set of elaborate costumes for the New Year's Day masquerade. We all won prizes, he as a frog, my mother as an Eaton's parcel, my sister as a snowman, I as Santa Claus. Mrs. Humby, the police inspector's wife, who ran the dancing class all the time she was in Dawson, held an annual gala at which her pupils appeared in costume to do the Sailor's Hornpipe or the Highland Fling or posed in one or other of the *tableaux vivants* so popular in those days. There I stood on the stage of the A.B. Hall, rigid as a statue, dressed as Gainsborough's "Blue Boy," wearing the long golden locks that Mabel Cribbs, the druggist's wife, had shorn when bobbed hair came in.

Of all the winter entertainments mounted on the Dawson stages, the minstrel shows were my favourite. They have become passé today, of course, and with good reason; but there was a time when the men about town — and the women, too — daubed their faces with burnt cork, adopted outrageous accents, and pretended to be comic Negroes. Oddly, I never connected these pseudo-blacks with real blacks. I played with a boy named Buster Hunter whose face was light brown and freckled, and I suppose I must have known that he was a "black"; but I don't think it ever sank in. We didn't use the word "black," of course; we said "Negro." I knew that Maggie Cobb was a Negro because she really *was* black, and I accepted the fact that Slivers, in spite of her yellow features, was a Negro because everybody said she was. But Mr. Martin, who cut my hair in the Royal Alexandra Barbershop, simply looked tanned, like Buster Hunter. Since I never heard either of them referred to as Negroes, I didn't think of them that way. Certainly they bore no relation to Billie Rendall and his twin brother, Charlie, up there on stage convulsing us with local jokes:

"Tell me, Mr. Bones, what is it that has two wheels and flies in the summertime?"

"Two wheels and *flies*, Mr. Interlocutor?"

"That's right, Mr. Bones."

"Well, sah, I would say that was Charlie McFarland's scavenger wagon!" (Laughter and pandemonium.)

Everybody was a performer in those long winter nights. Johnny Dines, the butcher, doubled as chief violinist in the minstrel shows, charming us children with a violin made from a cigar box that held real cigars. Charlie Mills, the hotel keeper, pranced across the stage in blackface, wearing a gigantic busby and singing "Alexander's Ragtime Band." One of the clerks from the Northern Commercial store joined the dredgemaster's wife in a sprightly duet of "In a Little Spanish Town." My mother sang at every concert: "The Little Hills of Duna," "Mighty Lak' a Rose," "Tommy Lad," and those eloquent if overheated Indian love lyrics, the ever-popular Kashmiri song ("Pale Hands I Loved Beside the Shalimar") and the stridently romantic "Less Than the Dust (Beneath Thy Chariot Wheels)." One hears them rarely now, these old concert favourites, for the "concert" itself is a thing of the past. But occasionally on some eclectic radio pastiche I hear a vagrant melody — "Christopher Robin Is Saying His Prayers," perhaps — and my mind goes back to those cold winter nights and those stifling interiors, when almost everyone in town, adults, children, even babies, made their own music.

When the concert was over, the floor was cleared and the adults danced the two-step and the one-step, the minuet, and the medley. The babies slept peacefully on the piles of winter coats in the cloakroom. And we kids raced round the upper balconies and onto the big stage, which had been cleared of cardboard props and curtained off for our own merriment, to be led home at two in the morning, crunching through the snow, with the mysterious green curtain of the aurora glowing above us in the velvet sky.

Dawson in winter was Christmas-card town. By mid-December, the snow lay thick in the vacant lots and on the sloping roofs, blotting out the blemishes, masking the tell-tale signs of decay. I remember somebody telling me — I think it was Billy Lowe, who was all-knowing — that there were places Outside where there was no snow at Christmas. I didn't believe it any more than I believed that Outside you could actually buy a bottle of pop for a nickel. If there wasn't any snow, there couldn't be a Christmas.

I remember how shocked I was when Billy told me there were places where people actually bought Christmas trees from lots, already cut. I could scarcely believe this and felt sorry for those people who did not live in a land where Christmas trees stretched off in every direction in a great undulating ocean of dark green. We didn't need to buy a tree in Dawson. My father and I went up the hill behind our house and cut our own, floundering through the drifts until we found exactly the right one. The powdery snow tumbled off the branches as we chopped away at the trunk.

The Christmas period lasted from about the fifteenth of December to New Year's Day. There was no fierce and long-drawn-out commercial build-up, no blaring carol music. "Silent Night" was heard only in church and in school. The week before Christmas the little stores put tinsel and toys in their windows; there were so few that every boy knew every toy in every window and the moment it disappeared. And there was only one Santa Claus, who made his appearance at the Community Christmas Party, arriving, believably, in a real sleigh from the North Pole, which we all knew was just over the rim of the horizon.

Christmas presents were not delivered by postmen but were brought round by hand on Christmas Eve. In our family, this was my task. Off I set after supper, with my little sled loaded with gifts and with my dog, Spark, at my side, moving from house to house, muffled to the ears, feeling the crisp crunch of the snow beneath my felt boots. And every

43

once in a while I would stop stock-still to cock an ear and listen. For all over that little town you could hear the cheerful tinkle of sleigh-bells. No Christmas music, recorded or taped or live from Hollywood, can ever equal that sound.

In the window of Madame Tremblay's dress shop one Christmas was one of the most magnificent toys I had ever seen — a clockwork device of great ingenuity. Little cars ran down inclines and were hoisted up a new incline and leaped gaps and finally did a loop-the-loop before repeating the circuit. We would stand in the bitter pre-Christmas cold, we boys, peering into the lighted window and staring at that marvellous toy, warmed by the scarlet and yellow of its paintwork.

The toy stayed in the window until the very last, and it was generally believed that Madame Tremblay, a plump, middle-aged Frenchwoman, could not bear to part with it and was saving it for herself to play with on Christmas Day.

But when I opened one mysterious and bulky parcel early on Christmas morning, there was the toy. I was stunned. I couldn't believe I could ever own a plaything of such magnificence. I looked at the card and I almost wept, for it had been given to me by my best friend, Alex McCarter. He and I had stood day after day marvelling at the toy, wondering who would get it. And at the last moment, he had spent all his money and given it to me, and I felt bad because I had not thought of giving it to him.

6 "The summer — no sweeter was ever!" Robert Service wrote of that bright, brief season when flowers and vegetables grew all night to achieve enormous proportions — cauliflower and cabbages a foot and a half across, beets the size of footballs, vegetable marrows as long as a man's arm — when the underbrush on the hills became a jungle, and when, to my dismay, the chickweed in the garden threatened to strangle us all.

We made the most of summer, the four of us. In those endless evenings we roamed the hills, picking raspberries and red currants in July and blueberries in August. We didn't own a car; not many did. Dawson was still a town of livery stables and blacksmith shops. We kids used to sit for hours watching Billy Bigg hammer red-hot horseshoes into shape, and when Dan Coates's big livery wagon rattled by we all made a rush to jump aboard for a free ride. The steam pumper, which sprayed a chemical foam on burning buildings, was also horse drawn. When the big whistle sounded in the firehall, the firemen slid down the brass pole as the harness automatically dropped onto the backs of the big drays. Moments later they were galloping through the streets with half the populace running behind.

Because of the horses, Dawson's roads were redolent with the odour of fresh manure and its hills scented with new hay, stacked in the tawny fields carved from the surrounding forest. There is one brief summer scene that comes back to me through a golden haze, like a dream. There we are, a group of laughing children — I have no idea how old we were then — scampering across one of those hay fields on the hill high above the town, flinging ourselves into the stacks and rolling about on the ground. For an instant I experience again the sheer exuberance of that afternoon — the warmth of the sun, the scent of the newly cut hay, and the freedom we all felt in those childhood hours. That's all — an instant's flash, nothing more. Like a dream, it vanishes before I can capture it. And yet of all the memories of my childhood this one is the most vivid, the one that warms me and that leaves me with the same sense of contentment I felt so long ago.

In those days, people were great walkers; we didn't need a car or a horse. I had my bicycle, but it was no hardship to use my feet. When my father courted my mother he used to walk to Dawson from Granville, a mining camp some forty miles away, in thirty-below weather with a pack on his back

— a thirteen-hour trip that caused him little concern. On Sundays the four of us hiked across the hills or out along the Klondike valley for miles, to return in time for evensong in St. Paul's Pro-cathedral on the riverbank. All the music of those times brings back memories. Whenever I hear that lovely old hymn "The Day Thou Gavest, Lord, Is Ended" I think of those Sundays in the wood — the smoky flavour of beans cooked over a fire of birch logs and washed down with cold spring water, the dry rattle of the trembling aspens, the pungent incense of the balm of Gilead tree, the chewy texture of spruce gum, and then later the vision of my mother in her surplice, joining her soft soprano to the voices of the choir, her face glowing from the wind and the sun.

I try not to think of the day when I, at the age of about nine, was invited not only to join the choir but also to lead it into the pews. I became confused, made a wrong turn, pushed blindly on through what seemed to be a labyrinth of benches with the entire choir following, until we were all inextricably mixed and had to be sorted out in full view of the congregation. It was my one and only appearance.

My father, on those hillside hikes, looked hungrily down at the river. He had no desire to own a car; but in the early days of his marriage he had owned a boat, and now he desperately wanted another one. He determined to build it himself.

He rented an old hotel on Front Street, near the church, and turned it into a carpenter shop. Every night after work and all day on weekends he worked on that boat. Lucy and I brought him lunch and sat for hours, watching as it slowly took shape. Occasionally we rummaged around the old building, which had been empty since the gold rush days. One afternoon, poking into a drawer in an old desk, we came upon a bundle of letters tied with a pink ribbon. We opened these and discovered to our delight that they were love letters from a miner out on the creeks to a dancehall girl in Dawson. I took them home to my mother who read them with interest, but none of us had any real sense of history at the time. To my eternal regret, these letters were discarded; I cannot even remember the details of what was written or the name of the man who wrote them.

It took my father a year to finish the boat, which he named *Bluenose* and powered with a Johnson Seahorse 12. It changed our life in the summers. The river became our second home. There was scarcely an evening that didn't find us out on the water, exploring the skein of channels, sandbars, and islands upstream from Dawson. (We rarely dared go downstream; if the motor failed, there was no way back.) When the water dropped in midsummer, more sandbars appeared, linking the islands together. It was on these that we camped and picnicked, splashing in the shallow ponds left on the sand spits by the ebbing waters.

The boat gave us a sense of freedom that we hadn't known before. Any island that we chose was ours by right of capture. We simply pitched a tent and moved in. Nobody bothered us; there were plenty of islands for all. Often my mother, Lucy, and I would camp for two weeks without returning to Dawson, while my father commuted to work by water.

My father was generous with his boat; indeed, he liked to show it off to visitors, for he was proud of it — a sleek, twenty-six-foot, round-bottomed craft with several inventions of his own: a pump system, for instance, that allowed him to draw gasoline automatically from the tanks in the bow to the motor in the stern. Visiting celebrities were given tours of the river and the islands in the *Bluenose*, and my own friends and Lucy's were invited along on picnics.

But my main memory of the *Bluenose* has to do with the Discovery Day race, which my father entered even though he had no hope of winning. His partner in the mining recorder's office, Phil Kelly, had a similar boat named *Shamrock IV* (named after Sir Thomas Lipton's famous

Shamrock III) with a Johnson Seahorse 14, which was certainly faster; but neither was as fast as some of the racing shells that bounced along the river powered by twenty-horsepower engines.

To my father it was the race that counted, not the prize. All the boats assembled at the dock, and at the opening gun their owners pulled on their starting cords and were off — all except my father. He pulled the cord; nothing happened. He pulled again; a cough of the motor, then silence. The other boats were far away, spanking along the rough water, heading for the turn. My father continued his attempts to start the engine. It was clear now that the race for him was over. Some of the boats were already turning back, speeding for the finish line. My father continued to pull on the starting cord, showing no embarrassment. The first boat crossed the line — a clear winner. My father still worked on the engine. The second boat dashed in, and then another. My father kept on. At last the motor turned over, caught, and spluttered into action. By that time the race was over; all the other boats had returned. None of this fazed him. Calmly and quite cheerfully, he set out to run the course alone. He completed it long after the others had left their craft; then he pulled up the motor, tied up his boat, and walked back up Front Street with a look of quiet satisfaction on his face. I had never been so proud of him as I was at that moment.

Those summers on the river gave him the release he needed from the routine of his job. In over a dozen years he had taken scarcely a single day's holiday and never a two-week vacation, to which he was entitled. Two weeks just wasn't long enough to go Outside, and the government recognized that fact, allowing its servants in the Yukon to accumulate their vacation time. By 1931 he had more than six months of holidays saved up.

All this time my mother had been working on her novel, to be titled "Then Alice Came Home." It was on her mind, and ours, almost twenty-four hours a day. She read great hunks of it aloud to the family — a titled Englishman takes a job as a hired man on a nineteenth-century southern Ontario farm and falls in love with the daughter of the house when she arrives home from the big city. That much I can remember, and I can also remember the opening line: "Mrs. Barnes was making cookies." I can remember it because it became a kind of catch-phrase with us. My mother repeated it over and over again, not without humour, and sometimes with a small giggle, so that I could never be sure whether she was spoofing herself or whether it simply ran through her head, like a melody that refuses to be expunged.

At last, when I was eleven years old, the novel was finished. Great excitement! I don't think it occurred to my mother that she could mail it to a publisher in Toronto. At any rate, she had no intention of doing that. We would all go to Toronto, and she would take the novel personally to one of the big houses. There were other reasons for the trip, of course. My father had left the Yukon only once since the gold rush of 1898 — for a three-year stint in the army. He hadn't seen his younger brother, Jack, since the war. But now he had accrued enough paid vacation time to allow him a winter in eastern Canada. My mother's father was reaching the end of his life; he was in his late eighties and almost blind from cataracts on both his eyes. She was anxious to see him again before he died. And it was time that Lucy and I saw something of the world beyond the Yukon hills — something more than minstrel shows and cowboy movies.

The decision was made. We would go Outside for the winter. For all of us it would be a glorious adventure. My mother would sell her book to a publisher and become a famous novelist. My father would be able to sit in on science lectures at the University of Toronto. My sister and I would become acquainted with our relatives, and, even more

49

important, we would be able to go to an amusement park, where strange devices whirled about and little cars ran down steep inclines.

We did not know then, as we climbed aboard the steamer *Casca* on September 1 and waved goodbye to our friends on the docks, that we were really saying farewell to Dawson City and that cosy little bungalow under the hill.

Chapter Two

On the Outside
1931-1939

1 *The Outside!* The words tell so much about life in the North before the days of modern communication. We on the Inside were cut off from the rest of the human race. Even the news arrived two days late. Reception was so primitive that scarcely anybody bothered to own a radio. The movies we saw were at least three years old and often older. Popular songs, women's fashions, dance crazes, even the argot of the day — "So's your old man!" "Gee whillikers!" "Get a horse!" — reached us only after they had become passé in the world beyond.

It was not easy to get to the Outside, even to Vancouver or Seattle. The steamboat trip up the Yukon to Whitehorse took a week in the autumn. Another day was spent travelling through the coastal mountains by narrow-gauge railway to Skagway, the Alaskan port on the Pacific. The journey to one of the West Coast cities occupied a minimum of five days. Toronto, of course, was another four or five days away. For my parents, both past middle age, with two unruly pre-teenagers in tow, the prospect must have been daunting.

To most of us boys in Dawson, the Outside was a mystery. People there used strange money — dimes, nickels, and pennies. They drank Coca-Cola, which we had certainly heard of but never tasted, and also something called a milk shake. (*Why would anybody want to shake up a lot of milk?* I wondered.) The streets were covered with cement, not gravel, and so were the sidewalks. There were coloured lights. People travelled by streetcar, and automobiles were driven all year round; in Dawson, the only car that ran in the winter was the milkman's Model T, which he was forced to crank furiously after each stop.

Some of these things I was dimly aware of because of an earlier trip with my mother and Lucy to Oakville, Ontario, to visit our grandparents. I was only five then, too young to comprehend the fairyland world into which I was suddenly plunged. It had been more like a dream. My first sight of a real locomotive terrified me; I thought it was a monster, determined to swallow me up, like the dredge. I faintly remember certain other marvels, the asphalt roads and cement sidewalks particularly. *Did the grass grow underneath all that?* I wondered. And a five-legged calf at the Canadian National Exhibition, which my mother refused to allow me to examine close up. Then there was the radio: my grand-parents didn't have one, but once, in a neighbour's home, I was allowed to put on the earphones to listen to a woman's voice carolling "The Last Rose of Summer."

That had been a winter of understandable confinement. Save for a couple of brief visits to Toronto we were rarely allowed to stray farther than the front yard of my grand-parents' home. The highlight of the whole vacation was a memorable voyage back down the Yukon to Dawson in a small poling boat christened *The P and L* after me and Lucy, a symbol of the affection our parents had for us. To me the Outside visit was a kind of blur; only the river journey stood out sharply in my memory.

By the time I had turned eleven, however, the Outside had become an obsession. Some new boys had arrived in town from the Outside and were full of marvellous tales of amusement parks, neon signs, huge toy departments, strange fizzy drinks with exotic names and flavours, bathing beaches, and a new movie cartoon character called Mickey Mouse, who they insisted was better than Felix the Cat or Oswald the Rabbit because the mouse actually talked on the screen.

It was this peek through the curtain that had begun to make me feel confined. The films we saw were so ancient that Fred Elliott didn't bother to send them back. He simply dumped them in an abandoned swimming pool, where they remained for half a century until a bulldozer unearthed them. It turned out to be one of the great film finds of all time.

The only gathering place for youngsters in Dawson was the B & F store (I have no idea what the name meant) where for two bits you could get a chocolate sundae or two ice cream cones made with condensed milk. The only restaurant was the Arcade Café, which we rarely entered. You could hang around the lobbies of seven hotels, with their black leather settees and their brass spittoons, but you couldn't enter the bar where illegal whisky was served. Those two emporiums of adult delights, Ruby's Place and Bombay Peggy's, were, of course, unknown to us. Dawson, in short, was a great place for a small boy, but not quite so great for a teenager. I was on the verge of outgrowing it.

The comic strips had helped to whet my appetite for the Outside. My grandfather sent me a huge bundle once a month. At first my parents refused to allow me to read them, believing they were a bad influence on a small, growing boy, but in the end they relented. I spent Sunday mornings on the floor on my stomach devouring "Tailspin Tommy," "Toots and Casper," "Elmer," "The Gumps," "Barney Google," and "Orphan Annie." The movies were less of an influence; we were allowed to go only rarely, and since they were mostly Westerns they told me nothing about the world beyond the Yukon plateau.

The first talkies didn't arrive in Dawson until just before we left. There we sat in the Orpheum Theatre, watching the words come audibly from the mouths of the stars on the screen. Billy Lowe nudged me. "That's the talkie you're hearin' now," he said importantly. I resented his patronizing and hated him for being so knowledgeable about the Outside. Lowe made me feel like a rube.

Fortunately that was about to end. We were going Outside, to that foreign world I remembered only dimly, where there were talking-picture theatres on every corner and banks of lights that dazzled the eye; and where, if Billy Lowe was right, the streets were so crowded that nobody bothered to say hello to every stranger passing by.

Considering my age, it's not really surprising that so many memories of that excursion should be gastronomical: the revelation, for instance, that you could order lamb chops for breakfast on *The Queen*, the ancient American steamship that took us on a leisurely voyage from Skagway down the coast to Seattle, picking up hundreds of Filipino workers who were leaving the fish canneries at the end of the season.

There were other lip-smacking discoveries: the plates of curled bacon served up on the monogrammed china and dazzling linen of the transcontinental CPR dining car, the realization that milk shakes came in many flavours and weren't shaken at all but churned up with ice cream and syrup in a machine. And my first Coca-Cola at Banff, a new and totally exquisite sensation that I have not been able to duplicate. First impressions can never be recaptured.

When we reached Toronto, we moved into my Aunt Florrie's house, a two-storey building of yellow brick on Huntley Street. Like so much else, bricks were new to me. So were the big stone mansions on nearby Jarvis Street.

When we first arrived in Toronto I felt almost as if I had come from another planet. What an incredible winter it was — everything so fresh, so strange! Looking back on it, I'm astonished that I was able to take it all in my stride; but then, for all growing children life is a series of discoveries.

In those days, Toronto really was Hogtown; most people considered it the dullest community in Canada. The time would come when I would agree. But to me in 1931, it was wonderland. Everything was so new, everything was different — from the orange Honey Dew signs that winked on and off to the policemen who stood in the middle of the main intersections twirling stop-and-go signs. (Traffic lights were just beginning to appear.)

It was the small, everyday discoveries that made the sharpest impact. I had never seen a milk bottle before; the milk in Dawson came round in beer bottles. I had never seen or tasted a toffee apple. I had never *heard* of roller skates. Ice cream tasted different, for it was made with real cream, not canned milk. Eggs were pale yellow instead of bright orange and had hardly any taste at all. After the twice-weekly *Dawson News,* the four Toronto dailies were astonishing: each contained two pages of comics. They changed their headlines almost on the hour and sometimes tinted their front pages, like the famous Pink Tely.

Even the school was different. I was enrolled in what was called the Junior Fourth at Rosedale Public, where all the boys wore berets on their heads. My mother was charmed at that old-world fashion, but I thought they looked like sissies. Within a month I had bowed to peer pressure and was wearing a beret of my own.

It occurs to me now that my father was as excited as I was about the smorgasbord of novelties being spread before us. He too had been cooped up for a dozen years, and so he too rode with us on the roller coaster at Sunnyside. And he was as fascinated as I was by the new neon signs, the milk shake machines, the miniature golf courses, the automobiles with free wheeling, the automatic popcorn makers, and all the other devices of the thirties.

That first week my parents went to a movie at the Uptown Theatre near us. It wasn't the feature film my father talked about with such excitement; it was the animated short, based on music from Camille Saint-Saëns's *Danse Macabre.* Some years passed before I realized he had seen the first of the Disney "Silly Symphonies" — the famous *Skeleton Dance.*

My parents saw the trip to the Outside as not so much a vacation as an education. They intended to try to cram into one winter all the experiences we had missed out on. It didn't matter to my father that we didn't start school until October 1 — a month late.

"When there's nothing else doing this boy will come to school," he told the principal, C.C. Swain. "But I intend to take him out when something more important comes up. He's got to see as much of the Outside as possible."

To his credit, the principal agreed; in the face of my father's firmness he had little choice. As it turned out, I had no trouble with my studies. Although the Junior Fourth was supposed to correspond to Dawson's Grade 7, I found myself taking subjects I had already mastered the year before and so, in spite of many absences, I romped through.

That winter was a whirlwind of excitement and discovery. We went on excursions — by radial streetcar to the Scarborough bluffs, rural in the days before suburbia, where we picnicked on the edge of the escarpment to watch the steamers in the lake below; to Niagara Falls by train to see the cataract illuminated at night, and on to Queenston Heights for Brock's monument and Laura Secord's home; to the Armouries on University Avenue to see the Queen's Own Rifles on parade; to the Royal Ontario Museum to marvel at the skeletons of dinosaurs and the mummies of ancient Egyptians; to a college football game at Varsity Stadium and a skating carnival at the new Maple Leaf Gardens; to the university to see the architecture, the legislature to view the politicians, and the High Park zoo to gaze upon the llamas and monkeys.

It was an eclectic experience, enlivened by my father's own commentary and occasionally by my mother's wry remarks. We took in both the trivial and the grandiose. We visited the magic shop in the Yonge Street Arcade, where I was allowed to purchase an explosive device to shock my friends; we soared more than fifty storeys in the Bank of

Commerce headquarters, then the Tallest Building in the British Empire. We visited the City Dairy to watch milk being pasteurized. At the Toronto *Star* building we saw the coloured comics rolling off the presses. I was even taken to Hamilton to watch steel being made. On Sundays we attended a variety of churches: St. Paul's, St. Thomas's, St. Mary Magdalene, and on one occasion St. Michael's, for my father felt we should take part in a Roman Catholic service.

Not everything delighted or amused me. I was bored by the Hart House String Quartet, even though my father told me it was one of the finest chamber orchestras in the world. I didn't care for the exhibition of the Group of Seven paintings at the Grange; they didn't look like "real" pictures to me. I was baffled by the Passion Play at Massey Hall because the entire performance was in German. And I wasn't crazy about Shakespeare's *As You Like It* at the Royal Alexandra, although I enjoyed looking through my father's binoculars to see what kind of food was eaten in the Forest of Arden; it turned out to consist entirely of chopped apples.

But I loved the performance of *The Mikado* at West Central United and Tony Sarg's wonderful marionettes at the Eaton Auditorium. And most of all I loved the talkies. Now that there was less danger of fire, my parents took us both to see the films of the day: George Arliss in *The Man Who Played God* at the Tivoli; *Penrod and Sam* at Shea's (together with eight acts of vaudeville); *Tarzan of the Apes* at Loew's; and *The Smiling Lieutenant* with Maurice Chevalier and Claudette Colbert, plus a newsreel, serial, two-reel comedy (*The Great Pie Throwing Mystery*) and a cartoon, Disney's second "Silly Symphony" called, I think, *The Clockmaker*, at the Hollywood.

The greatest entertainment, however, came in November, when we all went to the Royal Winter Fair at the Coliseum in the Exhibition Grounds to see a man actually shot from a cannon. My father, who explained everything, told us that in spite of the flash and the smoke, Zacchini "The

Human Cannonball" was actually propelled into the rafters by compressed air. No matter: there he was, soaring above our heads, doing a swan dive into a net at the far end of the building. Now, I thought, *I* will have something to tell Billy Lowe.

For all of us it was a learning experience. While we were at school, my father, who had enrolled at the University of Toronto, took lectures in physics three times a week with students forty years his junior. My mother gave lectures herself to women's groups about life in the Yukon.

Later that winter, my father took me to Ottawa for a week to meet his brother's family and to attend the opening of Parliament. The Speaker, George Black, MP for the Yukon, was an old friend. As he passed by in the lobby of the Parliament Building, in full regalia, walking behind the sergeant-at-arms and the great mace, he gave my father a prodigious wink.

That incident was less memorable than my discovery of French-fried potatoes. I had no idea what they were until Beth, my Uncle Jack's teenaged daughter, asked her mother, my Aunt Maude, to make them for us as a special treat. I never forgot that first batch any more than I forgot that first sweet sip of Coca-Cola. It seems trivial in retrospect, for great events were taking place at this time. The Bennett Government was in trouble. Unemployed men stood at the street corners selling pencils and shoelaces. Others were knocking on our door on Huntley Street, asking for handouts. My favourite uncle, Phil Thompson (who was at the time retyping my mother's novel), couldn't find work. But all this social ferment formed no more that a vague background to my days in Ontario. In the foreground were soda pop, French fries, and one-cent candy. My allowance then was ten cents a week, a generous sum that allowed me a stick of bubble gum, a licorice whip, a chocolate-marshmallow broom, a small root beer sucker, a set of peppermint paraffin teeth, and a toffee apple.

In Ottawa I was surrounded by cousins, all of whom seemed to be obsessed by the idea of pedigree, as indeed my father was. He was the proud possessor of the family Bible, a huge tome bought in London in the middle years of the eighteenth century by my ancestor Captain Peter Berton. I already knew that this Peter Berton was a grandson of Pierre Berthon de Marigny, a Huguenot from Poitou in France, who had fled to America by way of England and changed *his* name to Peter Berton immediately on his arrival in Rhode Island. I knew it because my father, in a romantic moment, had named me after him: Pierre Francis de Marigny Berton. The name haunted me at school, where I was the butt of many jokes. The time would come when "Pierre" would become acceptable, even popular, thanks to another Well-Known Personality. But in the Yukon, Pierre was a foreign name and "de Marigny" sounded too much like "dumbbell." Dumbbell Berton, the kids called me. *Why,* I asked myself, *would my father do that to me?* In later years I dropped both middle names and quickly discovered that "Pierre Berton" was a by-line that people tended to remember. Only then was I grateful to my father.

He was immensely proud of his lineage: Huguenot, and then United Empire Loyalist, thanks to Captain Peter Berton and the shipload of Tories he brought to Oak Point, in what is now New Brunswick, in 1783. As we crossed Canada and stopped at various towns, my father would rush to the nearest phone directory to see if any Bertons were listed. If there were, he would call them to find if they were related to us. They always seemed to be, or so my father believed.

2 I grew to know my mother's family more intimately. Her famous father, Phillips Thompson, whom she called "Pa," lived in Oakville with his second wife, Edith. We visited them regularly. I remember him as a very old

man with a fierce hawk's nose, a mane of white hair and beard to match, and those dark brown Thompson eyes, which my mother and I and five of my own children inherited. Those eyes were misted with cataracts by this time — he was eighty-eight years old — but he still worked away, dictating items to his youngest daughter, Maude (my other Aunt Maude), as he sat erect at his old rolltop desk. Later, in the sitting room after dinner, he would roar out work songs, such as "Drill Ye Tarriers, Drill," and radical songs — "The Red Flag" and others such as "One More Battle to Fight" and "Thirty Cents a Day," which he had written himself and published in the *Labour Reform Songster*.

This was the man whom the newspapers had begun to call the Grand Old Man of Journalism. They had not been so kind to him in his younger days when he had fought for so many lost causes. He had run for office on various socialist tickets and had always been beaten. He had championed a variety of reforms then considered radical but now taken for granted: women's suffrage, for instance, and the idea of Sunday streetcars. It's hard to realize that there was a time when the streetcars didn't run on the Lord's Day and anyone who advocated a change was considered a heretic. But my grandfather was ever a heretic. He'd been sent by the *Globe* to cover the Irish disturbances in the days of Parnell and returned a different man, changed forever by the plight of the Irish tenant farmers. In Toronto, he'd been writing a popular humour column, poking fun at the down-and-outs that crowded the police courts; he bitterly regretted that and never again made fun of the unfortunate.

At first he was lionized for his dispatches. Everybody wanted to hear him speak. But when it was revealed that he had become a radical and a socialist, he was reviled, attacked, and hounded. For the rest of his life he fought the good fight until the time came when he was suffered, tolerated — even indulged — and at last, when I knew him, had gained the country's respect.

Two stories about my grandfather illuminate his character.

In the early nineties, when, as usual, he was penniless, he sold the family home on Indian Road for a tidy sum. He did not bank it or invest it in stocks. Instead he took the entire sum and went off to England with his wife and three daughters. It was, my mother said, the most important and the most glorious period of her life — money well spent, for it introduced her to another world. She talked of it many times; it was clearly a milestone in her young life. It was the reason, I think, why she was emboldened to seize the chance when she was offered a teaching position in the Yukon. And it was also one of the reasons, I'm sure, why she wanted Lucy and me to have a similar experience on the Outside.

The other story is equally romantic. My grandfather's first wife died after the family's return, which meant that her unmarried sister, Edith, who had always helped keep house, could not remain under the same roof with a man now single; these were, after all, Victorian times. Off Edith went to work for another family in another town until, two years later, my grandfather received an urgent telegram: I CANNOT STAND IT ANY LONGER. PLEASE COME FOR ME, EDITH. He went at once and married her. I called her grand-mamma, though she was really my great-aunt — a warm, motherly woman, affectionate and indulgent to her grand-children and her husband. When she was taken to Charlie Chaplin's great motion picture comedy, *The Gold Rush,* she cried bitterly, believing it to be a tragedy. "Oh, the poor man! The poor man!" she kept saying as Chaplin teetered in his cabin on the cliff's edge or gnawed at his boots.

My mother's younger sister, Maude, lived with her parents at Oakville. She was a plump, rosy-cheeked woman, highly religious and more than a little eccentric. My Uncle Phil, her younger half-brother, told me with huge delight of a remark she had made when a picture of my

61

sister, holding a very large grayling, appeared in the Toronto *Mail and Empire*. "Teaching the child to torture animals!" Aunt Maude had cried out in a rage. On one occasion when she was taken ill, a neighbour, in a mistaken act of kindness, sent over a jar of calf's foot jelly. That also infuriated my Aunt Maude, who promptly sent the gift back, declaring that she was not an object of charity. But I liked her very much. She was fond of children and she loved the movies — the same ones I liked — and often took me on our visits to Oakville to see such thrillers as *Dirigible,* starring Jack Holt and Ralph Graves.

My Aunt Florrie, the eldest of the three sisters, whose house on Huntley Street we had rented for the winter, was even more eccentric than Maude. She was terrified of all dogs, from the tiniest dachshund to the largest Saint Bernard. She hated the idea of the radio, which she believed was about to destroy Western civilization, and she covered almost everything she ate (it seemed to me) with vast quantities of black pepper. I watched her blacken a plate of fresh peas in this manner during one of her visits and resolved to copy her. To my surprise, the result was tangy but palatable. Ever since I have thought of Aunt Florrie as I pepper my peas.

In spite of their fondness for one another, Florrie and my mother argued incessantly over any subject that came up. No matter which side Florrie took, my mother would take the other, and vice versa. I think it was on purpose, especially on Florrie's part. She liked to rile people, though I have no doubt her views were honestly held and often intelligent, if radical. My father kept out of it, merely inserting the odd mild comment, but my mother in her spirited way couldn't resist arguing with Florrie, in spite of the fact that she was something of a closet radical herself. My father's loyalty to the eternal verities amused her. When the national anthem was played he went rigid. Whenever a member of the military appeared he was instantly alert, especially if the officer was above field rank. "Watch your father," she said to me in an affectionate whisper one day when a khaki-clad general boarded a streetcar. And, sure enough, there was my father, eyes aglitter, leaning forward almost in an act of supplication.

The war had affected him as it had all veterans, not because it was such an appalling disaster, but because he believed that it had been a crusade, a war to end all wars. It was largely at his insistence that a monument to the dead was raised at Minto Park in Dawson. My mother took it all with a grain of salt, but she never ventured an opinion different from his. And so when Aunt Florrie railed against war, politicians, the military, the awful radio programs, the evil dogs that were allowed to roam free and attack defence-less women, my mother closed ranks and took my father's position, while my father, too much of a gentleman to attack a lady or an in-law, kept his silence.

There was also Aunt Sarah, who wasn't a real aunt but whom I liked very much because she always brought us candy. This, it developed, was in the nature of a bribe, for Aunt Sarah had written a poem in blank verse about the King, which she wished me to memorize and recite aloud to a large group of aunts, uncles, and cousins. I thought the poem quite dreadful but, plied with red wintergreen candies, readily agreed. The first four lines have stayed with me all these years:

The King! Honour the King!
The King is sacred to the nation's life
Not by pomp of power officially displayed
But by a higher power, God-given. . . .

Everybody applauded both Aunt Sarah and me, and since the candies kept coming, I didn't mind too much. Actually, I was beginning to test, a little gingerly, the chill waters of show business. At Rosedale School I came second in a public-speaking contest, again spurred on by both teachers and parents. I cannot say I disliked it. Each contestant was given a picture and five minutes to make up a story about it. My speech provoked some laughter and applause, and it may well be that I then first experienced the tiny tremor an actor feels when his efforts are rewarded. I was not yet hooked, but the hook was out and baited.

Something else was happening to me. I was reading the newspapers. My family took the *Mail and Empire,* but my Uncle Phil, who had worked on several papers, introduced me to the *Star* and the *Telegram.* Phil was in his early thirties and a great favourite with me and Lucy. He had an advanced sense of the ridiculous (Aunt Sarah's poem had reduced him to paroxysms of mirth) and a way with boys. He was his father's son — well read, sensitive, witty. He had an uncanny memory for dates and places — I never saw him stumped — and he was also a good cartoonist who inspired me to draw. He was my mother's favourite sibling, more like a son than a younger brother. She worried about him, for in those depression days he found it impossible to get work. It was Phil's strength as a human being and his tragedy as a professional journalist that he could never sell himself unashamedly to a prospective employer.

Of the two papers my uncle bought, I preferred the *Telegram* because it contained the Mickey Mouse adventure strip, starring those two villains, Peg Leg Pete and Sylvester Shyster. The papers, especially the *Star Weekly,* were full of wild tales about dinosaurs, bizarre murders, and the antics of Hollywood stars, as well as a good deal of humour including the weekly escapades of Gregory Clark and Jimmy Frise. I devoured them all.

In the classroom, half-listening to the history teacher, I found myself actually drawing up mock front pages, filling in headlines, and scribbling news stories about my classmates. In my spare time, I began to draw crude cartoons, copying the real ones from the comic pages. I found I could easily counterfeit some of the better-known comic figures, a talent that astonished and pleased my father. "Draw

Jiggs," he would say to me in front of a group. "Look at that," he'd say. "Isn't that talent? Now draw Maggie, boy." And everyone would oh and ah, more in deference to my father than in admiration of my crude artwork. Nonetheless, applause is an insidious virus, and it was beginning to work on me.

The very novelty of the Outside experience prevented me from suffering the loneliness of the stranger in town. For, though I had acquaintances at school, I had no close friends. I saw these boys at recess and in the classroom but rarely after hours. I once invited an acquaintance to come to my home after school and can still remember tidying up my room and then waiting expectantly for him to arrive. He never did. I was a foreigner who turned up periodically for class, never an intimate. Part of it was my own fault, for I was shy and small for my age — a skinny kid with a mop of red hair, unsure of myself in the big city, a fish out of water.

Lucy too had few friends. She was no longer my kid sister, tagging along behind me because my parents insisted that I look after her and include her in my circle of friends. There was no circle of friends, and so she became my best and only friend and constant companion, not out of duty but out of real need. We depended on each other, hiking off to school hand in hand and facing the terrifying traffic on Bloor Street together. Our parents bought us roller skates as part of our new education, and we spent almost every afternoon and most Saturday mornings skating together up and down Jarvis Street, once the classiest boulevard in Toronto. It still retained the old sandstone sidewalks, which were so much smoother and easier to skate on than concrete. No doubt this was considered very high class before the ladies of the night appropriated it as their own. When the snow fell, my parents also gave us ice skates and we skated together in the Lacrosse Park — or, I should say, stumbled about on the ice. It sounds odd — two kids from the frozen

North who had to learn to skate on the Outside. But there wasn't a smooth pond or stream in all of the Klondike; the rivers were a tangle of ice blocks; and the rink at Dawson had long since burned down. I never learned to skate properly and though I went to the YMCA regularly didn't learn to swim. I had been taught to fear the water, and I still feared it, even in the Y pool. I was especially afraid to tumble in head first and dreaded the instructors who tried to train me. To this day, I can't dive.

In Dawson on Hallowe'en, we'd gone from door to door with a gang all in costume. But there was no gang in Toronto — at least not for me. Lucy and I walked up and down Yonge Street with our parents, watching the crowds. That was all. I don't recall that I was in any way upset by this or in any way elated, either. It was a kind of ritual, nothing more.

Then, in December, we were both cut off from everyone by an attack of red measles. It was not unexpected. In Dawson there were almost no communicable diseases: no one in my day contracted measles, chicken pox, scarlet fever, mumps, or whooping cough. When I was very young I heard of one boy who died of diphtheria, but that disease never struck again. It was as if the germs could not travel over the mountains. Perhaps it had something to do with the climate. Mostly, I think, it was because we lived in something akin to an isolation ward.

The main diseases in the Yukon were pneumonia, influenza, and the common cold, all of which I survived. Alas, my mixed-blood friends from St. Paul's Hostel had no defences against influenza. When I was suffering from red measles in Toronto, my close friend Fred Watt was one of several struck down by flu in Dawson. We had built a raft together on the little slough that ran behind the hostel, poling our way through the muddy waters during the last hot days of summer. But by the time I returned to Dawson, Fred Watt and several of my other hostel friends were dead.

In those days before vaccination, people took measles seriously. A bold red placard was hammered onto our front door, announcing that the place was quarantined. We were held captive for more than a fortnight in a darkened room, unable even to read, our eyes smarting with the disease, our bodies prickly. In later years on the Outside all the other maladies were visited upon us. As late as 1958, on the very day I joined the Toronto *Star,* hailed as their newest columnist, I came down with an attack of double mumps. The paper carried my photograph with my neck distended, making me look like an escapee from a freak show. By then, fortunately, quarantine signs were artifacts of the past, and I was able to sneak into the office with my copy and no one was the wiser.

My father's leave was up in the spring. That meant we would have to take off in May before the school year ended. It didn't really matter. I had stood second in my class, and the principal was glad to give me a pass into Grade 8 in the Yukon. There was one last excursion — the greatest of all. My father took Lucy and me to Sunnyside Amusement Park and allowed us to ride on every ride: Roller Coaster, Carousel, Dodgem, Whip — everything. There was only one disappointment: nobody had offered to publish my mother's novel. She had seen several publishers, received a courteous reception, and been given a certain amount of polite encouragement but no offers. She bore her disappointment with stoicism. It was, for her, a temporary setback, no more. She was sure that with a little more work it would be accepted.

And so we said goodbye to friends and relatives and boarded the train to the West — the CNR, this time, for my father wanted us to see as much of the country as possible. The train had a fully equipped radio car. We sat on easy chairs with earphones on our heads while an operator at the end of the car fiddled with the dials. There was no music, only talk. I found it boring.

My sister and I wandered back to the Pullman. Above us, we noticed a long white cord that seemed to run the entire length of the train. To relieve the tedium, we swung on it. Almost at once the train lurched to a stop. Officials ran through the car and jumped down onto the tracks. Everybody then got off, milled about, and finally got on again, as the train once more got under way. It was all very strange; my sister and I couldn't make head nor tail of it. Nobody seemed to know what had happened and we, not knowing either, said nothing. We did not, however, tell anybody that we had been swinging on the white cord. Subconsciously, I think, we must have sensed a certain cause and effect. But it was years before I understood exactly what an emergency cord was for.

My father left us in Vancouver and headed north to the mining recorder's office in Dawson. He wanted to take me with him, for he had arranged for the *Bluenose* to be brought up to Whitehorse and had intended that the two of us would make the trip home by river. My mother, ever protective, vetoed the idea, a decision I went along with, for I was more excited by the metropolitan charms of Vancouver than the lonely river. But it was a choice I have since greatly regretted.

In Vancouver I had a chance to play on a real beach by a real ocean. I knew all about beaches, or thought I did, from the comic strips and the Outside magazines, but I was unprepared for the crowds that jammed the sands of English Bay. The pictures in the magazines had shown miles of empty strands framed by blue water, with a solitary couple strolling hand in hand in the middle distance. English Bay was an ants' nest. So many people lay sprawled on the beach that you could scarcely see the water, and when you got to the water there were so many people frolicking and splashing you could hardly find a place to paddle. In short, it was not the beach of my dreams.

But at night there were singsongs on the beach, sponsored by the *Vancouver Sun*, and crowds of youngsters of my own age. And so we ran about, larking and wrestling and singing "Let Me Call You Sweetheart" as twilight fell. A sturdy girl of ten bore me to the sand and pummelled me, a form, no doubt, of pre-pubescent foreplay. "Has your old man got a job?" she asked me between pummels. I assured her that he had, whereupon she pummeled me once more and said she didn't believe me. I think this was probably the first time I really became aware of the Depression — this fevered inquisition about a job. I couldn't understand it. Of *course* my father had a job! There might be hard times in the Outside, but in that secure enclave at the juncture of the Klondike and the Yukon there had never been a hint of unemployment.

I was wrong. The free-spending days we had enjoyed for so long and which had reached their climax on this expensive journey to the Outside were over for our family forever.

From the moment of our arrival at Dawson a fortnight or so later, we knew something was wrong. We could see the familiar crowded wharf, with half the population of Dawson on hand as usual to greet the incoming boat. I was aflame with excitement, nostalgic for Dawson, eager to greet my friends and boast about my adventures on the Outside. But as we stepped off the gang-plank, my father came out of the crowd, his face unusually grave, and took my mother aside. There were whispers, exclamations, long faces. What had happened?

When we reached our little house under the hill, we children were given the news. My father had been "superannuated." The phrase today is "early retirement."

My father didn't want to retire — couldn't afford to, really. His pension would come to less than fifty dollars a month, and although money had much more value then than it does today, that sum was scarcely enough with which to raise and educate a growing family. But the worst feature of the tragedy was the fact that though the government had known it must cut staff for some time, no one had thought to warn my father before he set off on an expensive vacation in eastern Canada. That had taken most of his savings.

The blow hit him with sledgehammer force. It had never occurred to him that his job would someday come to an end. I can remember my mother saying to him more than once, "What if you're fired, Frank? What would you do?" My father had always answered bluntly, "Well, I *won't* be fired. No chance of it."

But now he — a war veteran, "a returned man," to use the current phrase — was cut off from his job as mining recorder while his colleague, Phil Kelly, who had never borne arms in defence of his country, was to be retained. It was enough to shake his faith in the system. He was fifty-nine, with no prospects. He had no insurance, little cash. He had always been the kind of man who lived for the day, spending on impulse. His salary was modest enough — I think he made about three thousand a year with a cost-of-living bonus of perhaps five hundred — but it had been enough. Our wants in Dawson were simple. We had no car, no labour-saving devices except a sewing machine, no really expensive tastes. My parents rarely drank; entertaining was cheap. But the trip Outside had been costly.

We couldn't afford to stay in the Yukon on his pension, that much was obvious. Nor would it have been a good idea. The Yukon was a wonderful place in which to bring up small children, but it was no place for a boy growing into puberty. The educational facilities were limited; so were the jobs. Those of my classmates who remained in the North had little choice: most went to work for the mining company, on one of the big dredges. That was the limit of their ambitions.

Thus my father's superannuation came, for me, at exactly the right moment. The Yukon had been stimulating, but now, with a taste of the Outside, I was ready for a different and more sophisticated environment. The decision to pack up and leave did not affect me as it did my parents. For one thing, I had become used to leave-takings. My mother once said that living in Dawson was like being a passenger on a ship in which people were continually getting on and getting off. My closest friends were all gone. On a cold Easter Sunday the year before I had said goodbye to Alex McCarter. He and I had played together and exchanged confidences since early childhood. After I had watched him and his family board the Lockheed monoplane and fly off down the Yukon Valley I had felt a sense of emptiness and letdown. But now I was going to join him Outside, if not in the same town at least in the same milieu — the Outside where, alas, so many of the others I'd grown up with were also resettled. Strange new boys had arrived in Dawson during my absence. I felt no kinship with them. And so I faced the prospect of departure with mixed feelings: with sadness because I did not expect to see my home town again, but also with excitement because I knew that unknown adventures and strange encounters lay ahead. For me it was a turning point; for my parents it was shattering.

My father felt betrayed. He had spent thirty-four years in the North and loved every minute of it — the long walks in the hills looking for wildflowers, the endless summer evenings on the boat, the picnics on the islands, the fishing and hunting expeditions, the bridge parties, dinners, and entertainments that made up the close-knit social life, which was for everybody a kind of security blanket. Once he, too, had set off on a grand adventure into the Unknown, but that was long behind him. He had crossed his Chilkoot. I had yet to cross mine.

We were forced to sell or give away almost everything because of the astronomical freight charges. I kept a few books, nothing else. My mother kept her piano, two easy chairs, a Persian carpet, and two rugs made of wolf and bear skins. The house that had cost, I believe, around $700 in 1921 sold for the same price in 1932. It was very hard, I know, for my father to part with the *Bluenose*. The river had been his life, the boat his main indulgence. Now he was forced to sell that, too.

How blunt and brutal it all seems now, this sudden, frantic exit! Yet it was essential that we wind up our affairs before we were trapped in Dawson by the winter. If we were to move, we must get away before the school year began Outside. We were rather like prisoners who see a momentary opening in the iron gates and seek to dash through before they clang shut. And so, in late August, having celebrated our last Discovery Day, we took the steamboat upriver and retraced our route back down the coast to Vancouver.

We suffered one final blow the day before leaving Dawson, when Lucy complained of feeling poorly and was rushed at the last moment to the doctor. To my parents' dismay, they were taken aside and told that Lucy had a very weak heart. She would, the doctor said, be an invalid for the rest of her shortened life span and would never be able to lead an active existence.

They were devastated. On top of everything — this! On that last morning all we could think of was Lucy, pale and gaunt, probably in a wheelchair, living on gruel, raising one hand weakly to her brow like a sad Victorian heroine.

Lucy herself seemed totally unconscious of the tragedy that faced her. She raced up and down the deck of the *Casca* with me as if she didn't have a care in the world. She and I played the gramophone, scrambled up the gangways, leaped off the gangplank when the boat tied up to take on wood. I found it difficult to believe her heart was feeble; but the doctor had said so, and who were we to argue with the doctor?

In fact the doctor was wrong. All that Lucy had was the flu, and from that she recovered in twenty-four hours. As the days went by it became clearer and clearer that she was a perfectly normal eleven-year-old, full of so much bounce and energy that it became impossible to think of her as an invalid. I don't recall that my parents bothered to take her to a doctor again; no doubt they'd lost faith in the medical profession. At any rate, except for the mumps and the chicken pox, she has never had a sick day in her life. But this was in the future. As we made our way down the Alaska panhandle on the *Princess Louise*, Lucy's apparent affliction was never far from our minds. Our final destination was Victoria, the city where so many retired people go because the climate is warmer and life cheaper. We took the CPR boat across the strait from Vancouver, and then tragedy struck again — this time for me.

I was by this time feeling very much alone. For almost a year I hadn't had a close male friend. And now Lucy's days seemed numbered. In Vancouver I'd said goodbye, probably for years, to Alex McCarter. I had very little left to remind me of my home. Even my dog, Spark, had to be left behind. I had no one save for a small pet, a little turtle I'd acquired for fifteen cents in a Chinese shop in Vancouver. I called him Terry and on him I lavished all the love and affection of which I was capable. It was a strange alliance, a lonely twelve-year-old and a tiny reptile, and it didn't last.

I sat on the deck in the sunlight, playing with my friend. He was remarkably sprightly for a turtle. He crawled over my legs and shoes and out onto the deck, striking forward gamely on his own, warmed by the sun. And at that moment a strange woman came along, calling to a friend, stepped on him, plunging one of her high heels through his shell, and moved on, heedless of what she'd done. Terry died instantly.

I was inconsolable. The death of a favourite pet is a searing experience that most children suffer at one time or another. But it was more than that for me; it came at the climax of a roller-coaster year, a year of incredible highs and lows. I was faced not just with the finality of the life we'd

73

been leading but also with the finality of death. I couldn't stop sobbing. My father gently picked up my turtle's corpse, dropped it over the side, and sensibly left me alone.

In Victoria we booked into a cheap boarding house near Beacon Hill Park. The paint peeled from the walls; the rooms smelled of cooking gas. At dinner that night I still couldn't control my despair.

"She didn't even stop!" I said through my tears. "She just kept on going as if nothing had happened."

"Don't cry," said my mother. "We'll get you another . . ."

She was about to say, "We'll get you another turtle," but my father held up his hand to stop her in mid-sentence.

"That isn't the answer," he said, as I left the table to go to my room and sob the night away.

3 For the next seven years, from 1932 to 1939 — the years of the Great Depression — Victoria would be our home. My father sold all of his and my mother's nugget jewellery and went house hunting. For three thousand dollars he bought a two-storey frame dwelling on a double lot in the municipality of Oak Bay, a genteel, middle-class neighbourhood of quiet, tree-lined streets and stucco houses, squeezed between the ocean and the city.

I look back on my years in Victoria with great nostalgia. And yet as the years rolled on, I longed to get out. Vancouver in those days was the mecca. To a teenager, Victoria was a backwater, a dead town of titled Englishmen and former army officers who wore pith helmets and khaki shorts in the summer, of majestic Englishwomen in Victorian hats and voluminous dresses, of private-school youths in flannel blazers and little peaked caps. After the Yukon, Victoria was exciting enough, but by the end of the decade the excitement had faded and I felt, once again, that I was a captive in an enclave. We couldn't afford a cent for travel. Five years went by before I even saw Vancouver again.

My mother's greatest wish was that I attend a private school, such as Glenlyon or St. Michael's, whose neatly scrubbed residents seemed to me like strangers from a foreign land. My greatest satisfaction was that she couldn't afford to send me. I was as snobbish about the private school boys as I thought they were about me. I took my Grade 8 classes at Monterey Public School and then spent four more years at Oak Bay High, and I wasn't crazy about those schools, either. Fifty years later I was asked back, a Well-Known Personality, to address the graduating class of Oak Bay High. "Well," I told them, "this may not have been the worst high school in Canada when I went here, but I certainly *thought* it was the worst." The students cheered.

The problem was that I didn't play sports, and if you didn't play sports you were a nobody. There was nothing else to do after classes: no student council then; no plays or entertainments; no clubs; no official newspaper or school annual — nothing. My marks fell. I, who had been close to the top of my class in Dawson and Toronto, now dropped to sixteenth and lower. It wasn't that school was difficult; it was just boring. I lazed through without effort or enthusiasm.

My one great excitement at Monterey came when a small paper was started by two fellow Grade Eighters. It was printed on a hectograph press, the type faded and purplish, but I thought it was wonderful. It is hard to explain the thrill that went through me when I held that first edition in my hand, especially as I had had nothing to do with its publication. There was something magical about it, like my first ride on the roller coaster. I desperately wanted to be part of it and made some tentative moves toward that end, only to find the others wouldn't have me. I couldn't even afford to buy a copy because it cost a nickel, and the hard times had reduced my allowance to a cent a week. Somehow I scraped enough together to buy one issue, which I pored over until it grew ragged. My parents were baffled by this sudden obsession.

The Depression left its mark on everyone who lived through it, myself included. Nothing brought the times home to me more forcefully than my inability to spend a nickel on the school paper. To this day, like so many others who lived through the thirties, I engage in a curious kind of double-think when it comes to money. I am both a profligate and a skinflint, foolishly and recklessly indulging myself at one moment, hoarding carefully for the future at another.

The Depression made me this way, even though we children did not feel the hardships that others endured. It's true we couldn't buy much cent candy or go to the movies, and yet in Dawson we had rarely bought any candy — we hadn't been allowed it — while the movies were few and far between. It's true we didn't have a car or a radio in Victoria, but in Dawson we hadn't had them either. We couldn't travel or take expensive holidays, but we ate well enough, although never as well as we'd eaten in the Yukon, where game was available in the butcher stores and restaurants. I was used to moose, caribou, grouse, ptarmigan, and wild duck, which I thought of as plebeian dishes. Roast beef had been a luxury in the North, like chicken, which in that pre-Colonel Sanders era was another expensive treat. In Victoria we ate a lot of salmon, which *wasn't* a luxury item, and halibut. The word "pudding" has almost vanished from the language, for there are fashions in foods as well as in women's hats. In those days we ate suet pudding, cabinet pudding, rice pudding, bread pudding, tapioca pudding, blancmange, and junket — items that were cheap and filling and are now long out of the cuisine. We got bones from the butcher for a nonexistent dog and made soup out of them; everybody did that, and the butchers weren't fooled. We picked up our firewood from logs that had drifted onto the shore at Shoal Bay, and we gathered kelp from the same beaches to fertilize the garden that provided us with fresh vegetables.

A dollar was a lot of money then. A boy at school once

told me he'd spent two dollars the previous evening. I didn't believe him. How could he, when hamburgers were a dime and milk shakes — three and a half glasses — another dime? The movies were also a dime and sometimes even a nickel for kids; a triple-dip ice cream cone was a nickel; the most expensive dinner in town was sixty-five cents. How *could* you spend two dollars?

In those days I did much of the shopping for the family at the local Piggly Wiggly self-serve store. One day I was faced with a monumental decision when, at closing time on Saturday, I was offered a crate of overripe strawberries.

"Give you the whole crate for two bits, kid," the man at the cash counter offered.

I stood there in an agony of indecision; two bits was a lot of money, and it wasn't my money. Should I seize the bargain or play it safe? I took the offer, worried all the way home, and was relieved when my parents congratulated me on my foresight. It became a bit of a family legend, something we talked about for a long time afterward.

I have already written of the time my mother and I on the way to a movie found eighteen cents on the sidewalk. It seems such an inconsequential incident today; why should it bear repeating? Yet it was something my mother and I talked about for years afterward, that stunning moment of jubilation when we discovered the treasure, glittering on the concrete. The fact that we were on the way to a movie — an event that occurred about once in two months — added to the miracle. To my mother the money represented a pound and a quarter of stewing beef, or a loaf of stale bread plus two quarts of Jersey milk. And so in later years we basked in the warmth of that particular memory. "Remember when we found the eighteen cents on the sidewalk?" my mother used to say to me in her old age. "Oh dear, oh dear, oh dear; wasn't that a moment?"

I remember and cherish another scene from the early thirties. One afternoon my father came home, all agog over an amazing invention he'd spotted in the window of the Carmelcrisp Shop on Fort Street. What he described was a Silex coffee maker, something brand new to all of us. In the Yukon coffee had always been made in a granite pot bubbling on the top of a wood stove.

He had stood for some time, staring into the window, watching the coffee being sucked up and figuring out the scientific principle involved. He couldn't stop talking about the ingenuity of it and also the beauty — the bubbles reflecting the red glow of the heating elements as they rose to the surface. I suppose that everybody else, even then, took the Silex for granted, as we all do now, but to my father it was close to a miracle, and the following Saturday he took me downtown to witness the miracle for myself.

I can see us now, the small boy, the older man, standing outside in the cold, waiting for a fresh pot to be set on the element so my father could explain how the system worked. Suddenly he turned to me. "You know, I think it's worth just going inside for a bit to buy a cup of coffee and watch that thing in action," he said. And he added, "No need to tell your mother," for coffee cost a nickel and she would certainly consider that a dreadful extravagance.

And so we went inside, and my father paid his nickel and slowly sipped his coffee while the two of us watched, fascinated, as the red bubbles rose in the Silex. A cup of coffee costs a dollar these days, and sometimes three dollars in a tony restaurant, but as I gulp away at mine today I recall that scene, the older man savouring his coffee and explaining to a twelve-year-old, very seriously, the principle of the vacuum. It is one of my tenderest memories of the Depression.

My father, of course, had a great deal of time for me, much more than other boys' fathers, who were absent for most of the day at work. In the summer after our arrival in Victoria he took me on a two-week camping trip around the southern tip of the island. In those days you could camp anywhere: there were no subdivisions, no motels, few roadside stands. We simply took the streetcar to the end of the line and hiked off toward the wilderness.

We carried our food, blankets, and groundsheets on our backs, I with a small haversack, my father with a large one, using a tumpline, Indian fashion. We had no tent. When it rained my father built a bivouac, a lean-to of evergreens, and he taught me how to use boughs to make a spring mattress. By day he explained the geology of the country and named for me the trees and shrubs through which we trudged — hemlock, arbutus, salal, Oregon grape. By night he pointed out the stars and the constellations: the Pleiades, Andromeda, Orion's Belt. He did most of the talking; I listened. I wish now I'd striven to learn more about him, but I was diffident about talking to him on a personal level, shy of too intimate a contact. There was, after all, an age gap of half a century dividing us. I couldn't pour out my heart to him as I might to a close friend of my own generation. And even with close friends I was shy. My father, for his part, was too sensible to try to be a "pal" to me. He didn't want to be a pal; he wanted to be a father, and he was a good one.

Most of the time we were alone, following the tracks of the Esquimalt and Nanaimo Railway. But occasionally we met people. My main memory of those times is how kind these strangers were. One man, who worked for the big lumber mill, insisted that we should have something to read at nights and loaded us down with used magazines. There we lay in a tangle of bracken under a canopy of red cedars, devouring *Master Detective* ("Tracking Idaho's Mad Rapist"), *Modern Screen* ("Richard Arlen Confesses: 'I Was a Chump; Can I Come Back?'"), and *True Confessions* ("My Husband Made Me His Love Creature").

Once we camped near a strawberry farm. The season was almost over, and the farmer, who gave us permission to lay out our groundsheets on his property, invited us to pick all the fruit we could eat without charge. Strawberries were a novelty to us both. They were, of course, unknown in the Yukon save for the tiny wild variety. My father hadn't had many domestic strawberries. He talked about them with longing; to him they were the finest fruit ever grown. "You can't ruin strawberries," he used to say. "You can serve strawberries with anything; you can't hurt them." Now we could eat our fill, and we did.

Later, on the Island Highway, we stopped at a small, desolate café to ask for a glass of water. The place was run by a tired-looking, middle-aged widow and her daughter. It looked as though there hadn't been a customer in days. No matter; she took one look at me, skinny, mosquito-bitten, and unkempt, and insisted we sit down to a free meal of scrambled eggs with bacon. I can still taste them, hot and fluffy with crisp toast. "The boy needs fattening up," she told my father. These women were clearly having trouble making ends meet, but they refused to take anything for the meal, a piece of generosity that my father accepted with some relief, for I don't think he had any money left. I often wonder how long that restaurant stayed in business and what happened to that motherly woman and her daughter.

This trip was an even brighter interlude for my father than for me. For him, time hung heavy. He did not want or care for a life of leisure. He worked incessantly on our property, building rock gardens and ponds, putting up trellises and gates, planting trees, raising vegetables, growing flower borders. He joined the Royal Astronomical Society, mastered the new Culbertson system of contract bridge, which was rapidly replacing auction bridge, and tried without much success to find work. One Christmas he got a job as an assistant postman. For a time he advertised himself in the Classified section of the *Colonist* as an instructor in mechanical drawing. He actually got a couple of students but at a very inconvenient time, for it cut into our one holiday in a rented cottage at Shawnigan Lake. My father was forced to leave us in order to return to town to continue the lessons.

My mother worked miracles with a small budget, riding herd on all of us where money was concerned. I remember my father's efforts to build a hot air balloon out of tissue paper in our basement. One day he called me down secretly to see the results. "Had to buy a bit more paper for these last segments," he told me, "but I wouldn't bother to let your mother know about that." He never did fly the balloon. He was far more interested in the process than he was in the results.

My mother experienced one moment of madness that contrasted with her general parsimony. She had gone with me to an auction sale to pick up a few bargains, and to this day I don't know what got into her. She started to bid on everything and simply couldn't stop — it was as if she were infected by some kind of mysterious drug. Clocks, gramophones, bits of bric-à-brac, furniture, crazy quilts all fell to her with the rap of the auctioneer's gavel. She ended up stunned, with a mountain of merchandise she could ill afford.

"What got into me?" she kept asking on the way home. "What's your father going to say?"

My father said very little.

"We simply won't pay for it," he said. "They can whistle for their money."

My mother looked dubious. "It's a contract," she said. "I don't think we can get out of it."

My father marched down to the auctioneer's with me in tow. "My wife was carried away," he told the auctioneer. "We don't want this stuff. She didn't intend to buy it; I don't intend to pay for it."

The auctioneer said that was too bad; all bids were final. It was a legal obligation; we'd have to take it all.

"Nonsense," said my father, "we're taking nothing." And that's the way it was.

Well, almost. On Christmas morning, not long after this incident, Lucy and I were awakened to the sound of music:

somebody or something was playing "Adeste Fideles." We rushed downstairs to find my parents winding up the very gramophone my mother had bid on. Somehow they had retrieved this one item from the auctioneers. It came with a small pile of records, and for the next year, until we finally got a radio, we played that wonderful machine: "Three O'Clock in the Morning," John McCormack singing "When Irish Eyes Are Smiling," "Just A Wearyin' For You" — the songs of an earlier era preserved on bakelite.

We were not used to extravagant gifts during those times. I remember a boy at school asking me what I got from my parents one Christmas. I told him: *Popular Science*. "A subscription?" he asked. "No," I said, astonished, "just the one copy."

But when, with a nudge from my father, I decided I was going to be a research chemist, I began to get test tubes, an Erlenmeyer flask, a porcelain crucible, and a variety of acids and chemicals for the small laboratory I was setting up in our basement. In this my parents encouraged me and supported me financially. My father felt there was no greater calling for me than a scientific career. My mother did not disagree, though she felt perhaps I might make a good lawyer.

As my laboratory grew, my father felt it necessary to issue one warning. "Never, no matter what you do, never make gun-cotton," he told me.

Of course, I immediately tried to make gun-cotton, which is simply cotton soaked in nitro-glycerin, an awesomely unstable explosive made from nitric acid and glycerine. I had a good supply of these ingredients but no real ability to carry the process through. Luckily for me, the experiment was a failure.

Another explosive was more successful, since it simply required the mixing together of equal parts of sulphur and potassium chlorate. Under sudden pressure, this powder produced an acceptable Bang. Placed on the streetcar tracks at the end of the Oak Bay line, it could — and did — cause consternation. Fortunately, I was never able to make enough to blow the car off the tracks.

I fear that it was the show-business aspect of chemistry and not serious research that attracted me. Having become proficient in building a dust explosion, causing various liquids to change colour, and creating an enormous mass of ash by pouring sulphuric acid on sugar, I set up a stage in our empty garage, drew up some posters, and advertised a chemistry show on Saturday afternoon at a nickel admission. The results were wholly satisfactory, I netted a little over a dollar and felt, for once, in my element — a true ham, a future Personality.

4 Thanks to my mother's careful budgeting we finally got a small Philco radio, and I got a second-hand CCM bicycle with a coaster brake. The bicycle took me all over Victoria, to Elk and Beaver Lakes, Mount Douglas Park, and even, on one occasion, as far north as Duncan. The radio gave me a different kind of freedom. It dominated all our lives as it dominated the lives of everyone in those lean years. I still recall with great warmth those lazy Sunday afternoons with the rain pattering on the windows, when we would spend our time grouped around the radio with our friends. We did not stop for supper. My mother would prepare a big plate of sandwiches, cinnamon toast, and tea as we listened to Stoopnagle and Budd, Joe Penner, Wendell Hall (the Red-Headed Music Maker), Eddie Cantor, and, of course, the great Jack Benny.

Our conversation was peppered with meaningless phrases from those radio days: ''Wanna buy a duck?'' . . . ''Vas you dere, Sharley?'' . . . ''You really *minn* it?'' . . . ''How *do* you do?'' They sound so inane, rendered into type, but there was a time, long ago, when those lines, usually delivered in a comic accent, reduced us all to giggles.

We followed every episode of "One Man's Family," and I can still remember the awful moment when Mother Barbour almost collapsed when she heard (wrongly, of course) that her unmarried son, Jack, had actually moved in with his girl friend. We rushed home from school at lunchtime to listen to "Pepper Young's Family," "Ma Perkins," and "Vic and Sade." We bought Coco-malt because of Buck Rogers, Ovaltine in honour of Little Orphan Annie, and Wheaties for Jack Armstrong, the All-American Boy.

The voices of our time were filtered through the loud-speaker of our Philco: the odd, precise tones of H.V. Kaltenborn explaining what Hitler was up to; Walter Winchell, screaming his exclusives for Jergen's Lotion; John Nesbitt suavely telling his extraordinary tales on "The Passing Parade." Early each Christmas morning the King's voice ebbed and flowed and sometimes vanished in the static. Periodically, the President of the United States addressed us as "My friends." I remember no Canadian voices; the Canadian Radio Broadcasting Commission was a feeble thing: our loyalty was to the Red and the Blue networks of NBC.

The older people decried radio. The press and the clergy agreed. They said it was the greatest menace to hit the country since bloomers. They said it would ruin the next generation by preventing them from thinking for themselves. They said it would end conversation and turn us into weaklings by seducing us to stay indoors. They said it would cheapen culture, make us insensitive to the finer things of life and so lazy we would never do our homework.

In spite of all these warnings, we all listened to the radio, and that included the doomsayers. I remember my mother remarking that Jack Benny was an awful fool, but I also remember that she never missed a program. The only person I knew who really *hated* the radio was Aunt Florrie, who had moved out to Victoria, opened an antique store, and lived in a basement not far from our house.

"Oh, turn that dreadful machine off," Aunt Florrie would cry, whereupon my mother would nod at me sternly and the magical sounds would be stilled. I liked my Aunt Florrie but hoped secretly that a large dog would bar her way to us on Sunday afternoons, an eventuality that happily occurred more than once. "I couldn't come," she'd tell my mother on the phone. "There was a beastly dog. The brute was about to devour me."

I don't really know what my Aunt Florrie lived on — the interest, perhaps, from the sale of her house in Toronto. I believe my parents must have helped a bit. She certainly didn't sell many antiques. She lived like a bird and, I suspect, only ate a decent meal when she visited us. Years later, when I was a writer for *Maclean's* in Toronto, I arrived in Victoria and took her out to dinner at the Empress on my expense account. I never saw any woman, especially a frail, white-haired old lady in her mid-eighties, eat so much. She went through the menu from oysters, soup, and salad to a fancy dessert. She devoured a mountain of lamb chops. I egged her on; it delighted me to see her with such zest for food.

I've often wondered about her early life. What had it been like for her on the Left Bank? Were there affairs of passion? Possibly. There was a whiff of adventure in her past: she had gone to Buffalo before the turn of the century to sell knick-knacks door to door. When my grandfather heard about that he was scandalized; young ladies in those days could be nurses, teachers, or telephone operators, little else. But the way she attacked that meal at the Empress hinted at hidden passions. Had they been requited? I had never thought much then about her past, any more than I had thought to ask my father about his bachelor days in the Klondike. Children are remarkably incurious about their parents and relatives until it is too late. Shortly after that memorable meal my aunt died, her secrets, if any, carried to the grave.

Soon after we arrived Outside I plunged into the pop culture that had been denied me in the Yukon. I was like a dehydrated desert traveller who suddenly encounters an oasis and laps thirstily at the beckoning pool. I could now follow all the daily comic strips, from "Boots and Her Buddies" to "Alley Oop," many of which I clipped out and pasted in scrapbooks. I knew all the lyrics of all the popular songs, especially those on "The Big Ten," as the earliest of the charted radio programs (which pre-dated "Your Hit Parade") was called. (There weren't nearly enough ballads in those days to allow a Top Fifty.)

When my parents relaxed a little and my allowance was raised, I was able to buy second-hand pulp magazines, which we teenagers traded with each other. There were scores of these, occupying the position that comic books and the cheaper paperbacks occupy today — science fiction magazines, Western magazines, railroad magazines, crime magazines, airplane magazines, war magazines. I devoured them all: *Bill Barnes, Air Adventurer; Terence X. O'Leary and his War Birds; Dr. Death; Wu Fang; Nick Carter; Black Mask Detective; Amazing, Astounding,* and *Wonder Stories; Weird Tales; Street and Smith's Western*; and dozens of others, all printed on paper so coarse it seemed to have been manufactured by wasps, hence the name "pulps."

My favourites, though, were *Doc Savage* (whose eyes were like deep pools of gold dust stirred by tiny winds) and, best of all, *The Shadow*. Arthur Davies, the smartest boy in my class, was a *Shadow* addict, and so was my other high school friend, Ronnie Hines. We were experts on *The Shadow* — the magazine and the radio program. To this day when I hear the name of Orson Welles, I don't think of the Mercury Theatre or *Citizen Kane*; I think of him in his earlier role as radio's Shadow. Hines, Davies, and I all belonged to the Shadow Club, wore Shadow pins, and waited eagerly for the newest fortnightly issue to appear. In a small black notebook I scribbled down the titles of all the *Shadow* magazines I'd read so I wouldn't accidentally read one twice. Before I got tired of *The Shadow*, I'd listed seventy-two titles. All the Shadow stories came from the pen of the Shadow's ghost writer, Maxwell Grant, who, we were told, had access to his private annals. It awed me to realize that this genius was actually turning out two novels, each eighty thousand words long, every month. How could I know that one day I would actually meet and interview my hero on television? His name, it turned out, was Walter Gibson, not Maxwell Grant. Besides being a fast writer, he'd also been an advance man and press agent for several of the greatest magicians, from Houdini to Thurston.

On Saturday evenings we all played Monopoly, the Parker Brothers game that hit with terrific force in the thirties. It was made for the Depression, providing hours of enjoyment for very little cost — in the case of our family at no cost at all. We couldn't afford to buy a game, but that was no problem. I simply copied a borrowed Monopoly board, drawing the symbols and printing the names of the streets in various-coloured India inks. I pasted the result on a stiff sheet of cardboard while my father at his workbench carved out and painted all the hotels and houses and typed up the "Chance" and "Community Chest" cards. We'd play for hours, Lucy and I and our parents and other kids from the neighbourhood, on a homemade game that lasted for more than six years before it wore out.

In school, when the teacher was preoccupied, I drew cartoons, covering my exercise books with drawings and scribblings. I had the vague idea that one day I might even become a cartoonist. I invented a character in the Disney style named Pete the Pup. Since I couldn't produce animated drawings I contented myself with sketching in small posters with my character's likeness: COMING TO YOUR LOCAL THEATRE SOON! THE AMAZING ANTICS OF PETE THE PUP! I created an actual strip, on ruled paper, set in the jungles of darkest Africa and entitled "The Scarlet Scarab." I had no idea what a scarab was, but the name sounded suitably ominous. The strip was peopled with stick figures with death's-head faces creeping about the jungle in burnooses.

I also haunted the Victoria Public Library, gobbling up every kind of book, from the works of the great E. Nesbit, the consummate children's author, to the more sophisticated science fiction of Jules Verne and of H.G. Wells, whom my father admired as a writer but despised as a socialist. I had no idea what a socialist was, but when the CCF party was formed my mother took me to a political rally for the new party's nominee in the Victoria riding.

This was King Gordon, son of the Canadian novelist Charles Gordon, better known to his readers as Ralph Connor. Apparently socialists were hard to find in Victoria: King Gordon had been parachuted in from Winnipeg, and his picture was on every telephone pole — showing a dark, lean face with a small moustache and probing eyes. I found the rally dispiriting, probably because I had decided to be a Conservative, like my father. The shabbily dressed audience seemed curiously passive, and I cannot remember much fire in Gordon's speech. But then, Victoria was scarcely a hive of radicalism. It was a services town, full of retired officers from both the navy and the army. Anyone who'd acquired a rank above that of captain in the military, even in the reserves, continued to use it shamelessly. My father was in his element in Victoria. If he'd been one rank higher than lieutenant in the Royal Canadian Engineers, I'm sure he'd have put his rank on the door or at least in the phone book as the others did: Captain F.G. Berton.

When I reached fourteen, my father began to insist that I take a cold shower every morning. There is nothing I hate more, and I tried my best to squirm out of it, squeezing into a corner to prevent the full force of the icy blast enveloping me. But there were also cold baths, from which I could not escape. Soon my parents were insisting that I don shorts each morning and run around the block several times before breakfast. I found this embarrassing. None of the other boys were doing it — the jogging craze was two generations away. I was sure that people would stare, point, and laugh, but orders were orders, and for a time I trotted around dutifully, trying with little success to hide behind the holly trees that bordered St. David Street.

Why this sudden emphasis on athletics and cold water? I couldn't figure it out. Nor did anybody give me any reason except to say it was healthy. Years later it dawned on me: my parents were trying to protect me from the evils of masturbation, the dreadful vice that nobody talked about but that was supposed to weaken you forever, if it didn't turn you blind. Baden-Powell in his *Scouting for Boys* referred to it too, but in such euphemistic terms that it quite went over my head. (He called it "beastliness" and also advocated cold showers.) The treatment was finally allowed to peter out, to my great relief. It didn't work, anyway.

Nonetheless, sex in more specific forms was beginning to enter my ken. A new and illicit series of magazines could be obtained at the small U.S. ports of Bellingham and Anacortes. Of course, none of us had the means to visit these towns, but Captain Beaumont, an elderly philanthropist who owned a fine yacht, did. More than once he took our entire Boy Scout troop on a day-long cruise, which happily ended at one of these two towns — the Sodom and Gomorrah of Washington State.

We trooped off the sleek craft, clean-limbed youths in blue serge shorts, khaki shirts, and wide hats, and headed promptly for the nearest newsstand where we could purchase *Gay Paree, La Vie Parisienne, Spicy Stories,* and many other publications denied to all cloistered Canadians by an overprotective customs department. These marvellous magazines (there was even a *Spicy Western*) contained "art poses" of topless young women and mild tales with titles like "Sin on the Seine" that wouldn't raise an eyebrow, let alone anything else, today. But in 1935 they were much prized and well thumbed.

I was still a sexual innocent. My father had tried to tell me the facts of life when I was twelve, but his explanation of the process was so scientific that he had managed to make the sexual act sound like an exercise in pipe fitting. I had never heard of a brothel, even though there were several in Dawson, until my friend Barney Hager enlightened me.

"You've never heard of a whorehouse?" Barney asked me, as we sat in the sunshine on the rocks of Shoal Bay. I shook my head.

"Well," said he, "it's like this. Apparently there are some older guys who, you know, just *hafta* fuck."

I looked at him in astonishment.

"They absolutely *hafta*," said Barney, making it all sound like a dreadful affliction. "And so they've got these places for them to go when they hafta."

I formed a mental image of a spotless institution manned by clinicians in white, leading these poor, sad creatures who just hadda do it to a kind of operating room, where they finally achieved blessed relief.

5 I reached puberty late, around the age of fifteen, and at this critical period in my life, our family faced a difficult decision. My father was offered his old job back. His colleague, Phil Kelly, had died suddenly; there was nobody else who knew the ropes. George Jeckell, the gold commissioner, sent a terse wire to Ottawa: "MUST HAVE BERTON," with a copy to us. What to do?

We had three choices: my father could turn down the job; the whole family could move back to the Yukon; or my father could go alone.

The first two were unthinkable, or so we believed. My father desperately wanted a job — *any* job — but especially this one, which he felt was his by right. He could not bear to be idle, nor could he bear to live on his meagre pension. A job would mean that my sister and I could go to university and my mother wouldn't have to watch every cent. It meant also that he could indulge his own impulse buying from the *Scientific American*, which was advertising such things as bridge chips, plastic playing cards, and the new Schick electric razor, all of which he eventually purchased. But mainly, I think, it was a matter of pride. He didn't want to be part of the vast army of unemployed.

It was considered somehow shameful to be unemployed in those days, even though half the country seemed to be out of work. To be on "relief," as welfare was then called, was humiliating. I remember once walking up St. Patrick Street in Oak Bay and passing a group of relief workers digging a ditch. And there, half covered in mud, was my own Sunday School teacher! I averted my face, pretending not to see him. But he saw me.

"How come you didn't say hello the other day?" he said to me the following Sunday. He said it quite cheerfully, as if it was perfectly natural for him, a former business executive, to be digging ditches on the dole. I admired him for his nonchalance, felt bad for my own silliness, and determined to change my attitude. But the general feeling, as I remember it, was that it was something of a disgrace to be poor and out of work.

Could we have gone North again with my father? It would have meant taking my sister and me out of school, selling the house, pulling up our new roots, and going back to a community where there was no real future for young people. My father made the decision; he would go alone.

I think now it was a mistake. My father had an overactive sense of *noblesse oblige*. He was doing the right thing — in his eyes the *only* right thing. But we could have continued more happily, I think, with the family whole. I will not describe the wrenching leave-taking again — my mother confined to her bed with a psychosomatic case of nerves, we children crying at the boat. The scene is in *Drifting Home*. I found it difficult to write it then; I cannot bear to read it now. All that winter my mother wrote him love poems, which she insisted on reading to us before mailing. I found them affecting but also a little embarrassing. I had yet to write any love poems of my own.

So now I was without a father at the most sensitive time in my life. There were many temptations, and my mother was no match for my stronger will. I came and went as I pleased, tooling around town on my bicycle with a gang of cronies. We might have got into great trouble, though there was no hint of drugs in those days, or even of alcohol. But one thing saved me, and that was the St. Mary's Boy Scout Troop.

The Scouts filled a vacuum and gave me an anchor that the school system could not provide. High school was a washout for me. I had turned out briefly for the soccer team in Grade 8 but the result was disastrous. My position was Inside Right. To my delight I actually kicked a goal. Unfortunately, it was at the wrong end of the field. "You don't have to play any more," the coach told me bluntly. In those days the schools only cared about winners. You had to be a football hero, as the song went; otherwise you were a cipher.

At high school I tried on two occasions to organize certain extracurricular activities, both clandestine. My friends Ronnie Hines and Arthur Davies and I formed the PEST club, whose purpose, put starkly, was to pester everybody. The members all had military ranks, determined by the amount of pestering that went on. If you were kept after school or given lines to write or chastised by the teacher or sent to the principal's office, you were promoted. I had reached the giddy heights of lieutenant-colonel only to be surpassed by Ronnie Hines who, as the result of a wicked piece of ingenuity, was made a field marshal. Before class he dropped two matchboxes full of tent caterpillars into the teacher's inkwell. We watched in suppressed excitement as the insects crawled out of the ink and began to leave trails across the papers spread out on her desk. She was a grey-haired and humourless spinster — not our favourite teacher — and it took her some time to realize what was going on. By then several of the caterpillars had dropped off her desk and were crawling down the aisles, to the delight of the class. In the end the teacher screamed, the class tittered, Ronnie Hines got the strap, and the PESTs were dissolved.

The other clandestine operation was the school paper. I was in love with newspapers by then, and my experience at public school had convinced me that if I wanted to be involved I must start one myself. So I did.

The first edition was a little handwritten curiosity. You could in those days buy a cardboard package of five caramels called Tots for a cent. We ate the caramels and sailed the Tots boxes down Bowker Creek, which ran through the school property. I produced a newspaper, the *Daily Totsman*, to report on these nautical affairs. I drew the masthead in Old English as in the local newspapers, printed the stories in ink by hand, fitted headlines to them, laid out a front page, and even supplied a cartoon. The paper carried other school gossip and was passed around under desks and at recess. I quickly improved on this raw beginning, changing the paper's name to the *Schoolboy*, typing out several pages with one finger on my mother's Remington, making several carbons, and holding everything together with paper clips.

This was a lengthly and often irritating process. Quite often I put the carbon in the wrong way and had to begin all over again. I made many typing errors. I had to draw the headlines and cartoons by hand on each of several copies, as well as the masthead, which was done in green ink. I worked after school and long into the night. Once, my parents came home at midnight and found me typing away, my eyes red-rimmed. My mother sent me to bed and my father took over and typed the last few stories.

The paper was rented out for a cent a time. You could buy a copy outright for a nickel. It was still running when my father left home, and by then I was covering important stories outside the school ("CROWDS SWARM AROUND AIRFLOW CHRYSLER"). I received no encouragement from the school. The teachers were either indifferent or hostile to the idea. It didn't seem to occur to any of them that a school paper might be an asset to the institution.

When I was in my last year at high school, Lucy, then in Grade 10, was attacked for getting only 50 per cent on an exam that most of her class had failed. "Miss Berton," yelled the principal, "you have no business getting a mark like this — you're lazy, lazy, just like your brother." Lucy was outraged and so was my mother when she heard. She got on the phone to him and gave him a piece of her mind. "I don't care what you call her," she said, "but *don't* compare her to her brother." (Years later she encountered the same principal at a UBC summer school. I was by then writing major articles for *Maclean's*. "We always knew Pierre would do well!" he said smugly. His name was Harkness; why should I disguise it?)

The paper may not have done much for the school, but it did a great deal for me. It gave me what the football heroes had — status. Old enemies came to me pleading to be allowed to contribute. I remember one boy in particular who had constantly bullied me and now asked if he could be the paper's official correspondent for his street. I cannot say that I turned the other cheek; in fact, I revelled shamelessly in my new-found power and told him coldly that he wasn't qualified. It's probable that incidents like that helped to nudge me in the direction of my future career.

In contrast to the school, the Boy Scouts encouraged this kind of activity. The Scouts had their own status system based on different values. The kind of brains that produced cloistered scholars was not terribly important to the Scout leaders, nor was the ability to play football. The stress was laid on imagination, ingenuity, and a sense of humour. It was important that there was a badge for everybody — some for boys who were good with their hands, some for those who were good with their heads. Nobody was left out.

I had a wonderful time in the Scouts. Indeed, for all of the seven years I lived in Victoria, I lived and breathed the movement. Our Scout Hall was a second home to me. My closest friends were Scouts. Here I found myself excelling at all sorts of surprising things. To this day I can send a semaphore message or one in Morse code, tie a sheepshank, and make a sling to support a dislocated collarbone. I have never had to do any of these things and probably never will. But there was a time, long ago, when I did not believe I could be capable of such miracles. When I learned from the Scouts that nothing is ever as difficult as it first appears to be, I felt the first stirrings of self-confidence.

I spent almost as much time with the Scouts as I did at high school. There were patrol meetings on Tuesdays, troop meetings on Fridays, hikes every Sunday. There were camps at Easter and in the summer. There were rallies, fêtes, jamborees, garden parties, parades, banquets, tournaments, Monopoly drives, and every conceivable kind of social event.

Because of the Scouts, the awkward period of adolescence was for me a kind of idyll. That old song, "Till We Meet Again," always takes me back to the Scout version, sung around the campfire before Lights Out. The music conjures up a series of images: the glowing faces of my friends reflected in the leaping flames; Louis Durant playing the mouth organ as sweetly as any Heifetz; the dark, rustling wall of conifers at our backs; the lapping of water at the margin of the lake; the scent of hot chocolate; and the mingled feeling of mystery, friendship, and approaching adulthood stirring in me like the night wind in the pines.

As I rose from an ordinary Tenderfoot to a Patrol Leader with a King's Scout emblem on my arm, I learned something about leadership. I was also becoming something of a ham, again thanks to Scout training. I earned my Entertainer's Badge around the campfires at Sooke and Shawnigan Lake. Eventually I took on the role of a radio reporter, rapping out news from a fake microphone in the style of Walter Winchell. These reports soon became the basis for another newspaper, which I again drew and typed myself and pinned to the billboard in the Scout Hall. I became adept at using the age-old tricks of journalism. When Jack Fawcett, our troop leader, protested mildly about one of my stories, I ran a flaring headline in the next issue announcing that the freedom of the press was in peril.

Some of the things I learned in the Boy Scouts had nothing to do with the training manuals laid down by the movement's founder, Robert Baden-Powell. They were the fortunate by-products of a long and close association with boys of similar inclination and outlook. Perhaps the most useful piece of advice I've ever had was given by our scoutmaster one evening when the hall was about to close and some of us older boys had lingered behind to talk.

He had worked all his life for the government and now revealed that he had disliked every minute of it. There had been no day in his life, he said, when he had not crawled unwillingly to a job he loathed. He turned to us and said, very quietly and forcefully: "Boys, if there's one thing I want to leave with you it's this: never, under any circumstances, no matter what the pay, take a job you don't like doing. It just isn't worth it." I have always tried to keep that advice in mind.

By this time, we senior Scouts were fraternizing with our sister organization, the Girl Guides, helping out at charity garden parties, or "fêtes" as they were called in Victoria. We tended to sneer at the Guides, but I noticed that we all turned up at these affairs, outdoing ourselves to be notice-

96

ably helpful. The girls giggled and looked arch and occasionally poked us in the ribs, but most of us, I fear, were too young and inexperienced to recognize the beginning of a flirtation.

I cannot remember knowing anybody who had what is now known as a girl friend, in my circle at least. We went to the high school dances — there were only two a year — in groups, my sister and I and the neighbouring teenagers, and we came home in groups. The same group signed up to take dancing lessons from Dorothy Wilson, who at the age of ninety-one (as I write this) has just been made a charter member of the Dance Hall of Fame.

Off we trooped to Dorothy's every Saturday night, and there, as the Victrola scratched away, we stumbled through the continental, the tango, the barn dance, the foxtrot, and the waltz and other steps, most of which I couldn't do then and can't do now. The best I was able to accomplish was the box step for the waltz; but who can waltz today on the tiny, crowded dance floors of a new era?

It was expected that I would escort my sister to any dance or party that came up, unless, of course, she had a date. But neither she nor any of her girl friends ever had a date. Who among us could afford to date a girl in those trying times?

"Don't forget to dance with Lucy," my mother told me. I didn't particularly want to dance with my kid sister, who was two years behind me in school. She had developed into a leggy teenager, with big brown eyes and dark hair that hung down to her shoulders — an attractive girl, no doubt, but still my sister. On the other hand, I didn't have the wherewithal, let alone the nerve, to ask a "real" girl out.

I was secretly enamoured of a dark little thing named Wanda Ross but could never screw up enough courage to talk to her, much less ask her to the high school dance. As I pedalled down Hampshire Road or Oliver Street on my CCM bike I would spot Wanda walking home, books under her arm. "Now's my chance," I'd say to myself. "I'll just

97

slow down and greet her casually — maybe make some kind of conversation about the weather or Grade 9 or something." Of course I did nothing of the sort. Long before I came abreast of Wanda I began to pedal furiously — eyes straight ahead. I zipped past Wanda without so much as a wave of the hand — P. Berton challenging Victoria's own Torchy Peden, the world's champion six-day bike rider.

One day I was inveigled into a game of Post Office at the home of a high school friend. To my horror, Wanda Ross was invited, too. *Oh Lord,* I thought, *sooner or later I'm going to be "it." There'll be a letter for me, and Wanda Ross will be at the top of the stairs, waiting for me to post it.* Which, of course, is exactly what happened. Up the stairs I went, knees trembling. There, at the top, stood the delectable Wanda, looking remarkably composed. I blushed; she didn't.

"Look," I said. "Let's just stand here for a moment and then I'll go back downstairs again. Okay?"

"Okay," said Wanda.

That was my first and only conversation with her. Back down I went, cursing my lack of enterprise, to be greeted with knowing grins, I felt like an imposter.

At the high school dances I held my partners at arm's length, terrified, perhaps, that they might break easily. Lucy was more sophisticated than I. All the girls that year had purchased identical shiny ballroom gowns from the Hudson's Bay Company for the scandalous price of five dollars apiece. They came in five colours — sea green, robin's egg blue, lemon yellow, peach, and pale pink. Lucy's was blue, and she looked quite fetching in it. Now, as I bounced her awkwardly about through a sea of shimmering pastel, she decided to give me some sisterly advice.

"For God's sake," she told me, "you've got to squeeze your partner a little! Get your arm around her waist like this and hold her tightly. See what I mean?" And she seized me in a furious grip, a kid sister no longer, older in some ways than I.

I decided to follow Lucy's advice. At Mrs. Wilson's final class, a celebration complete with non-alcoholic punch, a girl actually winked at me; and so I screwed up enough courage to ask her for a waltz. Off we tottered across the floor, she floating in my arms, me still struggling with the box step. One whirl too many and she fainted dead away.

Here was my chance! A girl collapsing, waiting to be revived and taken out onto the balcony for a breath of fresh air. Alas, the opportunity passed me by. I was struck dumb, all my Scout training in first aid forgotten. I stood there, gawking, as she slipped out of my arms onto the floor. Almost instantly, Edgar Dickson oozed in, revived her, picked her up, and swept her out to the balcony. The songs of the day bring it all back now: "Blue Moon," "These Foolish Things," "I'm in the Mood for Love" — background music to my lost opportunity.

I lived vicariously through the radio. Now that my father had a job we all had a little extra money. I accumulated twelve dollars and spent it all on a second-hand desk model. My mother was scandalized that I should commit such a sum without her okay, but I didn't care. I *had* to have a radio of my own. This one was so ancient it didn't even have a modern dial, but it was loud and clear. At night, when the others were in bed, I'd switch it on low and listen to the music of dance bands all over the continent. In those days the bands played live, always from some mysterious nightclub or ballroom. "Ladies and gentlemen," the announcer would say, "it's the music of Carl Ravazza coming to you from high atop the beautiful St. Francis Hotel overlooking Union Square in downtown San Francisco," and I'd hear the clink of glasses and the chatter of cheerful voices, behind the theme song, "*Vieni Su.*"

I had, of course, never seen a nightclub. I knew of them only from radio and the movies. In my imagination they were marvellous rooms, all white and gold Art Deco ("modernistic," we called it then), with men in long tailcoats and white ties proffering gold lighters to elegantly coiffured women in Ginger Rogers dresses.

Would I ever enter a real nightclub? I wondered. I saw myself at some future time at one of these tables, as acquaintances dropped over to say a few words of greeting and waiters popped champagne corks. On the cavernous dance floor (as big as the one in Al Jolson's *Wonder Bar*) couples swirled and did the box step and Carl Ravazza, smiling, acknowledged my presence from the podium.

But in the winter of 1936-37, I still lived with my dreams. That was the winter of Roosevelt's landslide victory over Alf Landon, the winter of Edward VIII's abdication, the winter that saw Benny Goodman introduce swing music.

Change was in the wind for me, too. It was my last year of high school and the end of my campfire summers. When school finished in June, my life took on a new direction.

Chapter Three

Keep the
Water Running
1937-1939

1 By the spring of 1937, my parents had been apart for two
years and my mother was desperate to see my father. She
had dyed her prematurely grey hair since the age of twenty-
five. Now she allowed it to go white. It was, I think, a symbolic act, a statement of her grass widowhood. She was still
a lively and handsome woman, who kept her figure and held
herself erect — a fetish with her. Often at public functions she
would give me a fierce stare and throw her shoulders back to
indicate that I, now a gangling six-footer, should pay more
attention to my own posture. "Bad posture! Bad posture!" my
mother would say reprovingly. She was also an advocate of
deep breathing and a confirmed believer in the healing properties of a glass of hot water before breakfast, not to mention
the many advantages of chewing each mouthful of food
thirty-two times.

Her main emotional outlet was in her writing. She had put
aside her novel and was now trying to write short stories,
which she read aloud to me. She was anxious for my approval
and accepted my criticisms meekly. Apart from the Scout and
high school newspapers I had done no writing of my own,
but that didn't stop me from being a critic. I was, I fear, unnecessarily harsh. I remember tearing one of her favourite detective stories apart.

"I'm tired of hearing about detectives and 'crooks' as you
call them with ridiculous names such as 'Classy Carson,'" I
told her. "If you can't pick a better handle you'd be better

writing Sunday School stories. Just because a man is a crook, he doesn't *have* to have a nickname."

The literary environment in our house had its effect on me. My mother was a member of the executive of the local branch of the Canadian Authors Association, which often met in our living room. The members were mainly middle-aged women, many of whom wrote unpublishable poetry, which they read aloud to each other. I listened in and was fascinated. There were talks and discussions on the writer's craft, which I absorbed almost by osmosis. By the end of my last year in high school, I understood something of the nuts and bolts of commercial publishing. Phrases like "narrative hook" and "plot twist" were familiar. I had also soaked up a good deal of elementary information that surprisingly few novices understand to this day — matters as simple as how to prepare and submit a manuscript to a publisher.

My mother's head was crammed with plots, most of them highly melodramatic. Years later, however, one of these that I never forgot formed the basis of Charles Templeton's best-selling novel *Act of God,* the story of a priest coping with the awesome discovery that Christ was mortal.

I remember another plot she outlined to me.

"It's about a married woman in the prime of life," she told me. "She meets, quite by accident, an attractive man who wants to take her away for a weekend to another city. There is not the slightest chance of discovery for her husband is temporarily absent — no one will ever know of the escapade. She's intrigued, of course. The story hinges on how she grapples with the decision and how, in the end, she turns it down."

"But wouldn't there be more to the story if she actually agreed to go?" I asked.

"No, no," said my mother. "She couldn't go. She *wouldn't* go. She might like to, but she wouldn't. *That's* my story."

And of course it *was* her story, although that didn't occur to me at the time. Years later, thinking back on that conversation, which had stuck in my head for so long, I realized that almost certainly she's been talking about herself and the kinds of decisions that she'd had to make in those lonely months in Victoria. The story itself never got written.

She couldn't stand another year alone. Now that we'd saved some money it was financially possible for her to spend the summer in Dawson, especially as I was planning to go north as well. My father, who knew most of the executives of the Yukon Consolidated Gold Corporation, had written that there was a job for me out on the creeks.

So our family was partially reunited that summer. My mother went north immediately, in May. I boarded briefly with friends and followed in June. Lucy stayed behind as a paying guest with another family. There wasn't enough money to take her along. My mother was still counting every cent.

Standing on the pier at Vancouver, waiting to board the *Princess Louise*, I felt a sense of mounting excitement. After five years, I was going home! The pier was crowded with Yukoners, some waving goodbye to friends, others boarding the vessel; I knew most of them — steamer crews, old-timer Dawsonites, and others, like myself, expecting to get jobs. I climbed aboard with my sleeping-bag and my kit — hobnail boots, wool socks, Caribou-brand work clothes, denim shirts — a skinny kid not yet turned seventeen, part of a man's world at last.

On deck a band was playing. Long streamers of paper hung from the railings. People shouted goodbyes. A young girl on the deck sobbed and waved back at her boy friend as the ship pulled away into the night. I shouldered my kit and descended into the bowels of the vessel where I found a spot on one of the double-tiered bunks in the hold. I was, of course, travelling steerage. The following morning I was shaken awake at six for a rough-and-ready breakfast. I wolfed it down and rolled back into my bunk.

A little more than a week later I stood with the crowd on

103

the prow of the *Casca*, my heart thumping as we approached the Dawson bluff. The trip downriver, on the crest of a seven-mile current, had been swift. Now, all the familiar landmarks of my childhood were unwinding past me like paintings on a Chinese scroll: the mouth of the Indian River and then Swede Creek, where we had once fished for grayling; Chicken Billy's Island, where we'd pitched our tent on those warm July weekends; and the hay fields at Sunnydale. I knew this part of the river as well as I knew the streets of Oak Bay; at any moment I half expected to see the *Bluenose* chug by, with my family aboard. But the *Bluenose* was no more — sold long ago by my father and sunk somewhere on the lower river.

At last the *Casca* rounded the bluff and gave the three familiar blasts on its whistle. And there was my home town, sprawled out for a mile and a half along the right-hand bank.

There was Lousetown, where we'd played on the old train as kids. There was the mouth of the Klondike and, a bit farther on, St. Paul's Church, where my mother had sung in the choir. There was the hotel where my father had built his boat, and there, beyond the Administration Building, was our old home.

For the first time I was seeing Dawson through adult eyes. How old and decayed it looked after the well-scrubbed profile of Victoria! Cars and wagons clattering along the roads raised clouds of dust. Paint peeled from the façades of the abandoned buildings. Log cabins seemed to be crumbling before my eyes. Front Street was still a Hollywood set, but a very old and decrepit one.

My father waited on the dock to greet me, with my mother. He too looked older and also smaller. I towered over him, astonishing him with my height. He had left a small boy beyond; now he was faced with a six-footer. He paraded me about town with great pride, making the same joke to everyone he encountered.

"Got to get a ladder to talk to this fella," my father would say, over and over again. I grinned sheepishly and tried to chuckle, as if hearing it for the first time.

My father took me in to see an old friend, Mr. Haliburton, the local jeweller.

"He'll be going out to the creeks," my father told him.

Mr. Haliburton looked sceptical. "Let's have a look at your hands," he said. He found no calluses on my upturned palms and looked even more sceptical. "Do you think he'll make it?" he asked. "A lot of them don't, you know. It's no disgrace."

"Oh, he'll make it," my father said. I felt a vague sense of unease. What was I getting into? What if I didn't make it? It sounded very much as if it *was* a disgrace not to make it. I had no idea what kind of a job I was going to get on the creeks, but the hint that I might somehow fail the test and thus shame my father disturbed me.

The following day I went down to the offices of the Yukon Consolidated and registered for work. Then, with scores of other young men hoping for a job in Dawson, I waited. Some of the transients occupied the waiting period profitably by panning under Dawson's wooden sidewalks for gold dust, a surprising amount of which had sifted down from the pokes and pockets of the oldtimers. One pair actually took a lease on the floor of the Bank of Commerce building, while it was under repair, and netted, it was said, fifteen hundred dollars.

Some of these men had travelled three thousand miles in the hope of getting a job. Most succeeded, for the company required close to one thousand labourers that summer. The Yukon Consolidated controlled all dredging in the Klondike and Indian River watersheds, and also the hydro-electric and telephone systems that serviced its own operations as well as those of the town.

I lived with my parents in a rented house on Seventh Avenue. Every morning I went down to the company office to see if my name was on the bulletin board, assigning me to a job. The apprehension I had originally felt turned to

105

frustration as the days went by. Long lists of names of men to be hired appeared every morning; mine wasn't among them.

In the late afternoons and on the weekends, the three of us went for walks in the hills and out along the Klondike Valley, as we had done in my childhood years. It wasn't quite the same. On one hike out to Bonanza Creek my father suddenly suggested we take a breather. I was eager to push on; I wanted to find the old handcar we boys had played with so many years before. My mother put a restraining hand on my arm. "Your father needs to rest for a moment," she said, and for the first time I realized he was mortal.

Then on July 12 I stood in front of the company's bulletin board and saw that my name had come up at last. I felt a surge of excitement, turned about, and dashed up the hill to Seventh Avenue to get my kit together. It was my seventeenth birthday.

I caught the look of disappointment on my mother's face but paid no heed to it as I began to throw clothing into my dunnage bag.

"Do you have to rush off so soon?" she said. "It's your birthday." She had planned a small party for me — the first since 1934 that my father had been able to attend.

"The truck leaves at eleven," I said breathlessly.

"But I'm making your favourite coconut cake! It's almost ready."

"No time! No time!" I said. And there was no longer any time: no time for childish diversions; no time for the rites of passage. I can still hear the touch of panic in my mother's voice, the sense of disappointment, sadness, and a touch of pride, too, as she realized at last that I was no longer her little boy. I felt for her. She would miss the birthday party more than I. But I was eager to be on my way.

No greener kid ever boarded a Dawson truck to go to work on the creeks. My destination was a construction camp on Dominion Creek, some thirty-five miles from Dawson. When we stopped at the Bear Creek headquarters a few miles out of town one of the clerks hung a tag on me marked "Middle Dominion Camp." I was too ignorant to remove it. I thought they tagged people the same way they tagged supplies. The story made the rounds of the creeks and was never forgotten. Four decades later, on a return trip to my home town, I ran into the same truck driver who had taken me on that birthday ride to Middle Dominion. "Remember when they put that tag on you?" he said. How could I forget?

Dominion Creek had not been extensively mined since the gold rush days. Now the company proposed to strip away the valley floor, thaw the ground to bedrock, and dredge up the gold the earlier prospectors had missed. As the truck rattled down the long hill from the Hunker summit, I could see the black scars left by the big nozzles that were already tearing away at the over-burden.

We came to a stop at a tottering roadhouse — a two-storey frame building with a false front and a covered porch, another relic from the stampede days. This served as a temporary bunkhouse and cookhouse for the construction crew that was building a new camp as well as for the brush cutters and the men who worked the big nozzles.

The building was empty, except for the cook, a cheerful Austrian, who met me at the door and showed me to a bunk, one of several in a room on the upper floor.

"Look at this, " he said to the driver as I stood there awkwardly, the tag still on me. "Now they're tagging human beings as well as provisions. Doesn't that beat all!"

The following day I went to work on the construction gang building a new camp a couple of miles upstream. I was to be a jack-of-all-toil: carpenter's helper, digger of postholes and deadman pits, carrier of dressed lumber, dauber of pitch. For a boy just turned seventeen, almost six feet three inches tall, but only one hundred and sixty pounds in weight, the ten-hour work day was a tall order. There were no holidays, no weekends off. Sunday was just another day. The pay was $4.50 a day with board. We had to be on the job at seven after the two-mile hike to the new camp site. We worked till noon, hiked back again on our own time, wolfed down a huge lunch, and were back on the job by one. We worked until six, devoured another meal, and shortly after that flopped into bed.

It was a lonely, primitive existence. The other workmen were much older than I, and most had accents. George Lund, my boss, was a Dane. Jimmy Shugar, the partner with whom I worked, came from Eastern Europe. Ole Oleson, who handled one of the big nozzles, was Norwegian. The bull cook was Swiss — or said he was; it was not politic in 1937 to say you were German.

For the first time I came into contact with men who had more than a nodding acquaintance with the dismaying international scene. I remember the cook telling the story one night of how his uncle had been arrested in Vienna for displaying in the window of his haberdashery shop ties with red stripes. This was before Anschluss. The government, so he said, considered his uncle a closet Nazi because the stripes were the same shade as that displayed on the flags of Hitler's Third Reich.

These were all older men, most of them in their forties. Some looked even older; they had worked like this all their lives and had no other future. I got on well enough but had no real point of contact with them. There was nobody of my own age to talk to, and I couldn't help thinking wistfully, as I toiled away, of my friends who would now in late July be enjoying Scout camp on an island in Shawnigan Lake. What a contrast to this cheerless wreck of a building, devoid of all facilities! We had no baths, no showers, no common room. We washed on a bench on the porch; by August we were breaking the ice in the metal basins each morning. We slept, several to a room, in narrow bunks. We didn't bother to shave. In all that time I never had a real bath.

But we ate well. I can recall, with some awe, the size of my own breakfast; several bowls of preserved fruit, then a couple of bowls of porridge followed by four fried eggs and a mound of bacon, and then five monstrous pancakes swimming in butter and syrup followed by a heap of toast. It was never enough. By mid-morning I was half famished and soon learned to grab a few extra pieces of toast at breakfast, layer them with bacon, and wrap them up to go in my pocket for a ten-o'clock snack.

We were building three bunkhouses, a mess hall, shower stalls, and a couple of smaller cottages for the bosses. The carpenters with whom I worked had achieved an interesting lifestyle. Each summer they toiled in the Yukon; each winter they went off to Tahiti. It was, they explained, a paradise, the landscape unspoiled by the ravages of the twentieth century, the women equally unspoiled. They lived for the winter and talked constantly of sex as they hammered away on the roofs of the bunkhouses while I dumped piles of shiplap before them. They talked of sex en route back for lunch and they talked of it again in the evenings. Each man had several girl friends on the islands, and they all worked like demons, lured by the prospect of another elysian, sex-filled winter in the South Seas.

Occasionally, one of the company's survey crews would stop overnight, young engineering students, working their way through college. For the first time I had friends my own age. They taught me to play solo whist, and I could hardly wait for the day to end for the game to begin. Exhausted as I was at the end of a gruelling day, the prospect of companionship was even more welcome than the prospect of sleep. But these intervals were rare.

For me, the summer never seemed to end. Because there were no holidays there was nothing to look forward to at the end of the week — only that far-off September day when I could take the stern-wheeler back upriver. It sometimes seemed as if that day would never come.

As I grew more accustomed to the work and a little less weary at night, I'd spend an hour or so before bedtime

109

reading or walking down the great valley of Dominion Creek, which was almost a mile across. Here was all the refuse of the gold rush — a tangle of old cabins and caches, sluiceboxes and shafts, rusty boilers, picks, shovels, and wheelbarrows by the hundred. In the cabins were old newspapers and magazines, some dating back to the gold rush years, not to mention tin pans, basins, coffee pots, crude furniture, handmade bedsteads, and rotting mattresses.

For the first time I was looking at the Klondike experience through new and different eyes. Phenomena that I'd taken for granted as a child now seemed extraordinary. The history of man's ingenuity in seeking for gold was everywhere. At one point the valley floor had been scraped as flat as a pool table, as if a gigantic paw had levelled it with some monstrous piece of machinery. And, indeed, I came upon that machinery — gigantic scrapers that had once been attached to cables strung across the valley. They had never worked. One memorable night on a longer walk I came suddenly upon another cumbersome device: a landgoing dredge towered above me, sitting abandoned on its rails, its bucket-line only half full of moss-covered earth. That hadn't worked either.

All this debris of a vanished era caught my imagination. For the first time I was able to stand back from the bricks of history and see the edifice, to realize what a remarkable epic had been acted out here in these broad valleys. What a magnet gold was, to draw men here to this forsaken corner of the world and cause them to toy with these useless Rube Goldberg devices — these mammoth scrapers, this towering mechanical digger!

And now they were at it again, scything away every scrap of foliage, every wildflower, every birch and spruce, alder and willow; tearing down the old cabins and sluiceboxes; clearing the mountains of shovels, picks, wheelbarrows, and cribbing to make way for the hydraulic monitors, the great nozzles that ripped off ten feet of frozen muck and

110

sent it coursing down the creek and eventually into the Yukon River.

The monitor men, who lived in our roadhouse, were rarely seen, for they worked a twelve-hour day and spent most of their free time sleeping. It was gruelling work, tearing away at the rock-hard soil, hour after hour. I wondered how they could stand it, working that nozzle all day with only a cold lunch, eaten on the job. They were wet most of the time from the spray. And the water pressure was awesome. Ole Oleson told me it would rip a man in half. He amused himself tearing gophers to bits with his jet; it helped break the monotony.

As I sloshed tar on the footings for the new mess hall I could see the stripping gang at work below me. The landscape they were creating might have come from one of the illustrations for *Astounding Stories,* my favourite science fiction pulp. I looked down on a weird and forbidding realm — cliffs of black ice glistening in the sunshine, jagged peaks and valleys, gnarled and misshapen, half torn away and reeling under the nozzle's pounding. By the end of the season this whole section of the valley was a black, uneven scar of frozen silt. In the autumn, when the aspens turned a flaming yellow and the buckbrush on the treeless peaks went purple, the contrast was jarring. The dark wound crept up each side of the valley for ten feet to the level of the original floor.

This is where I would work the following summer — in this stark moonscape, ice cold, thick with gumbo. I can't say I looked forward to the prospect, but I knew that I would have to come back, reluctantly, to the Yukon as my father had before me, and for the same reasons. In those Depression days a job was a job, and anyone who had employment was lucky. Meanwhile, college beckoned and my work was at an end. I picked up my pay, climbed aboard a truck, and went into Dawson, feeling more than a little elated that I had stuck it out, if only for a couple of months, and hadn't disgraced my family by quitting.

2 I returned to the Yukon the following May after a year spent at college in Victoria. The ice on the Yukon River was still frozen and so I took a Ford tri-motor monoplane to Dawson. The trip of less than three hundred and fifty miles took four hours. The plane rose slowly into the sky, hit an air pocket and dropped with sickening speed, to rise again, then plummet, hour after hour without a break. I had never been so sick in all my life and never so glad to set foot firmly on hard ground. My father met me and took me to the Arcade Café ("Home of Good Eats"), where for a dollar you could get an enormous meal of soup, salad, moose steak, and Yukon blueberry pie. I couldn't eat any of it.

I went to work on June 2, living in one of the bunkhouses I'd helped build the year before. This time the season stretched ahead for almost four months without a break; but thanks to my earlier initiation I was better prepared for it.

It was wet, filthy work, and there are many days now when I wake at 6 a.m. and thank whatever gods there be that I don't have to do it any more. It was also silly work. Here we were, hundreds and hundreds of men speckling the Yukon hills and valleys for more than fifty miles, slaving away in the muck, tearing the countryside to pieces in order to extract from the depths of that mutilated landscape gold that would eventually go back underground again in the vaults at Fort Knox, USA.

Still, it was a job, and jobs were scarce. When I came back from the Yukon after my first year and told some of my friends that I'd made $4.50 a day, they wouldn't believe me. Nobody made that much money! Their attitude was the same as mine had been toward the boy who claimed he had squandered two dollars in one night! Actually, after paying for my kit and fare I had no more than broken even that first season. But now I had an extra six weeks ahead of me to make, at the very least, my college and university fees. Mercifully, the pay had been boosted to five dollars a day and the work day lowered from ten hours a day to nine.

Essentially I would be doing the same work that my father had done a quarter of a century before — helping to thaw the ground down to bedrock so that the dredge could dig its way through. In my father's day the work was wet, hot, and filthy. For me it was wet, cold, and filthy. My father faced the danger of being scalded by live steam. I lived in peril of drowning and freezing in the heaving man-made swamp that we created that summer. Steam was no longer used to thaw ground in the Klondike district because the hills had long since been denuded of fuel to feed the boilers. We used cold water, millions and millions of gallons of it, pumped under pressure deep into the earth's bowels. Day and night for the entire season the water was forced underground, through thousands of pipes known as "points." All over the valley you could hear the dissonant clang of hundreds of slide hammers as the point drivers pounded away.

I didn't drive a line of points; that task was reserved for older and tougher men. I was a member of the gang detailed to build the vast latticework of pipe that fed the points and then to keep it in shape as the ground crumbled under the terrible assault of the water. Our first job was to assemble the segments of the main pipeline. Four of us gripped the ropes of a wooden battering ram and hammered the male end of each segment into the female end of the next, slamming it against a steel plate that, to complete the sexual metaphor, was known as a maidenhead. I found it hard going, pounding away, hour after hour. It was a relief when my turn came to straddle the big pipe and hold the maidenhead steady while the others whacked away at it.

The main pipeline slithered down the centre of the valley like a gigantic prehistoric serpent, its tentacles trailing off in every direction. It was broad enough to act as a pathway and later as a bridge when the rest of the landscape, bloated by water, fell away. The first time I negotiated it I almost slipped and dropped fifteen feet into a morass of water and slime. Only then did I realize that I had chosen the wrong footgear

113

for the job; I should have had rubber shoepacks, not hobnail boots. But it was too late to buy a replacement, and so for the rest of the summer, I slipped and slid over that narrow steel highway, always fearful that I would tumble into the murky depths below.

Once the main line was complete we drove feeder pipes at right angles, bolted together, and from these feeders smaller and smaller pipes, held in place by baling wire to make them flexible when the ground collapsed under them. Day after day we worked until the entire valley was a spider's web of pipes, all carrying water to the point drivers for the single purpose of turning the landscape, to a depth of thirty feet or more, into a mire.

One late evening at sunset I stood on the back porch of the bunkhouse looking out over that ravaged valley. An orange glow was spreading across the naked hills as one of the point drivers, an Irishman named Paddy, came out and stood beside me. Paddy was a devout Catholic, the butt of many jokes, all of which he took with great good humour. Now he attempted to proselytize me.

"Look at that, Pete," said Paddy, pointing to the glowing hills. "Look at that! And there are some who would have it that there is no God!"

But I dropped my eyes to the valley itself, caught in the last roseate rays, and wondered why, if there was a deity, He had allowed His handiwork to be so devastated. The spectacle was Satanic: the incredible checkerboard of piping, the spaghetti-like tangle of the hose connections, the forest of steel points poking up from the glistening muck like the coarse hairs on the body of some supernatural beast. Through this insane mesh of steel and rubber a night shift of men known as "point doctors" roamed, checking the lines, crimping the hoses and putting their ears against them for all the world like physicians listening for a pulse, to make sure each point wasn't clogged. If it was, it would have to be hauled up and cleared, the water spurting in every direction and soaking the point doctors. We became used to the phrase "You got to keep the water running." It was a kind of slogan, a mirthless joke tossed around the bunkhouses at night when the point drivers sat on their bunks, trying to straighten out fingers rendered rheumatic from the constant wet and cold. The water never stopped. Men could get trapped to the waist in gumbo or topple off the pipeline into one of the pools that suddenly appeared like a magician's rabbit, or even break down from the constant pounding with the slide hammer; but the water must be kept running.

In spite of the mud and the filth I wasn't able to have a real bath until July 1, when the showers were finally completed. The hot water did more than cleanse; it helped to soothe my aching muscles. My legs ached, my back ached, my arms ached. I can remember one night sitting on my bunk trying to open my left hand, which seemed to have become permanently curled through gripping a long-handled shovel. My right shoulder was scarred from carrying loads of steel points, which tended to roll against each other, pinching the skin as I walked warily along the pipeline.

I thought I would never get used to it, but I did. I was rather like a lifer who has come to terms with his predicament and decided to make the best of it. The comparison with prison is not exact, but there are similarities. Except for a few prospectors there were no neighbours, no other signs of civilization, and, of course, no women. The company provided no recreational facilities — no movies, no library, no central gathering spot. Dawson was more than thirty miles away, too far to reach at night. The job stretched on day after day, week after week, with only the autumn release to look forward to. "Thank God it's Sunday," one wag used to shout when the bull cook's triangle sounded at six o'clock on the morning of the Lord's Day. All we could do was groan as we prepared for nine more hours on the mud flats.

In the early weeks I came back to the bunkhouse after dinner almost too tired to stand. But, as the only college student in the camp, I had more work to do. The others could play pinochle or penny-ante poker or pan the old tailings for a few colours. I was faced with the prospect of ploughing through *Kenilworth* and *The Vicar of Wakefield*, not to mention my French and physics texts. There was no privacy in those thirty-man bunkhouses. As I struggled away with Scott and Goldsmith, men sang and shouted, pummelled each other, boasted of their sexual exploits, or snored on their bunks.

Everybody but me, it seemed, was an expert on the subject of sex; and sex was the chief topic of conversation in that womanless environment. One of my Dawson contemporaries, whom I'll call Charlie (it was, in fact, his name), was positively eloquent on the subject, a gift that astonished me for he hadn't been eloquent on anything in grade school, invariably standing at the foot of his class. Now here he was, engaging in a kind of informal debate with his neighbour on the next cot on the advantages of prostitution over any other form of sexual encounter.

"I say you can't beat a whore," Charlie was saying. "I don't honestly know why you guys bother with anybody else. Me, I've never had anybody but a whore. They're the best. With a whore you're sure of what you're going to get. There's no trouble, no fuss, no fooling around. You pay and you get your money's worth."

His opponent shook his head sadly. I believe his name was Ben — I can't remember his surname — but I can still see his face: a young, sad face burned by the sun, his blond hair cropped short, and a distant look in his eyes as he tried to explain to Charlie that in this area the amateurs had it all over the professionals.

"I don't see it," Charlie kept saying. "I just don't see it."

"You don't see it because you never had it," said Ben. "But I've had it once, and it was sweet."

The faraway look in his eyes increased the melancholy cast of his face.

116

"Yeah. I remember once me and this girl, we went swimming. There wasn't nobody else around, just the two of us splashing about in the lake. And when we came out of the water into the sunlight, all goosepimply, you know, we kinda cuddled up there on the grass, quite natural, and then we fooled around a bit, and then we did it. And oh, it was sweet ... so sweet. Not like a whore, Charlie. Not at all like a whore."

By this time the entire bunkhouse was listening, basking vicariously in Ben's encounter, thinking no doubt of their own sweet moments, in another place and another time far removed from the grim prison of the mining camp. All but Charlie.

"Well, I can't see it," he said. But there was no doubt who had won the debate.

I was still the youngest in the camp and certainly the most inexperienced. On my eighteenth birthday a present arrived from Lucy: two books, some packages of gum and Lifesavers, and some film for my camera, all, to my horror, wrapped up in red tissue. I looked about quickly, saw that nobody was looking, tore off the birthday wrapping and hid it away, terrified that somebody would see it and I would get a razzing.

The older men in the bunkhouse treated me with consideration; it was the ones closer to my own age who tormented me. The youngest of all, next to me, a boy of about twenty-one, insisted on calling me "Peterkin." Nothing galled me more than this infantile nickname. I dearly wanted to have it out with him, to punch him in the face or perhaps break his arm with an iron bar. But he was big-chested and hard-muscled; he could have clobbered me with a single blow. A nasty fight would have got us both fired, and I couldn't afford to be fired. Besides, he always spoke to me so genially that it almost seemed as if he was my best friend. I decided to ignore the name; but it rankled all that summer and it rankles to this day. My greatest regret is that I didn't steal a sixteen-foot point from the pile on the edge of the flats and break both his kneecaps.

The rest of the camp called me "Pete" or sometimes "Pointhole Pete." The description was apt, for I was one of the pipeline gang who constantly faced drowning as we tried to maintain the network of pipes in the face of appalling hazards. As the weeks wore on, a pool formed around each point, and the land began to fall away. The pools joined to form vast ponds, or "point holes," which grew vaster almost by the hour. By the end of the season the valley had taken on a nightmarish quality, like a battlefield pocked by shellholes and mine craters, all full to the brim with ice-cold water.

My boots were almost always filled with water as I struggled through this frozen quagmire. We propped up the smaller pipes with wooden blocks and rewired the connections while water squirted in our faces from the gaps in the line. We kept the flange feeders rigid by driving pilings on both sides for support. Often I'd feel the ground heave under my feet; if I was lucky and quick, it dropped away behind me; otherwise I got wet. There was no machinery. I stood on the top of a high, unsteady step ladder and hammered away at the wooden posts with a forty-pound maul. We propped up and bridged the main line with high scaffolding, held in place by cables attached to "deadmen" — logs sunk six feet below the surface in unthawed ground. Digging a six-foot hole in permafrost is rather like trying to dig a grave in a piece of the Canadian Shield. I can remember flinching each time the hard chips of frozen clay sprayed skyward at the blow of the mattock.

The weather, as always in the Yukon, was unpredictable. One day we'd shiver until our teeth rattled, as an icy wind howled down the valley. The next the temperature would rise into the mid-nineties, and we'd gasp for water, our shirts sticking to our backs. This would be followed the same week by a dreadful downpour soaking us to the skin in icy water. There was, of course, no shelter. Blackened by the sun, maddened by hordes of mosquitoes and blackflies, by turns frozen, soaked, and broiled, I toiled away in the ankle-deep mud with only the distant prospect of my September release to cheer me.

Nonetheless, I determined to stick it out. There were days when I thought I'd be fired for incompetence. Somehow I hung on. Others quit or, in the phrase of the day, "went down the road." I didn't. One of my Dawson contemporaries, an older boy named Jack Cody, whose father worked for the Northern Commercial company, gave up. He'd lost most of his wages on penny-ante poker in the bunkhouse. I'd also lost but quit after a couple of hands and never played again. Jack didn't quit playing poker; but the points were too much for him, and off he went, back to Dawson.

Big Jim, my straw boss on the pipeline gang, used to shout cheerfully at me when the wind grew chill and the rain washed the mud flats. "Don't worry, Pete," he'd say, as we struggled with a heavy pipe, "autumn's coming soon. Before you know it, you'll be sittin' on the deck of the *Casca*, smoking a big seegar and watchin' the river go by."

There were times when I thought that day would never come, and when it did, I wasn't sure what would follow. I would go back to my second year at Victoria College, but what then? What was I going to do with myself? No doubt I would work eventually in an office of some kind, in some minor position. But what? The only office I had ever really seen was my father's. He sat in his shirt-sleeves, with a green eyeshade on his head, recording mining claims and, with his engineer's training, drawing new surveys of old creeks. I knew I couldn't do that. What could I do? As I teetered along the big pipe, a 125-pound load of steel pipes rolling on my shoulders, I tried to envisage my future office. Would it be like my father's? Would it be for me alone, or would others work beside me? What would I *do* in an office? I didn't really know.

"Stop that goddam whistling," the straw boss shouted, "and get on with it." I hadn't realized I'd been whistling, but I knew I'd been daydreaming and dragging my feet. So I got on with it.

3 The contrast between my summers and my winters during these mining camp years was nothing short of bizarre. From May to September I was locked away from the world, my only home a spartan bunkhouse, from whose back porch thirty strangers urinated each morning until the ground below became a stinking mire. For the rest of the year I found myself taking classes in a fairyland castle of Corinthian columns, terra cotta chimney pots, marble tiles, Spanish mahogany, and stained glass.

This was Craigdarroch, a handsome sandstone pile whose seven chimneys, soaring for seventy feet over steep, irregular roofs of Vermont slate, provided a touch of fantasy for Victoria's otherwise mundane skyline. In this romantic building with its thirty-nine rooms and eighteen fireplaces — conceived by a coal baron to fulfil a promise to his wife — I spent two college winters. I cannot say that I treated it with the respect it deserved. Like those of the others, my boots tore into the parquet floors and my penknife dug into the panelling. Now that the building has ceased to be a college and has become a tourist attraction restored to its original beauty, only a few traces of those student days remain. But some of the names are still to be seen; my own is still shown to visitors, notched into the frame of a bay window on one of the upper floors. Such are the dubious by-products of notoriety.

In the two years I studied there, the college was more like a glorified high school. There were just two hundred students and the curriculum covered two years only. We were expected to take our junior and senior years at the University of British Columbia in Vancouver, with which the college was affiliated. Meanwhile, it was cheaper in those lean times to live at home and bicycle each day from Oak Bay to the castle on its hill overlooking Fort Street.

Here, for the first time, I got some encouragement from the faculty. The principal of Oak Bay High had gone out of his way, in front of my classmates, to announce loudly that I would never make anything of myself. The following year, after I'd left, he repeated this canard in front of my sister, bringing her close to tears. But in college we were treated as young adults. It was assumed we were going somewhere. Now for the first time I began to get good marks in English. This was due to the influence and encouragement of an elderly spinster, Jeannette Cann, a formidable-looking woman with bristling eyebrows and iron-grey hair, brushed straight back. Actually, her main interests were in modern art, and much of the class time was often taken up by lectures on the work of such painters as Georgia O'Keeffe. She once urged me to buy work by Emily Carr, explaining that it would be extremely valuable within a few years. I believed her but didn't have the price, which was one hundred dollars.

Miss Cann set us to writing essays on subjects of our own choosing, a sensible idea, since that is the way most professionals operate. I chose to write about the Yukon — about the Last Boat, the ice breakup, life in a trapper's cabin. For these I got A's and A Pluses, together with Miss Cann's benediction and encouragement.

Our French professor was a tiny, white-haired, and eccentric Frenchwoman, Madame Sanderson-Mongin, a great fixture at the college and also a great favourite. I did not do well in French in spite of my name. My father had struggled to teach me the language without success. But I liked Madame, and I especially liked her one night at a college dance.

There we were in what had been Robert Dunsmuir's ballroom, now transformed once again from lecture hall to dance floor, the orchestra playing "Love Walked In" or "That Old Feeling," we males all serged and starched and clustered at one end of the dance floor, the girls crowded together at the other. Not a soul stirred. The girls engaged their neighbours in animated conversation, never so much as looking at the boys as if dancing were the last thing on their minds.

The boys, hands shackled to pockets, scuffed tiny dust specks from the floor or stared fixedly at the ceiling, whistling

121

tunelessly to the music. A few hardy souls actually danced, sophisticated youths who had come in their parents' cars and seemed to know instinctively how to do the foxtrot even if they hadn't been to Dorothy Wilson's classes. The rest of us stood there trying to get up courage to cross the floor in such a fashion that the object of our attention would never realize, until the last moment when we blurted it out, that we were actually there to ask for a dance.

What held us back? Partly, I think, the fear of being refused. My face had broken out in adolescent pimples — or "hickies," as they were then called — and in spite of the thousands of packages of Fleischmann's Yeast I devoured (the ads in the comic pages showed miraculous cures followed by miraculous love affairs) I could not clear up my complexion. I was convinced that all women considered me incredibly ugly, rather like Boris Karloff in *The Mummy*. What if I asked a girl to dance and she turned away coldly? What if she fled into another boy's arms?

But here came Madame, in a long, glittering gown, crying out to all of us. "Dance!" she cried. "Dance, you fools! You have so little time!" And she began to seize each one of us by the arms and propel us toward the girls who, to my astonishment, affected to be, if not delighted to dance, at least not too bored to decline. And so, little by little, the sexes came together, and Madame no longer needed to break the ice at the affairs that followed.

I was doing well at Maths and Literature, badly at French, poorly at Chemistry and Physics. The two subjects my father had wanted me to master were my worst! Nor had I paid any attention to the chemistry lab in my basement for more than a year. In fact, I had lost all interest in science and was feeling guilty about it. What was wrong?

The answer was that I was spending more time on the college paper than I was in the chemistry labs, and when I should have been studying my physics texts I was actually typing out stories and drawing cartoons. The paper was a bulletin-board affair called the *Microscope*. I didn't start it. Two of my classmates, Harold Parrott and Ivan Mouat, were entirely responsible for the first edition. I wasn't aware that they'd launched it until I saw it tacked to the bulletin board — two pages, each containing two columns of typed news, with headlines, rather like the paper I had once produced for the Boy Scouts.

As I stood in front of the bulletin board, reading the new paper, a variety of conflicting emotions consumed me. The paper excited me, but why wasn't I part of it? At Monterey Public School I'd tried to join in and had been rebuffed. *Dammit*, I thought, *this time I* won't *be left out. I won't ask anybody. I'll simply jump in with both feet, unasked.*

The great thing about a bulletin-board newspaper is that you can tack up more pages beside it, and that's what I determined to do. I went home and produced a third page in the same style and tacked it onto the bulletin board with the other two. It has long since vanished, which is just as well. I wince now when I recall that I actually used such clichés as "these halls of learning" and "our fair city" in my column "Craigdarroch Comment."

In spite of these gaucheries, I was welcomed into the fold by Parrott and Mouat and made the third member of an editorial triumvirate. From that moment on I lived and breathed the *Microscope*. The paper was, of course, iconoclastic, as most college papers are (or should be). Poor John Meredith, the president of the student council, as decent a gentleman as ever walked through Craigdarroch's doors, took an awful drubbing. We referred to him invariably as "J. Roger Meredith," which made him sound far more pompous than he was. At the college there was a different attitude as far as newspapers were concerned. Unlike my high school teachers, several professors took a genuine interest in the *Microscope* and in me.

There were, moreover, several extracurricular activities besides the inevitable sports. I was a member of the editorial board of the college annual, a vice-president of the glee club, and a founding member of a short-lived organization known as the Anarchophiles. This last was the brainchild of my friend Bruce Mickleburgh, whom I had supported ineffectively for student council president against the more conventional J. Roger Meredith. Mickleburgh was a flamboyant figure with an unruly shock of black hair, a huge snub nose, dark staring eyes, and a weird sense of humour. Our campaign, I fear, was far too eccentric.

Mickleburgh wasn't really an anarchist; he was well on the way to becoming a Communist. His father was president of one of the local Conservative associations and Mickleburgh insisted he was actually a Tory spy among the Reds — "boring from within" as he put it. Nobody believed him.

Victoria, in those days, was a hotbed of political and religious non-conformists of all hues: Rosicrucians, British Israelites, Trotskyites, Technocrats, Four Square Gospelists crowded into the city, attracted no doubt by the mildness of both the citizens and the climate.

I remember at one meeting Mickleburgh pointing out a lean-faced youth in a dark shirt whom he identified as the leader of the Young Fascists. I looked at him with awe, expecting to see horns pop from his head at any moment.

In Professor Farr's history class we argued the pros and cons of Chamberlain's deal with Hitler. The professor praised Chamberlain as the man who had brought peace in our time at Munich.

Mickleburgh stood up and damned the British prime minister. Chamberlain, he said, would have to go.

"And who," said the professor sarcastically, "would you have replace him?"

"I would suggest Winston Churchill," said Mickleburgh, but Professor Farr was not convinced.

The Anarchophiles held one meeting only, a short one. Mickleburgh had singled out John O'Donnell, a diminutive scholar whose deadpan face belied a dry humour, as chairman. O'Donnell was known as Honest John O'Donnell, and on this occasion he lived up to the billing. Since any political structure was inimical to anarchist principles, Honest John ruled, it would not be possible for the Anarchophiles to have a chairman, let alone an executive. Therefore, he said, he was stepping down immediately. The meeting broke up in confusion and we all left for the Royal Dairy on View Street, where the ten-cent milk shakes were so thick you could actually stand a spoon in them.

It was during Bruce Mickleburgh's ill-fated campaign for president of the student council that I came to a decision about my life. I cannot now remember the details, only a heated discussion that spilled out of the classroom where one of our rallies was taking place. Somebody on the opposite side asked me just who I thought I was and what I intended to do with myself. Without stopping to think it over I found myself saying, "I'm going to be a journalist."

There; it was out. I had ignored science classes to work on the college paper. Obviously, then, if that's what I enjoyed that's what I should do. My scoutmaster's words of warning had taken root.

My mother was appalled when I told her. She had long memories of her own family's penury when her father had moved from paper to paper, fired often enough for his opinions and never paid more than a pittance.

"You'll live all your life with frayed shirts and worn trousers," she warned me.

I said I didn't care.

"I'm told that some people make eighty dollars a month in research chemistry," she told me. "You're throwing all that away."

But there was no moving me, and having noted my determination, she accepted my decision, unhappily but gamely. So did my father, when he was told by mail. Their boy wasn't turning out quite as they'd hoped, but if that was what he wanted, then they were prepared to back him up.

It was all very well for me to announce that I was going to be a journalist. But how was I to do it? The University of British Columbia had no journalism school; indeed, no Canadian university had one. But UBC did have a student newspaper, the *Ubyssey*, whose twice-weekly editions I devoured as soon as they reached the college library. I soon became familiar with the names of the editors and the staff and also with the by-lines that appeared on some of the feature stories, not knowing that some of these campus journalists were to become lifelong friends and that one would become my wife.

I noticed something else. The top editors on the *Ubyssey* all seemed to get jobs in the Vancouver media after they graduated. This was especially true if they'd been hired during their college terms as freelance campus correspondents. The paper carried stories about *Ubyssey* graduates who'd made good on the dailies: Himie Koshevoy and Stu Keate on the *Province*, Dorwin Baird on radio station CJOR, and many others. It was obvious what I should do: go to UBC, work hard on the *Ubyssey*, try for a job as campus correspondent, and get my foot in the door of a real newspaper.

I went to see Sydney Pettit, the college librarian, who had shown an interest in me. What courses would he advise me to take?

"For God's sake, don't specialize," he told me. "Take a bit of everything. Don't bother to go for honours. What you want is a broad general knowledge." It was good advice.

I drenched myself in the romance of newspapers — or what I thought was romance. I read every library book I could find, from technical journals such as *Editing the Small City Daily* to the memoirs of such big-time journalists as Stanley Walker and Emile Gauvreau. I was heavily influenced by Hollywood movies in which lone reporters solved crimes single-handed and rushed through the city room shouting, "Stop those giant presses!" I saw myself as Scoop Berton, a hard-drinking, hard-driving reporter with a hat on the back of his head in the band of which was inserted a large white card bearing the magic Open Sesame: PRESS. I actually bought myself a fedora, but all it had in the band was a feather; nor, in all my years as a journalist, have I ever encountered anybody with a press card in his hat.

It was at this stage, in the spring of 1939, that I took my first drink. After all, if I was going to be a newspaperman I would have to learn to handle liquor. My researches into the Fourth Estate in Chicago had made it clear that no self-respecting reporter was ever without a flask on the hip.

Four of us took part in the escapade that followed: we needed a drink, in truth, to carry out the criminal act that we'd planned. For we had decided to celebrate the end of our college year by painting the Pandora Street Lighthouse red.

What was a lighthouse doing in the heart of the city, a mile from the water, not far from the Christian Science temple? Only in Victoria would you find the city fathers erecting such an absurd monument to mark the town's seventy-fifth anniversary. Built of white stucco and outlined in flashing neon, it had been the subject of heated controversy for years.

Its chief critic was Bruce Hutchison, then a columnist for the Victoria *Times*. Bruce has always been an influence on me, and that influence began when, in the mid-thirties, I started reading his column, "Loose Ends." I thought then and think now that it was one of the best newspaper columns ever published in Canada.

Hutchison had two campaigns going. He wanted to abolish the lighthouse, which he called "a simple abortion," and he wanted to release from its cage in Beacon Hill Park a rare white bear, captured on the Queen Charlotte Islands and named Ursus Kermodeii after its discoverer. It was Hutchison's argument that the little bear was completely harmless and should be allowed to roam the streets like any other honest citizen. Little did the columnist know what he had wrought. Here was a group of his fans, enflamed by his rash words, determined either to release the bear or to disfigure the lighthouse. We chose the lighthouse. To be honest, we were, in spite of Hutchison's assurance, a little afraid of the bear.

We planned our exhibition with care. One of us was detailed to get a can of red paint and a brush. Another somehow procured a bottle of rye. None of us had ever before taken a drink so, not wishing to run short, we ordered twelve full ounces. The price was eighty-five cents, which was about all we had among us.

The details of that memorable midnight are misty, possibly because of all the rye we consumed. The impact of the first drink still lingers in my throat. Had I drunk turpentine by mistake? I did not yet realize that rye comes in various grades of smoothness.

I remember we laughed a lot, sang, giggled, fell down, bumped against lampposts, and played poker awhile with matches. Then we drove to Six Mile House in Esquimalt in Honest John O'Donnell's father's car to squander ten cents on one glass of beer among the four of us, feeling like devils because the foolish waiter apparently believed we were all over twenty-one.

On the way back to Pandora Street a policeman pulled us to the side for speeding, whereupon Dick Maclean announced he was going to punch the policeman in the nose. Two of us sat on him and muffled his threats while Honest John O'Donnell, at the wheel, talked to the officer.

"You are quite right to stop us, sergeant," said Honest John, in his deadpan fashion. "There is little doubt in my mind that we were exceeding the lawful limit and it would be dishonest of me to deny it for an instant. Put it down, pray, to an excess of youthful high spirits occasioned by the sudden release that comes after weary hours spent mastering the theorems of Euclid and the couplets of Pope."

The officer gave us a warning, and we sped off to further crimes. Like so many others of that generation, John O'Donnell was killed in action a few years later, and a great talent was lost to the world.

It was not as easy to cover the Pandora Lighthouse with red paint as we had supposed. It takes a great deal of energy and a great deal of paint to deal with stucco. By 1 a.m. we were out of both. The lighthouse, indeed, seemed to be immune to paint. At last, two of us managed to daub on the façade a large but ragged swastika, the only symbol we could think of that was suitably rude. We had little doubt that Bruce Hutchison, the famous columnist, would be proud of us.

We went back to my house for a brief snack. My mother and sister were asleep, so we tried to be as quiet as possible, whispering *Ssh-hh!* in loud sibilants every time we stumbled across a chair or knocked over a lamp.

The following morning, Lucy discovered me seated at the breakfast table, my head in my hands.

"If I didn't know better," she said archly, "I'd have said you were drunk last night."

She offered me bacon and eggs, which I refused. My mother had a more sensible comment.

"I don't know whether you were drinking whisky or not last night," she said, "but if you were, I hope it was a well-established brand. Always drink a good brand, never cheap whisky. It just doesn't do." And those were her only words on the subject.

I scanned the newspapers that day for word of our escapade: nothing. Surely Bruce Hutchison would make something of it in his column! But the great man totally ignored the incident. I searched the editorial page expecting some kind of a comment. The editorials were all silent. Was our act of defiance, then, to pass unnoticed?

Events moved slowly in Victoria in those days. Three days went by before a small item finally appeared on one of the inside pages: POLICE SEEKING SWASTIKA VANDALS.

The story that followed said that police were seeking a gang of hoodlums who had desecrated a city monument on Pandora Street, but refused to give credence to a report that

129

the signs revealed the presence in town of a well-organized gang of Nazi blackshirts.

"It's only a bunch of college students blowing off steam after the exams," the chief was quoted as saying.

That was all. Three paragraphs, nothing more — no editorials either attacking us as barbarians or praising us for striking a blow for good taste, and not one single word of praise, damnation, or even puzzlement from the man who had instigated, albeit unwittingly, our act of iconoclasm. Even the police seemed curiously passive. No attempt, apparently, was made to follow up the chief's theory. No further news stories reported on the progress of the crime investigation. As for me, I was preparing to bid Victoria goodbye. A few days after the incident I was on my way again for a third season at Middle Dominion Camp. Somewhat to my surprise, I found that I was actually looking forward to it.

4 When I arrived back in Dawson in May 1939, I found my father much changed. He had been told by his doctor that winter that he was suffering from angina pectoris, and his reaction was, in my opinion, unnecessarily extreme. He no longer hiked in the hills to look for wildflowers. He never again enjoyed an outing on the river. The boat that he had bought on his return to Dawson was first put away, then sold. He walked to work so slowly it was painful to watch him. He seemed to feel that any extra exercise would put him in his grave. What he really needed, I think now, was a complete rest and then some carefully accelerated exercise. It was a tragedy that a single diagnosis should have turned him from an active and lively personality into a bent old man.

And yet he had not given up on life. All that winter he had spent grinding, polishing, and silvering the mirror for a reflecting telescope, which he intended to build. It required both skill and patience to achieve the proper focal length with a device of his own invention and to finish off the task with jeweller's rouge. Again, it was the process that interested him, not the result. He completed the job and produced a flawless mirror. But he never bothered to build the telescope.

It was Lucy's turn to go north and look after my father. My mother should have gone too, but she did not feel she could afford more than one fare, especially as my father intended to leave the Yukon in September. Money was still tight and if Lucy and I were to move to Vancouver and attend the University of British Columbia — as I would do in the fall — then every cent counted. And so the three of us had a brief reunion in Dawson until my name came up on the company board and I again made the long journey to the mud flats of Dominion Creek.

I was still the youngest in a camp where everybody under the age of thirty was known as "kid." But now there were many closer to my own age, a friendly, cheerful group, full of fun and glad to have a job. A good many were immigrants, including one little Italian who smiled and grinned a lot but didn't speak a word of English. Some of the Germans were committed Nazis. Two were very hard characters indeed. I remember the pair of them walking down to work, swinging a live rabbit by the tail and banging its brains out against a tree for the fun of it. They were not popular. Another, Hans, was more genial if naïve. He kept showing me photographs of Hitler's autobahn, which he seemed to feel excused the dictator's many excesses.

We had one fanatical anti-Semite in our bunkhouse: Karl, a Scandinavian, not a German, known as the Danish Prince, a derisive nickname. When Karl railed against the Jews each evening, blaming them for all the world's troubles, the reaction among the Canadian-born was either laughter or anger. The world was about to go to war against men like Karl, and most of the young men in the bunkhouse sensed it. None had got past high school, but all had read the newspapers. When Art Webster did a devastating imitation of Neville

Chamberlain's famous "peace in our time" speech after returning from Munich, he was applauded and cheered.

The worst epithet you could hurl at a man in the company's camps was to brand him a "highballer" — a man who works too hard and never takes a break or stops for a smoke. Nobody at camp that summer shirked his task, but no one was anxious to work a sixty-three-hour week at an insane speed. The highballers were despised, but short of murder nothing could slow them down. The only answer was to let them work at their frantic pace without attempting to compete. After all, the company couldn't fire the entire camp. It was no accident that almost all the highballers were immigrants. All of us needed work, but in those grim times the immigrants needed it most. They were terrified, no doubt, of losing their jobs or being laid off in the first batch when the approach of winter slowed down the work.

The two tough Nazis were among the chief highballers in the camp that season. It didn't help them. When war was declared in September, the Mounties interned them both.

I actually enjoyed myself during this third season. The big dredge that had been under construction the year before was now in operation. In Dawson it was accepted that the dredges were the prime source of employment for boys who finished high school. Now several of my former classmates were at the camp, working as oilers, winchers, or deck-hands on Dredge No. 10. These included Percy de Wolfe and Alex Van Bibber, mixed-bloods with interesting pedigrees. Percy was the son of Percy Senior, known to all as the Iron Man of the Yukon. For years he had been mail carrier between Dawson and Eagle, Alaska, enduring great hardships and adventures, detailed each winter in the pages of the *Dawson News*: Percy de Wolfe falling through the ice and saving his sleigh and dogs; Percy de Wolfe breaking another record; Percy de Wolfe in an encounter with a grizzly.

The Van Bibber clan on their father's side went back, so it was said, to Daniel Boone, himself. I had known them all. Helen Van Bibber often stood ahead of me at school. And I still remember, when the first airplane flew into town, how little Jay Jay Van Bibber had thought it was a bird or a butterfly and tried to catch it. His older brothers, George and Alex, carved replicas of it overnight and sold them to us white kids for two bits apiece.

Charlie Mills, another contemporary, was also at the camp. His father, Charles Senior, ran the Central Hotel, sometimes known as the Bucket of Blood, and was a frustrated music-hall entertainer — the same man who had pranced across the stage in the days of my childhood singing "Alexander's Ragtime Band."

I no longer tumbled into bed, exhausted, an hour or so after dinner. I can scarcely believe it now, but with the help of one of the point drivers, Ron West, I actually started a camp newspaper.

Why did I do that at the end of a long day — sitting in the mess hall, typing it all out on foolscap, ruling the columns, drawing the cartoons, printing the headlines by hand, just as I had at college and in the Scouts? The only sensible answer is that I was obsessed by the idea of expressing myself in print.

The paper was called the *Pipeline*; its motto: "Keep the Water Running." It carried an editorial page, a social column, a poetry corner, a serial story ("Murder on the Mud Flats"), and even a STOP PRESS section. To say that the contents were corny would require a new and more extreme definition of that overworked word. The humour was laboured, the spoofs far-fetched, the gossip puerile, the jokes ancient, the cartoons crude, the columns overwritten. In short, it was everything that a paper of this kind should be, and when its five typed pages, two columns to a sheet, went up on the bulletin board in the mess hall, a crowd gathered to read it. It helped give me a little status in the camp where, in spite of two years' experience, I was still thought of as a green kid.

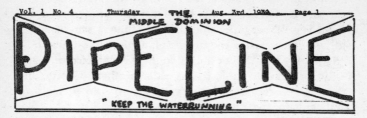

THE MIDDLE DOMINION PipeLine

"KEEP THE WATER RUNNING"

TRUCKS ANTICIPATED FOR CELEBRATION

ONE NITE STAND

According to unimpeachable sources, members of Middle Dominion Camp will be able to whoop it up in Dawson during the Discovery Day celebrations without serious loss of work, (but not without loss of sleep.)

High sources are quoted as saying it is "extremely probably" that trucks will be on hand to rush the boys in on any of the three Big Nites. They will return to camp early next morning with their load (slightly the worse for wear, but doubtless happy) in time for work at 7 a.m. sharp.

Large numbers have already indicated their willingness to enjoy this opportunity of taking in some of Dawson's gay Night life.

THOMAS WALLNUT TO PULL UP STAKES

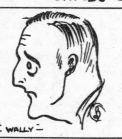

: WALLY -

Tom Wallnutt, ace point driver, better known to his brother point

Continued on next col.

YUKON WEATHER LOWERS SOFTBALL HOPES

GRANVILLE "SCARED"

Old Man Yukon tightened his grip last week and a continued series of thunderstorms have been rendered such things as ball fields and roads well nigh impassable. No change was made in the mud flats, which are impassable anyway.

With the softball diamond closely resembling a point hole, practices have been few and interest in the game is slowly dying. Karl Kaiser has laughed off all bets, Reggie Young has once more resumed his usual scowl, Lauronz Obermaier has gone back to a diet of Horseradish, Thomas Wallnutt is about to leave in disgust while Art Hagen piles on shirt after shirt and still shivers.

Rumour rears its ugly head to say that the Granville team has the wind up. We heard from a high source that the Mud Flashes have the Granville team scared.

Granville attempts to increase morale by whipping Middle Sulphur in a game last night. It is hoped that they will screw up enough courage to invade Dominion in the near future

Meanwhile Karl Kaiser, thawing ass., is training to be a relief pitcher. But practice makes perfect and as everybody knows, Karl is a persevering young man. (e.g. lettuce patch.)

drivers as "Doc" and "Wally" expects to leave shortly for the outside.

In a press interview Wally stated that he had seen the last of the Yukon "They should give it back to the Indians and apologize for taking it!" he is alleged to have said.

Continued on Page 4 Col. 2

"THE BACK PRESSURE HERE IS SOMETHING TERRIBLE!"

50 YEARS FROM NOW ?

Possible items from news papers fifty years hence.

Dr. Phineas Horseradish, who is conducting an archeological survey of the once densely populated Middle Dominion Mud Flat area, has exhumed the skeleton of a man of the Dark Ages, believed to have died of mud poisoning. The deep creases in the fore part of the skull indicate that these are the bones of an early time point doctor.

In a statement to the press this morning, Dr. Alexalo H.H. Storn, who has enjoyed a long and successful career as a music critic, said that he is of the opinion that swing has come to stay. This, despite the fact that Dark Cloud Young, his equally famous contemporary, insists that it is nothing more nor less than one of the growing pains of music. Both critics received their early training in Northern Mining Camps, listening to primitive musicians.

‒NOTICE‒

Mr. George Ramsay wishes to announce that he is authorized to take subscriptions to all magazines AND Vancouver Sun.
A SNAP! Colliers and American to one address for one year - $3.75.

JOAK

1st. point doctor - They say I'm bushed. That's silly.
2nd. Ditto- Let me test you. What have I got behind my back?
1st. Ditto - A bulldozer.
2nd. point doctor - You cheat! You saw me pick it up!

"You'll go far, Pete," the blacksmith, Jimmy Struthers, said to me one day when in his cups. "The rest of us ain't goin' nowhere, but you'll go far." *What did he mean by that?* I wondered. *What was "going far"?* The best I could hope to be — indeed, all I wanted to be — was a reporter on a city newspaper. Struthers made it sound as if I was going to be a politician or a business tycoon.

There were other after-hours diversions that year: softball games between a team from our camp and another from the Granville camp, some ten miles away — all to be cheered and reported in the *Pipeline*. And, having learned to drink (after a fashion), I would sometimes stroll five miles upstream to Fraser and Rusk's roadhouse for a hot rum or two. The roadhouse was all that remained of the old community of Paris, where several hundred Frenchmen had lived in the gold rush days. My father had at one time taught school there. Now there was nothing, save for the big false-fronted emporium where George Fraser and Bob Rusk sold groceries and dry goods and dispensed strong drink to all and sundry, following a kind of unwritten police tolerance that allowed anybody with a beer licence to sell anything alcoholic.

Fraser was a wiry man with a white handlebar moustache and a wheezing laugh that welled up from his Adam's apple until it became a coarse guffaw. His partner was plumper and quieter. These two old prospectors had lived at Paris since the stampede and still took a few ounces of gold regularly from their claim. Bob did most of the mining while George drove his Model T around the company loop, selling everything from chocolate bars to workshirts. Farther than that he never ventured.

"When was you in Dawson last, George?" somebody asked him as we sat sipping hot rums.

"Now, lemme see," said George, tilting his bowler back on his head. "That would be 1922, that last time."

"You mean you haven't been in town for *seventeen years*?"

"Never been back," said George Fraser. "Too many bright lights for me."

Bob Rusk, it turned out, had never visited Dawson since his arrival in Paris.

On the other side of the camp, a mile or so downstream, lived a sturdy Italian prospector named Pete Nazarino. He too seemed to have been rooted in Dominion from time immemorial, hauling out pay from his shaft, sluicing the gold free, and piling up each year a small stake that, as regularly as the ice breakup, he would squander in Dawson.

When Pete Nazarino hit town, after a few drinks he became a wild man. He actually lit cigars with twenty-dollar bills and once, it was said, bought himself a fine suit of clothes and burned it on the spot. Crowds would follow as he flung the loose change from his pockets until a group of sharpies got him into a blackjack game and fleeced him of his spring cleanup. But Pete Nazarino wasn't dumb. Before he took a single drink he always bought himself a grubstake for the coming season. Only after that did he run wild. Why? Perhaps because there was nothing else to do.

"How much do you figure you take out in a year, Pete?" one of the boys asked him.

"Maybe thirty-five hundred dollar," said Pete Nazarino.

"Hell, Pete, with a claim like yours, you could do a lot better."

"But why?" asked Pete reasonably. "I'd only burn it up in one weekend there in Dawson."

For Dominion Creek was still rich. It had been worked over by individual miners, some of whom, like Pete, were still making living wages from it. Their primitive methods had no more than scratched the surface. When the dredge came through there would be plenty left for the company, which would, of course, have to share its take with the owners of private claims.

The dredge was an awesome sight, lurching forward a few feet at a time on its thirty-ton spud, swinging from side to side on its cables, its bucket-line gouging deep into the bedrock. It was actually a floating sluicebox digging its own pond as it went, leaving behind those long mountains of gravel tailings that choke the valleys of the Klondike today.

As a child I'd feared the dredge. Now I respected it. I was glad that I didn't have to work as a dredge-hand, my ears assailed by the screeching of its cables and the whine of its engines — a cacophony that made normal conversation impossible. All of us that summer had heard the chastening story of Chris Bredenburg's accident on the dredge at Eldorado. His arm had been accidentally caught in the moving belt and twisted out of its socket as he hung from the stacker. Dropped onto the tailings thirty feet below, unable to make himself heard over the screeching of the dredge, Bredenburg was forced to stumble around the monster to attract the dredge master's attention by waving his remaining limb. Nobody thought he would survive, but he did, to marry his nurse.

Another event took place near us that summer — one that had all the elements of a scene from a B Western. A couple of miles upstream lived a crazed prospector. This was not as unusual as it sounds. Most men who lived alone, summer and winter, were at the very least slightly daft. It was true not only of solitary miners but also of some partnerships, which often broke up because two men living together in a single cabin found they couldn't stand one another. No winter in my childhood seemed to pass that Sergeant Cronkhite of the Mounted Police didn't come into town with a miner in a strait-jacket on his sled.

I cannot remember the name of the crazed miner on Dominion, but I am safe in calling him crazed because of what happened. He had taken a definite dislike to George Fulton, the mail carrier, who drove his truck around the creeks once a week. To lure Fulton into a trap he spread some newspapers on the road, apparently in the belief that the mailman would stop to read them. Fulton took one look and jammed his foot on the accelerator as a series of bullets whizzed over his pick-up. The prospector barricaded himself in his cabin, and a gun battle followed with the Mounted Police. It ended when he was killed. We were told his body was riddled with bullets. Being a crack shot, he might have taken some of the policemen with him, but fortunately, in his dementia he had raised his sights so high his rifle didn't find a target. Such was the atmosphere in which we toiled and sometimes caroused in that last pre-war summer.

5 On the twenty-first of June, 1939, the night of the summer solstice and the occasion of the Klondike's biggest seasonal ritual apart from Discovery Day, I got into trouble. In Dawson people were heading for the Midnight Dome in the mistaken belief that they would see the midnight sun. About fifteen miles upstream from our camp, another dome-like mountain known as the King Dome was a similar mecca. From this eminence most of the gold-bearing creeks of the Klondike and Indian river watersheds flowed out in every direction, like the spokes of a wheel. Did that mean that the fabled mother lode lay deep within the bowels of the mountain? If so, no one had ever discovered it; nor have they since. But on the longest day of the year people for miles around headed for the King Dome to watch the sun set just before midnight and rise not long after, and to toast it with bootleg whisky in Joe Fournier's roadhouse, which sat not far away on the crest of the divide between Hunker and Dominion creeks.

By this time I was ready for a break — any break. So were we all. We sat on our bunks, a dozen of us, talking wistfully about the celebration we knew would be taking place that night at Fournier's.

Then, at about nine, just as we were getting ready to turn in, a truck screeched to a halt on the road below.

"Anyone for Fournier's?" the driver called. We tumbled

139

from our bunks, dashed down the slope, and hurled ourselves onto the truck, already half full of celebrants. One of the strangers had a pinch bottle of Haig and Haig — nothing but the best. It was passed around from mouth to mouth in the Yukon fashion. Somebody handed it to me.

"Here, kid. Have a drink!"

I hesitated. I'd never drunk Scotch whisky — never drunk much of anything, really. "I don't think so, thanks," I said.

"*Have a drink!*" The order was unmistakable. It was an insult to refuse. I drank.

I did not know then that whisky could be drunk from a glass and mixed with water or soda. Nobody seemed to take it that way in the Klondike that summer of 1939. They swallowed it from the mouth of the bottle, like Coca-Cola. By the time we reached Fournier's, I was already half gone. Within an hour I was roaring drunk, even though Fournier was notorious for watering his bootleg booze.

I was tossing billiard balls around the poolroom when one of our gang suggested we go down the Hunker Valley to the roadhouse at Gold Bottom, where a dance was in full swing. It seemed like a wonderful idea. Since we had no transport of our own we appropriated Joe Fournier's pick-up and headed off at top speed, downhill all the way.

At Gold Bottom, the world was a-whirl. In the crowded roadhouse they were dancing schottisches to the music of an accordion, and I hadn't seen a woman since I left Dawson. I lurched over to a group on the sidelines — me, a raw, unkempt youth, still in my working clothes with seven days' beard and a pronounced stagger — and asked for a dance. I was coldly rejected. I drank some more from a proffered bottle. I may also have danced a little on my own, doing the box step as taught at the Dorothy Wilson school of dancing. I'm not sure; much of that evening remains foggy.

Back we went in Joe Fournier's borrowed truck up the Hunker road to the summit. By now it must have been three or four in the morning. We bumped around a turn, slid off the gravel, and found ourselves careering down the bank and into the trees. All of us jumped clear, so relaxed from drink that not a bone was broken. But the truck lay on its side in the bush.

Suddenly, I found myself sobering up. Camp was a long way away, and I was due on the mud flats at seven. Nobody else felt like going back and nobody else did go back that morning. But again I was terrified of being fired and disgracing my father. How could he face his friends, including those company executives who had been persuaded to hire me? Besides, I needed the money.

And so, still sodden from drink and shaken from the accident, I stumbled off, reached the summit, and headed on down that long, fifteen-mile slope that led to the camp. My chances of making it by seven o'clock were slim; I knew that. I broke into a run: I was in good condition and it was all downhill. I swayed as I ran, weaving from side to side, and kept on in this fashion, alternately running and walking. And then, from some miles behind me, I heard the rumble of a truck. I was saved!

The driver picked me up and deposited me in front of the Middle Dominion mess hall. It was just ten minutes to seven and the gang was already heading down to work. There was no time for breakfast; I couldn't have eaten it anyway. I staggered along and joined the pipeline crew on the mud flats. One of the flange feeders was about to burst open. Wooden piles had to be driven to keep it level. Without a word, Big Jim handed me the forty-pound maul. I climbed the ladder and began to pound away. Each blow, it seemed, matched the throbbing in my head.

Since that night I've never been able to taste Scotch whisky without making a face. It was years before I could even manage it with soda. And what I did not know, as I swung the big maul and felt the pangs of hunger overtake me, was that Joe Fournier, the most litigious man in the Yukon, was about to attempt court action against the men who had taken his pick-up. Most of these were strangers, who had no intention of identifying themselves. But one face from the past, one son of the North, was more than familiar, and that was me.

In spite of this sobering incident, which I duly recorded, with some gusto, in the pages of the *Pipeline* — thereby giving Joe Fournier hard evidence against us if he were bright enough to realize it — my spirits remained high. Rather than dampening my enthusiasm, the brief adventure had whetted it. By mid-August, with two more months of seven-day weeks behind me and Discovery Day in the offing, I was again feeling festive.

The Brains, as the chief executives of the company were called, looked with a certain indulgence on Discovery Day. They allowed us no paid holidays — we had to keep the water running — but they knew they couldn't stop most men from roaring into Dawson for a couple of days, without pay, to celebrate. The Brains were all friends of my father. I had been in the homes of several. But on the mud flats they took on a different character, awesome and distant. From time to time I would spot one of these Brains walking the pipeline with Walter Troberg, the camp boss. I found it hard to realize these creatures from the higher stratosphere were the same quiet figures in tweeds and flannels to whom my father had introduced me.

They could fire us on whim, or so it was whispered. The tale was told, almost certainly apocryphal, of the Brain who had seen a man in the distance apparently idling. "Fire that man," the Brain was supposed to have thundered, "he hasn't moved in half an hour!" Later it developed that the poor wretch *couldn't* move; he was stuck up to his hips in mud.

The chief Brain was a tiny, white-haired creature with the appropriate name of G. Goldthorpe Hay. He came out from London once a year, visited the various camps, and walked the pipeline wearing a wing collar and foulard tie with his formal suit, the trousers of which were tucked into a pair of rubber shoepacks.

I thought it ironical that they had hired Chester Henderson's father, Grant, a great bear of a man, to carry the little chairman around on his shoulders, piggyback, to keep him out of the mud. The symbolism of that spectacle — the head of the great company riding on the back of the son of the original discoverer of gold — was not lost on some of us.

In spite of the Brains' indulgence regarding the August 17 weekend, all of us who had gone to the Summit on June 21 swore we wouldn't repeat our folly. Why, if we went to Dawson we would, like Pete Nazarino, blow all our hard-earned money.

We all agreed there were too many temptations lying in wait for men who had been cooped up all season. Terrible tales were told of those who had gone into Dawson on previous Discovery Days and were lost for a week. I hadn't forgotten the spectacle of my construction foreman, George Lund, returning from a binge in 1937, pale and shattered, sitting with his head in his hands at the breakfast table, unable to speak. That wasn't going to happen to me; I needed every cent for college.

Then why did I look forward so avidly to Discovery Day? Why, when the truck came by, did I join in the stampede to jump aboard? I was like an alcoholic who swears off the bottle but has one hidden in the chandelier. In spite of the fact that Scotch whisky made me gag, I cheerfully took my pull on the Haig and Haig when it was passed around. One of the gang, Art Hagen, announced that he intended to take my sister to the dance. He was a handsome Irishman with a Clark Gable moustache and a swagger to match it. I was horrified. Suddenly I was her big brother, protective of her honour, terrified of what might happen to this fragile and sensitive girl in the hands of a sex-crazed monster from Middle Dominion. I tried to dissuade him. "You wouldn't like her," I said, "She's not your type." But he persisted.

I went briefly to my father's rented house in the north end of town. He and Lucy greeted me warmly. I don't think they cared much for my attitude. I swaggered about, talked with a rough accent (there were so many Scandinavians in the camp that I had developed a Swedish lilt), and railed against foreign highballers, an attitude that disturbed my father, who was the most tolerant of men. Then, to cap it all, I announced I wouldn't be going to the big dance that night with them; I'd join my own gang downtown.

Looking back on that evening, not without shame, I am amazed at my father's forbearance. He did not attack me for my insufferable posturing or order me out of the house. He only remarked, mildly, that he was sorry he wasn't going to see much of me.

At this point the telephone rang. It was Art Hagen, inviting Lucy to the dance. She seemed flattered, my father delighted.

"Lucy's got a date!" he told me. I already knew.

"I'll see you both there," I said, and off I went to the Bucket of Blood, bellied up to the bar, and allowed Charlie Mills, Sr., to sell me a brace of Tom Collinses. I found them delicious — a contrast to the straight Scotch I'd been drinking. The gang arrived and announced that we were all going to a whorehouse. A little tingle ran through me, compounded partly of trepidation, partly of excitement. At nineteen, I was a sexual novice who had only rarely dated a girl. That clearly bothered my father, who kept asking me, during my stays with him, if I wasn't interested in having a girl friend. It occurred to me, years later, that he was terrified I might be homosexual. It wasn't that; it was just that I could never summon up enough courage in Victoria to approach a girl and ask her out. Besides, I had little money and no access to a car.

Fortified by Charlie Mills's gin, I tramped off with the gang along Second Avenue to the north end of town, where the weeds and willows half covered the old sidewalks, until we came to a small log cabin rented by two women who had come up from Juneau especially for Discovery Day. I joined the mob of men seated on stuffed couches in the tiny parlour.

144

As the men engaged each other in a kind of artificial badinage, the two girls bustled about with drinks and then indulged in a ritual. Each would sit on a man's knee for a few moments, fluff his hair, whisper in his ear, and drag him off to one of the two bedrooms. Five minutes later the man would emerge, looking sheepish, and the girl would follow shortly after to sit on a new knee. Finally, the moment came when one sat on my knee.

I can't remember much about it because it all happened so quickly. One moment she was sitting on my knee, the next she was scrubbing my genitals in a china basin in the bedroom. I flung myself at her, more to cover my own embarrassment than to display any lust. "Not that way, sport," she said, and showed me the proper way. Two minutes later she was calling her associate, who arrived with a fresh basin and towels, and I was back in the parlour with my friends.

At the dance that night, through a misty sea of gin, I spotted my sister arriving late on my father's arm. Where was her escort? What had happened? I looked around for Art Hagen and found him at last dancing with a pretty little girl whom I recognized instantly as Bertha de Wolfe. Hagen had switched sisters. Instead of taking mine to the dance, he had taken Percy's. I looked over at Lucy and felt a wave of guilt and compassion, for she looked more than a little downcast. I box-stepped her across the dance floor, making sure to grip her tightly as she'd taught me. "You're well out of it," I told her. "He wasn't for you. You wouldn't have liked him."

She looked at me dubiously. "I waited a long time," she said, and my heart went out to her. "Fellow's a bit of a cad," was the way my father put it.

I did not indulge in further sexual adventures, although there were many temptations. Ruby and Gabby — the two best-known whores in Dawson — were holding court, and so was the notorious Cross Fox, so called because she had two contrasting shades of pubic hair. It wasn't that I didn't want to go. It was simply that I couldn't bring myself to squander another ten dollars of my hard-earned funds. I rejoined my father and sister and, forty-eight hours later, returned to camp to finish out my season.

When word got around that I had actually been to a whorehouse, there was great interest and no little curiosity. It developed that a good many of the others who had bragged so constantly about sex had not had the experience. "What was it like? What did you do?" asked Ron West, co-editor of the *Pipeline,* who'd also gone into Dawson but had declined any sexual adventure. I shrugged nonchalantly, said it was nothing, really, and pretended it was old stuff to me.

I made no more than a veiled reference to the event in the *Pipeline.*

EDITORS COVER 17TH CELEBRATION

Ron West and Pierre Berton, editors of the Middle Dominion Pipeline, lost valuable sleep and time in a martyr-like effort to cover the Discovery Day Celebration. The effect was unsuccessful owing to the fact that their reports differ widely in several of the important details.

The editors stated that it was impossible to give an accurate account of the Crowning of Miss Dawson, etc., as the whole thing was too colourful.

"The Dawson papers have said all there is to say," Berton is quoted as saying. "Besides, we had important business elsewhere." Anyway, it was a good excuse.

By this time the flats on which we toiled were an unspeakable mess. The ground crumbled beneath our feet, water spurted up in all directions, ponds formed suddenly, others expanded until they joined a string of pools to create a labyrinth of mud and water. We worked from rafts and duckboards, fighting to keep the pipes straight, wiring and rewiring, doused regularly with cold spray. The points were all down to bedrock by this time. Now each point driver's job was to keep the water running in his line. I too could sometimes feel the rheumatism in my hands; it was a decade before the last traces of it vanished.

One late-August day, the first group of men was laid off. I was one. I heaved a sigh of relief, for I had had enough. I wanted to get on with my university career. And so, for the last time, I took the company truck back over the divide to Dawson and stood once more on the Hunker summit to look down on those famous gold creeks that radiated from the King Dome like the spokes of a wheel. Forty-seven years would go by before I would stand again on this post. By then the dredges would be long gone, the tailing piles would be furred with new growth, the naked hills would be clothed once more in birch and poplar, and Joe Fournier's roadhouse would be a ruin.

In Dawson, I joined my father and sister for a leisurely dinner. They, too, would be leaving Dawson — forever. I tried hard not to wolf my food, but old habits died hard. Meals at Middle Dominion had been swift and silent. It was said that if you stumbled on the mess hall steps going in you got caught by the rush coming out.

"Slow down," said Lucy. "You're not at camp now. You've got me all out of breath."

I paused in mid-forkful just as a knock came at the door. My father rose to answer it and there, framed against the autumnal sky, resplendent in scarlet, stood a constable of the Royal Canadian Mounted Police. He handed my father a document. It was a summons for me. Joe Fournier had charged me with theft.

6 My father took it all remarkably well. He didn't chastise me or tell me I was a goddam fool. I think he knew that I already realized that. Perhaps in his youth, right here in the Yukon for all I knew, he too had sown his measure of wild oats. Perhaps he secretly admired me for getting into a scrape. All he said was, "Well, I guess we'd better go down tomorrow morning and look in on Charlie McLeod."

Charlie McLeod was the town's leading lawyer, in fact the only lawyer, because the other one, George Black, was not in Dawson that summer. He was also the company's lawyer and an old friend of my father.

He listened with some amusement to my story.

"Joe Fournier, eh?" he said. That seemed to please him. He turned to my father.

"The first thing to do," he said, "is to get this boy out of town."

"I was going anyway," I said.

"Good," said Charlie McLeod. "I'll handle this, Frank."

And that was the last we heard of the matter. Forty years later, John Gould, a classmate of mine, gave me the brief details of what happened when the case came to court.

"The judge looked at the docket and then took one look at Joe Fournier who, as you know, had appeared before him many times on the wrong side of the law. 'Get out of my courtroom,' he shouted. 'Case dismissed.'"

And that was the end of my criminal career.

I cannot say that the prospect of a court trial perturbed me greatly as I sat on the deck of the *Casca* watching the river go by — just as Big Jim had predicted. I did not know it then, but this was the last time in my life I would be able to enjoy a steamboat journey up the Yukon, with the birches and aspens golden against the pale blue of a September sky. The river today is silent; the steamboats are no more. But in those days there was no voyage like it. It was a unique experience to lounge in the forward saloon of the *Casca* with my father and Lucy, listening to the slap-slap of the paddlewheel, watching the forest unwind around each bend of the Yukon.

It was a leisurely, almost dreamlike voyage. The water was so low that it took twice the normal time for the stern-wheeler to force her way upstream to Whitehorse. At Five Finger Rapids, where five separate channels of white water were squeezed between four massive blocks of conglomerate, she had to be winched through, a process that took several hours. There were regular stops along the way to take on birch wood, piled up by woodcutters on the high banks. We travellers wandered about, picking wildflowers, as the deck-hands sweated to load the boat with more fuel.

One of the several sounds associated in my memory with river travel was the thunderclap produced when each deckhand, racing down the gangplank with his load of cordwood, pivoted at a ninety-degree angle and hurled his load into the well of the engine room. All this stretched out the journey to a week, but nobody minded. We were on northern time, moving at the unhurried pace that had long been mandatory in that realm of dogsleds, steamboats, stagecoaches, and sudden unexpected vagaries of weather.

We reached our destination on the very day that war was declared in Europe. Whitehorse was then a sleepy hamlet of about three hundred. Dogs were snoring in the dusty main street when a man crossed over from the White Pass station to tell my father that the British were determined to fight over Hitler's invasion of Poland. We had been a week without news, but I cannot recall that this information in any way surprised me. It all seemed so far away; no cannons boomed for us beyond those smoky hills.

Yet the war would change Whitehorse more than most Canadian villages. Before it ended, this would be a raucous community of perhaps fifteen thousand, an anchor point on the Alaska Highway, which in 1939 was no more than a concept. It would mean the end of the steamboat era and the end of Dawson as the territorial capital. But all that was in the future as we took the train to Skagway and boarded the *Princess Louise* for the journey to Vancouver.

In the first-class lounge, the orchestra was playing the new songs: "Roll Out the Barrel," "Sunrise Serenade." My father and sister travelled first class; I was down in the hold with my friends from the mining camps. We steerage passengers had the run of the ship, though not the first-class dining room. Emboldened by the memory of Madame Sanderson-Mongin's words, or perhaps by my adventure on Discovery Day, I had met and taken up a pretty waitress from the Lake Bennett mess hall named Aggie, several years older than I. My father was delighted. "He's got a girl!" he told my sister jubilantly, forbearing to add the phrase, "at last." But it hung there unspoken. *At last*, I wasn't queer after all!

It was a memorable trip. Besides my friends from the Yukon, there were college students returning to UBC who would soon be my classmates. In Juneau, Alaska, one of the coastal stops, a motherly woman stuck her head out of an upper-storey window and hailed us. "I've got a nice girl here, lads," said she.

"Well, see that she stays that way," someone shouted back, as we headed for the nearest tavern.

We wanted no more illicit adventures. One of our number had contracted gonorrhea, almost certainly as a result of that visit to the little cabin in the north end of Dawson. The rest of us escaped. Luck was with me then, as it has been for most of life — luck, and a certain amount of prudence; I had tested the waters but, in the interests of financial stability, had declined to take a second plunge. "You are probably the most conservative man I know," my mother once told me — an odd remark to make about someone generally considered a radical. But I think I knew what she meant — that I was careful, even at times cautious.

When we reached Vancouver, I took charge and helped my father off the boat with his luggage. It was almost as if I had become *his* father. My mother was visibly alarmed at his appearance — he looked so old and so grey, and he moved so slowly. She was also more than a little baffled when I announced that I would not be staying at the Grosvenor with the family but at the more plebeian Dunsmuir with my friends. I must say my parents took this new-found independence with good humour. The following day they left for Victoria, but I decided to stay for a while in the bigger city.

We went to the Cave, my first nightclub. It wasn't a bit like the ones in the Hollywood films, but under the influence of sloe gin, the only palatable alcoholic beverage I could find, it took on a certain aura.

A few days later I turned up in Victoria with Aggie in tow. Our relationship was warm, friendly, and even passionate, but never carnal, largely because I couldn't summon up the courage to enter an Owl Drug Store and ask the girl behind the counter for a package of condoms. Aggie stayed at a hotel; I lived at home. My mother was clearly worried but tried not to show it. Years later I learned that she was convinced I was madly in love and would run off with Aggie, thereby wrecking my career. I had no such intention.

Aggie was invited to tea with Aunt Florrie and the family. Everyone seemed to be walking on eggs, overly polite, incredibly solicitous. It was as if they were leaning over backward not to offend my young lady, knowing that this would provoke an opposite reaction from me.

I took Aggie back downtown and returned to Oak Bay. "Well," said my mother, "what did she think of us?"

I replied truthfully: "She said you were all cute."

My mother's face was a mask. "Cute," she said. "Cute. Well!" And that was all.

It was never a torrid romance and remained platonic largely because of my own inhibitions. We both went back to Vancouver, I to university, Aggie to a job as a housemaid in a big home in Shaughnessy Heights.

I remember once, on a visit home to Victoria, my mother asked about Aggie.

"I see her on Thursdays," I said.

"Of course," said my mother, "maid's day..." she stopped and bit her tongue.

We drifted slowly apart. To be honest, I too was more than a little snobbish about Aggie. There were dances at UBC to which I could have taken her; but I wouldn't, perhaps because I thought she wouldn't fit in with the sophisticated fraternity men or the pert young things in saddle-shoes and bobby sox, or perhaps because I thought I'd be looked down on for bringing a mere housemaid to a college hop. I regret it now, for she was a good friend who always made me feel grown up. "You're quite the ladies' man," she used to say, gazing at me with those round blue eyes and crinkled snub of a nose until she almost had me believing it.

My father took this photograph of me before I was two years old, with
our husky dog, Grey Cloud. We had no photo labs in Dawson in 1922
and, from the look of things, no diapers either. My father processed
his own pictures in a makeshift darkroom while we kids looked on.

I hated this hair-do so much that, at the age of five, I tried to cut it off when this formal portrait was made. The damage I did is easily visible.

Lucy, at four, was a chubby girl with big brown eyes that she inherited from our mother, who got them from her father. My granddaughter, Elora, has them, too.

Our house in Dawson still stands, but it doesn't look like this any more. My father had planted canary vine along the east wall, and the tourists who came to visit Robert Service's cabin across the road were charmed to find such jungle-like growth in the frozen North.

Dawson in winter. My sister and I are in the sled, Grey Cloud pulling.
Note the woodpile – the only fuel we had in those coal-less days.

There's my grandfather at eighty-eight with my Uncle Phil and
my grandmother in the rear. One of my many great-aunts, Allie, is
on the left.

I know that this family photograph was taken in 1925 because my mother has yet to follow fashion and have her hair shingled. The fringe of pansies and the window boxes of nasturtiums on the front of our house establish the month — July, about the time of my birthday.

My sister, Lucy, and I — two chubby moppets screaming with laughter — roll about in the wet snow, beads of which cling to the soft wool of our outfits.

Lucy in her fairy costume. Her dance teacher later moved to Fernie, B.C., where my future wife, Janet, wore a similar dress.

Here we are, anchored in Swede Creek, downriver from Dawson, on the boat my father built himself. Being a New Brunswicker, he named it *Bluenose* and painted the prow the appropriate colour. We're angling for Arctic grayling, which, being cold-water fish, are very fine eating indeed.

This is me as a Second-Class Scout in Victoria. Later I rose to be a King Scout and leader of the Seagull Patrol, St. Mary's Troop.

The student editor emerges from the offices of the Publications Board at UBC, doing his best to look like a a real journalist.

My first broadcast on CJOR as a member of the UBC Radio Society. I look calm, but actually I'm shaking like a leaf, not yet having conquered mike fright.

In her teens, Lucy looked a bit like Hedy Lamarr and was often mistaken for the movie star by some of my own reporting staff.

BEAST STALKS CAMPUS, the headline read in the *Ubyssey's* "Goon Issue," spring, 1941. I'm the beast, and this is my college swan-song. But they still use that photograph.

Remember those street photographers? This one caught my mother and me in Vancouver in the days when a fedora hat was very much the style.

The year is 1941, and by this time I *am* a real journalist, editing copy and answering the phone at the cluttered city desk of the Vancouver *News-Herald*. Hollow-cheeked from lack of sleep, I weigh only 165 pounds; but at least I've got hair, even if it isn't brushed.

Driving pipe on the mud flats of Dominion Creek in the Klondike in the summer of 1938. I'm the kid in the rear. The cushiest job was to sit atop the pipe and hold the iron "maidenhead" while the others banged the male end into the female end – a sexual metaphor in a womanless community.

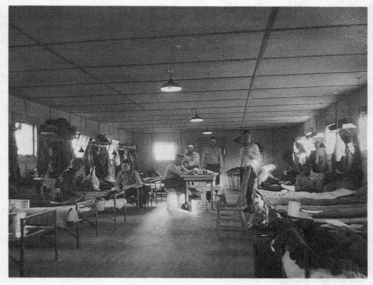

In these Spartan quarters I spent my summers. I'm not in this picture because I took it. Otherwise I'd be on one of the bunks, flat on my back, exhausted from the day's labours. After we finished work, scrubbed our clothes, and wolfed down dinner, it was generally time to go to bed.

Life on the mud flats. I'm in the foreground, helping lug a heavy valve for one of the flange feeders, which will control the flow of water to the smaller pipes lying across our path. Once that starts, this hard-packed clay will become a sea of mud and the pipes will start to bend and break.

I always looked a bit of a mess in the mining camp. After nine hours of hard labour, I wasn't too keen on doing laundry.

But I was keen on three square meals a day. This is our mess hall; I helped build it. They said if you stumbled on the steps going in, you got caught by the rush coming out.

Those tall pipes with the tangled hoses were known as "points." There were hundreds of them, and the water poured through them, deep into the earth's bowels, day and night. That's why I'm working in pools of mud and slime. The ground is already starting to fall away as the bedrock thaws.

First Lieutenant Berton leads his men not into battle but on one of the bond parades that were a feature of the war years. Since only one division was in battle when this photograph was taken, we had very little to do except to march through the streets of Calgary.

As a private soldier at Vernon, B.C., I signed up as a Seaforth. I didn't make the regiment, but I got to wear the Balmoral.

I look keen and competent on my Indian motorbike during a driving and maintenance course, but you'll notice it isn't moving. Actually, I failed dismally.

Army or no army, I couldn't leave the typewriter alone. I started two army newspapers and contributed to a third. On my leaves I sometimes visited my old paper (as shown here) and even contributed a column under a pseudonym. I cannot recall that it created so much as a ripple among the readers.

Janet Walker was my closest friend in Vancouver – but not yet a girl friend. Still, she helped me pick out my uniform when they made me an officer.

As soon as I became a leader of men I grew a moustache just like Errol Flynn's. The idea was that it might make me look older than my callow years and impress the troops.

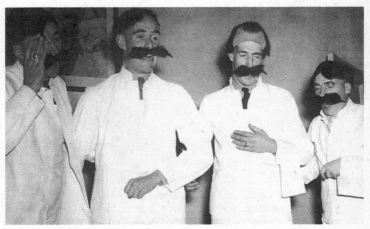

The army brought out the ham in me. Here my buddy, Stretch Colville, and I, flanked by two others, are singing "The Trouble With Women" from the Broadway musical *One Touch of Venus* in the Officers' Mess at Calgary. We are supposed to be singing waiters; I'm the waiter second from the left.

There was some talk of wearing formal clothes when Janet and I got married on March 22, 1946. But that came to nothing when we learned there wasn't a dinner jacket in town that would fit the best man, Harry Filion (rear). So I put on my only good suit and let Janet do the dressing up.

We called this a "gag photo" on the *Vancouver Sun*. That's Evelyn West, the Hubba Hubba girl, whose hubbas were insured by Lloyd's.

At the Fourth Estate Frolic with my new bride, Janet, who's better dressed and coiffured than I am. But then, I've spent most of the day chasing a pig.

The great Hal Straight, riding high, urges on his painted steed. Jack Scott (centre) and I are right behind him. Harry Filion took the picture. There was method in Straight's madness. He liked to help us blow off steam because he knew we'd work better together as a team. And he was right.

The promotion department loved this photograph taken just after we landed in the South Nahanni. Russ Baker, our pilot, is in the centre, and that's Art Jones, our photographer, on the right. The plane is a Junkers designed before 1920. It can be seen today in the air museum at Ottawa.

This is the photograph that Harry Filion gave to Janet and me when we left Vancouver in June of 1947 for Toronto. That's his wife, Veryl, in the centre, and little Vicki bringing up the rear. (Now she's Vicki Gabereau, Well-Known Personality.) It made us both very homesick when we opened it.

Chapter Four

Halcyon Days
1939-1942

1 The campus of the University of British Columbia was vast and, to me, a little terrifying. I had never seen so many students — more than two thousand. (Today, when it has more than ten times that number, I find it even more terrifying.) I was confused, bewildered, and elated all at the same time.

I gave little thought to lectures or curriculum but instead went straight to the offices of the Publications Board, where the *Ubyssey*, the *Totem* (the university annual), and the *Tillicum* (the student handbook) were all produced. At the front counter I received a warm smile from a pretty girl with cherry lips and dark brown eyes. This was Janet Walker, editor of the *Tillicum*, also in her third year. Her name was familiar to me from my study of the paper during my last year in Victoria. I thought her smile was a special one for me and believed myself to be in love with her. I didn't realize that she smiled cheerfully at everyone, for she had a sunny disposition and a warm heart. She still has. Seven years later I married her.

The *Ubyssey*'s editor-in-chief was John Garrett, who'd been a class ahead of me at Oak Bay High. He was a bantam cock of a man with a crisp accent, part English, part Victoria, who gave the impression that he was surrounded by idiots and morons. His main purpose, he announced, was to raise the intellectual standard of the university by at least 10 per cent, using the *Ubyssey* as his instrument. In that, I fear, he failed signally.

The snobbishness of the Publications Board was a

reflection of Garrett's own personality. The staff of the paper invariably referred to him as "God," a title he clearly relished. Budding journalists like me he treated as insects, useful for fetching Cokes and chips for the seniors on the staff but far too inexperienced to be trusted with any kind of assignment. If that was his way of getting rid of those who joined the paper for glamour rather than journalism, it worked. But one or two of us hung on, and after a fortnight of being ignored I was at last handed a list of books the library had purchased that week and told to write a paragraph about it.

My first assignment! I sweated for hours over that paragraph — the first story of mine to see real print.

I wrote: "A new and exciting series of titles will grace the library shelves as a result of shrewd purchases by the librarian, John Ridington. . . ."

And I wrote: "Librarian John Ridington today revealed the acquisition of valuable volumes for the university library. . . ."

And I wrote: "Library shelves bulged today with six newly acquired tomes. . . ."

And I wrote: "Cost is no object with genial John Ridington where good literature is concerned. Throwing caution to the winds, he has spared no expense to acquire six new volumes. . . ."

It finally came out as: "The following six books were purchased this week by the library. . . ."

I can still remember the moment when the paper came out and I snatched a copy off the pile, turned to my own story, and read those printed words over and over again. NEW BOOKS ON LIBRARY SHELVES. *Beautiful!*

Two more weeks dragged by without an assignment. I continued to hang around the office, fetching more Cokes, and trying to strike up a meaningful conversation with the girl who kept smiling at everybody. Finally, I decided to do something about both: the paper first, the girl second.

154

I was living at Salisbury Lodge, a boarding house within the university gates on what is known as the University Endowment Lands. We feuded in a friendly sort of fashion with the theological students resident in the nearby Union College. One day, a group from Salisbury Lodge fell upon some of these theologs in a dark wood near the college and scared them silly.

The following morning I wrote the story — or part of it — an attack by "unknown assailants" for the *Ubyssey*. It was a slow week. My scoop became the lead story on the front page; DASTARDLY ATTACK AT UNION COLLEGE. The three members of the *Ubyssey* staff who also acted as campus correspondents for the downtown dailies rewrote it immediately.

The following day I wrote what is known as a "follow-up," revealing that the escapade had been a student prank. Again my story made page one: STUDENT ATTACK PROVEN HOAX. I was commended for my enterprise, and from that point my rise was rapid. I had learned a cardinal principle of journalism: Don't wait for the news to come to you; go after it, and if necessary make it up.

Thus I kept my eyes out for interesting, out-of-the-way stories and was often rewarded for my curiosity. Once while walking down the Mall I encountered a young Norwegian who asked me the way to Professor John Irving's office. Of course I asked him why. He explained that Irving was an expert on the Kwakiutl Indians, who, he believed, were related to the Polynesian tribes of the South Pacific.

I took him over to the *Ubyssey* office and interviewed him at length about the year he and his young wife had spent on a cannibal island — Fatu Hiva in the Marquesas. His name was Thor Heyerdahl, and nobody, including the downtown press, had heard of him. The famous "Kon-Tiki" raft trip that would make him famous was eight years in the future. We became good friends, and when he went to Victoria he spent many evenings with my parents. Meanwhile I had a strong feature story for the *Ubyssey*.

About this time I began to date Janet Walker, creating something of a sensation in her boarding house when I sent her a three-dollar orchid corsage on the occasion of the Arts-Aggie Ball. None of her roommates had ever received an orchid, and a great fuss was made over me when I arrived to pick her up. Actually, I didn't know the name of any other exotic flower; I simply blurted out to the florist the only one I could think of.

Janet seemed to be involved in everything and anything on the campus. She was an associate editor of the *Ubyssey* and editor of the student directory, a member of the Radio Society, the Student Christian Movement, the Big Sisters, the Social Problems Club, the women's organization known as Phrateres, her own sorority (Alpha Delta Pi), and, from what I was able to discover, half a dozen other organizations. She was, in short, gregarious to a fault, always smiling, ever cheerful, continually in demand.

She also seemed to know everybody and everything about everybody on the campus. She had the happy quality of remembering people's names, and because she was genuinely interested in those she talked to — not as a journalist seeking a story but as someone who cared about the human condition — people told her everything. She was the perfect candidate to inherit the *Ubyssey*'s innocuous gossip column, which she wrote under the house pseudonym "Mary Anne." This was a potpourri of short, chatty advertising copy interspersed with nuggets of anonymous tattle ("What football-playing senior has taken his pin back from which blonde Delta Gam?"). To the frustration of the rest of us, Janet's column turned out to be the most popular feature in the paper.

She had no shortage of dates, but she kept them all guessing. She was everybody's sister, nobody's girl friend. Sometimes she allowed *two* escorts to take her to a college function. One of them, on occasion, was me. It was not a happy experience. We two males exchanged pleasantries through gritted teeth, each trying to outdo the other in civility. Janet knew how to keep a man at arm's length in those critical moments on the doorstep when one did one's best to stretch the goodnights into a passionate embrace. I tried to kiss her on one occasion, but she sidestepped neatly, leaving me lunging at the door frame. "It's raining," she said apologetically, hoping that flimsy excuse would salve my feelings. The next time out she had an equally brilliant excuse. "It's too cold," she said as I leaned toward her with puckered lips. *Too cold!* Ye Gods, I was burning with frustration. But she had popped inside the door of her boarding house before I could remonstrate, and all I could hear were the faint giggles of her roommates.

And so we danced to all the great songs of those days: "Harbor Lights" and "Moonlove" and "All the Things You Are." Eventually I went on to other girls, she to other boys; but we remained good friends, part of the same gang, moving with the *Ubyssey* crowd from Cokes and fries in the cafeteria to beers in the basement of the Georgia Hotel, and to Howard Mitchell's print shop on Pender Street, where the paper was published that year. We were a tight-knit group. Only a few belonged to any Greek-letter society. But, like the fraternities and sororities, we had our own table in the cafeteria — bold was the stranger who tried to sit at it — and the sure knowledge that our place at it was earned through ability and not social status.

I paid no attention to my appearance on the campus. I had one dark suit, which I kept for special occasions. The rest of the time I wore a cheap, light blue jacket, green checked trousers, and a maroon shirt, which I occasionally washed by hand, set off by a yellow tie in the McLeod tartan. I was always rumpled and could not understand how it was that people like Ozzie Durkin, a Big Man on

157

Campus who was, among other things, editor of the *Totem* and author of the university song, "Hail UBC," could look so neat. Ozzie's pants always had knife-sharp creases; his jacket was free of wrinkles. Finally I asked him how he kept his clothes that way.

"I send them out," said Ozzie.

I didn't know what that meant. *Out?* Out where? In all those years in Victoria we had never sent anything to the cleaners or the laundry, and it took a little while to digest Ozzie's curt remark. Finally it dawned on me: Ozzie actually *paid* to have his pants pressed. I was impressed, too.

I couldn't afford such luxuries, but I was having a wonderful time. "Make the best of these years, my boy," adult friends of my family would tell me during my visits home to Victoria. "These are the best years of your life. You'll look back on them, some day." I didn't need to be told that; I *knew*. This was one of those times when I was able to look at my situation as if I were an old man gazing back fondly on my youth. It is a trick I have often employed, and when I bring it off the sky always looks bluer and the grass greener.

I can still remember one sunny spring day when a group of us wandered across that beautiful sea-girt campus, arm in arm, intoxicated with love and life. We walked through the trees that bordered the ocean, clambered down the slope to the beach below, and gambolled for a while in the sand. We climbed back up and romped along the centre Mall until we reached the farmlands of the Agricultural Department, where cattle lowed and chickens squawked. We skipped along to the Dolphin Tea House overlooking the strait and ordered Viennese coffee, thick with whipped cream, and Viennese cake, heavy with dark chocolate. And I thought then: *Remember this day. It will never happen again exactly like this; save it for your later years because you may never again have it so good.* From time to time, I retrieve that scene from the filing cabinets of my memory to caress it once more and think back to those golden afternoons when life lay spread out before us like a welcoming carpet and anything seemed possible.

I saw little of my family in Victoria that fall, and I was too bound up in campus activities to write regularly. In my wallet I carried a photograph of Lucy, looking alluring with her pageboy haircut and her long eyelashes. Nobody would believe she was my sister.

"Come *on*! That's not your sister. That's your girl friend, and you've been hiding her."

"I tell you it *is* my sister. You can see the family resemblance."

"Family resemblance! You've got to be kidding. She's too beautiful to be your sister."

"Well, she is so my sister."

"Honest to God, Berton, I can't figure how you got yourself a girl friend that good looking."

In November, I got my first break. Jim MacFarlane, who had been the *News-Herald*'s campus correspondent, decided to give up the job because his low marks were worrying him. He recommended me as his successor, and I was accepted. This was a memorable moment. At last I had my foot in the door of a real newspaper! Down I went to the *News-Herald*'s offices in a small two-storey building on Hamilton Street, climbed the outside stairs to the editorial department on the second floor, and entered the newsroom. It wasn't quite like the ones I'd seen in the Hollywood movies, being small, dingy, and overcrowded, but to me it was glamorous beyond description. Shirt-sleeved men hammered away at typewriters. Others in green eye-shades sat at a big desk in the background, shuffling through mounds of copy. In the background I could hear the rhythmic clatter of the British United Press teletype.

Nobody paid the least attention to me. I found an empty desk and began to type out my first story from the campus. I had hardly begun when a youngish woman in mannish tweeds, looking more than a little dishevelled, seized me by the shoulder and gave me a push.

"That's my desk and my typewriter," she said. "Find your own." I retreated meekly, not having a place of my own, and waited until another machine was free. Her name, I learned, was Evelyn Caldwell, and she wrote a column on the editorial page titled "Sauce for the Goose." In spite of that unpropitious beginning we were eventually to become lifelong friends.

The *News-Herald* paid me twenty cents a column inch to report on university happenings that might have some interest to the outside world. I made the most of it, entering into a see-saw battle with the city desk over the length of my copy. I wanted to write the longest possible stories; the paper wanted them short, in the interests of space as well as budget. In order to work in as many valuable column inches as possible, I learned to write the uncuttable news story, stringing the paragraphs together in such a way that each depended on the preceding and following ones. Everett Leslie, the city editor, quickly spotted this artifice and ordered me to confine all my stories to a single piece of copy paper. I responded by securing a typewriter with small type and by abandoning all margins, thus making one page carry enough words for two.

We three campus correspondents — Patrick Keatley for the *Vancouver Daily Province*, Wally Gillespie for the *Vancouver Sun*, and I — traded our stories, deciding in advance on different leads so it wouldn't look like collusion. My paper wanted short, quirky stuff. Once, in class, I remember a professor remarking casually that co-eds at UBC tended to waddle rather than walk because of the way they carried their books. This piece of nonsense made a box on the front page, and such stories became known as "waddlers." "Got any waddlers today?" the city editor would ask.

In our struggle to get our copy into print we all went to

extremes. I described one minor fraternity row as "a battle that has shaken the campus to its foundations." Everett Leslie peered at me owlishly over his glasses. "Come off it," he said. "Shaken the campus, my ass!" And he threw my story into the wastebasket.

Then one day in March I got a by-line. *Ecstasy!* In those days by-lines were few and far between, doled out like candy to small children (the simile is not inexact) as a reward for a well-written or exclusive story. It used to be said, not entirely without truth, that the papers paid their reporters in by-lines instead of money; certainly they were much sought after. I couldn't get over my name in the paper in eight-point bold-face caps above a small two-column story about some campus incident that I cannot now remember. I left the *News-Herald* lying open at the proper page on the breakfast table at Salisbury Lodge in the hope that one of my friends would notice the by-line and comment on it. But nobody did. Most reporters in those days had an overinflated belief in the value of by-lines. They didn't create instant celebrity. Most readers scarcely noticed them.

2 My hope was that the *News-Herald* would hire me for the summer when my university year ended — the *Colonist* in Victoria having already turned me down. But I hadn't expected that I would be plunged into a kind of sink-or-swim contest, pitting my wits and experience against a horde of other would-be reporters. Robert Elson, the new managing director, took on about a dozen of us and let it be known that after a fortnight's trial he would retain only two. Somehow I managed to cling to the job by my finger-nails, along with a newcomer to the business named Ralph Daly.

Daly was the most enthusiastic reporter I've every known; that's how he kept his job. There was nothing of the

161

jaded scrivener about him, perhaps because he'd never before worked on a newspaper. He'd been secretary to one of the CPR executives, not the best training for journalism, but he'd steeped himself in the lore of the newspaper business, as I had, and knew all the jargon about "follow-ups" and "subleads" and "angles." He couldn't resist telling about his triumphs, which would include the smallest two-paragraph throwaways in the paper. Assigned to the police beat, he'd come into the office literally spewing out news of the amazing things he'd discovered. "I've got the meanest thief!" he'd cry, or "I've found the stingiest housebreaker!" or "I've got a lulu — I've got the unluckiest burglar!" A sharp man with an angle, Daly, and a hard worker. In those days you had to be to hang on to your job.

And so, at last, I was a real reporter, covering city news, not minor stories about fraternity squabbles and waddling co-eds. It didn't matter that the *News-Herald* was by far the smallest paper in town, with circulation hovering around twenty thousand; the *Sun* had four times that, the *Province* five or six times. The hours were long — as long as twelve hours a day, six days a week — and the pay, at fifty dollars a month, wasn't much. I didn't give a hoot. I loved every minute of it.

The staff was a motley group, for the *News-Herald*, because of its wretched pay scale, had to take on newcomers like myself or old hands who had seen better days. There were several ancient reporters in the small office, all crammed together and tapping out stories with two fingers. The city hall reporter was a small neat man with a white moustache and a florid face who impressed me by typing his own by-line — H. Cromar Bruce — on everything he wrote, an unusual privilege. Then there was T. Harry Wilson, a courtly and earnest journeyman of considerable bulk who, it appeared, literally knew everything. The paper exploited his phenomenal knowledge in a front-page feature called "Ask Mr. Green." You could phone up with a question and if T. Harry, *aka* Mr. Green, couldn't answer it in five minutes, you got some sort of prize. He was rarely stumped.

T. Harry had once committed a dreadful gaffe, the story of which pursued him to his grave. It dealt with the sinking of the CPR's *Princess Sophia*, a dreadful tragedy on the Alaska coast in October 1918 in which every soul was drowned. T. Harry was active on one of the papers at the time and actually handled the story, which was exclusive. But when the next edition appeared, no one could find it. With perfect logic, Harry had placed it on the Marine Page under the heading "Shipping Notes."

Then there was Evelyn Caldwell, who wasn't ancient at all, only poor. In later years when she was better paid, she began growing visibly younger, a transformation that startled her colleagues. She was, as I'd already discovered, as tough as any man. Once during an argument I saw the copy editor flee from her to try to hide in the men's lavatory. That didn't faze her. She followed, climbed over the partition, dropped into the cubicle he was occupying, and bopped him on the head with a Coke bottle. Her adventures were legendary. She was once assigned to do a story about a Norwegian freighter docked at the waterfront. She did not return to the office. Three weeks later a cable arrived from Oslo explaining that she'd signed on as a member of the crew.

I boarded that summer in the same house as our entertainment reporter, Christy McDevitt, who had free tickets to everything. A former carnival press agent, he had a saying: "When in doubt, lose the elephant." That stunt had always stood him in good stead when the circus came to town on a slow day. Now he applied similar techniques to his newspaper beat.

We didn't have Associated Press or Canadian Press, which were considered almost essential for any self-respecting newspaper. Instead, we settled for British United

Press, a livelier service in those days and more in keeping with the *News-Herald*'s raffish nature. The local manager, who managed himself, since he had no other staff, was Charles Lynch, blond, smoothfaced, bespectacled, and only just learning to play the mouth organ.

I was more in awe of Al Williamson, who cut a dashing figure with his flannels and tweeds and the silk handkerchief flowing from his breast pocket. A handsome man with a pencil-line moustache, he was always preceded by an enormous pipe that seemed to me to appear around corners, signalling the presence of its owner before he came into view. Al was a man in the know; he seemed to know everybody — the rich, the powerful, the political. "Al has wonderful contacts," I was told soon after arriving at the paper. Certainly he knew all the inside stories, the scandal, the gossip, and the political secrets. Unfortunately, he could not commit any of these fascinating and exclusive tales to print. "Al can't afford to lose his contacts," they used to say.

There was also a charming man named Benny Pastinsky, a former reporter turned jeweller, who filled in on occasion when the police reporter was sick. I don't believe Benny had ever actually written a news story in his life. He dictated from the police station, always in the first person, usually from the point of view of the victim. "I am a corpse," Benny would say. "I am lying in a cheap room in the Niagara Hotel with a knife in my gullet . . ." I always thought Benny's stories lost something in the rewrite.

Later a shaggy man with a sad, hound's face turned up. This was George Wright, who would shortly write a column of elegant prose. He was preceded by a considerable reputation, as much for his drinking habits as for his style. Apparently this problem had caused him to leave Montreal for Vancouver. It was said that he was always drunk, and it is certainly true that he shuffled into the office at a kind of forward slant, like an Arctic explorer struggling through impassable snows. But he never actually fell down, and I

164

was not able to tell from his speech, which always sounded as if it were filtered through mush, whether he was loaded or not. Certainly drink had no effect on his work.

The *News-Herald* office catered to night people and other hangers-on — press agents, old newsmen hoping for a job, friends of friends, small-time entrepreneurs — who made the city room a kind of second home. The one I remember best was Lily Laverock, a lavender ghost of a woman who floated into the office just before midnight to read the files of the three Vancouver dailies. Lily was a theatrical impresario of indeterminate age whose aristocratic features and upper-class English accent belied her poverty. She always wore a hat complete with veil perched atop her greying hair, and she worried constantly about the young women reporters who were forced to make their way home late at night through the seedy district in which we laboured. These concerns did not extend to herself, and, in truth, I could never imagine anybody attacking Lily, defenceless though she clearly was; there was a genteel shabbiness about her that defied assault. She had a connection with the Hurok office in New York and regularly brought the great artists of the day to Vancouver, but there was little profit in it for her, possibly because she handed out so many passes. It was said that her business manager had to stand behind her in the box office to prevent her giving away every seat in the house.

At these concerts and recitals one could always spy in the lobby a tall, threadbare man with gaunt features and a grizzled moustache, looking about him with a fierce stare. This was Professor Francis, a Vancouver fixture. He went to every concert in town but never paid; it simply didn't occur to anybody to charge him. It was said that he had once been a great musician but had suffered a nervous breakdown and could now play exquisitely the first few bars of any classical number but nothing more. I never learned if this romantic story were true. Oddly, in my time nobody on any paper thought to interview Professor Francis or write something about him. Perhaps we all thought the story had been done to death. Perhaps it had. Vancouver was full of eccentrics in those days, like the pigeon woman, who walked the back alleys feeding the birds. They had all become part of the scenery.

One of my many tasks was to cover the service clubs. That meant I ate at least six free meals a week, lunching or dining in the Hotel Vancouver or the Georgia with the Rotary, Gyro, Lions, Kiwanis, Kinsmen, or Optimists, the Ad and Sales Club, and many others. Although meals were cheap by present-day standards — a small steak at the Niagara Sea Foods was only a quarter, while four lamb chops could be had with chips at Louie's Lunch across the road for forty-five cents — the club luncheons still represented an important saving. Unfortunately, the meals were all the same. If the hotel served the Gyro Salisbury steak on Monday, the Kiwanis got exactly the same thing on Thursday. To protect myself from what was then known as service club stomach, I investigated the system and discovered, gratefully, that anyone who didn't want the regular menu could substitute either bacon and eggs or fruit salad. It was a happy compromise since, as I was a morning paper reporter, luncheon was breakfast for me.

I worked eagerly and hard, milking every incident for its optimum news value. I remember being sent to cover some kind of convention at the Hotel Vancouver. I hustled about interviewing everybody and turned in seven different news stories to the paper. The two reporters from the evening papers were severely chastised when each turned in a single piece of copy. It occurs to me now that I was doing the same thing as the highballers at Middle Dominion Camp, and I marvel at the forbearance of my two colleagues, one of whom was Charles Woodsworth of the *Province,* the son of the CCF leader. Charlie didn't seem in the least offended by the fact that I had outpaced him. "It's our own fault," he said. "We were jaded and lazy and you showed us up. Good for you."

The *News-Herald*'s new boss, Robert Elson, was the former managing editor of the *Province*. A burly man with a bold, pugnacious face, Elson was a mass of nervous energy. In moments of high tension he chewed copy paper as if it were lettuce. He had left the larger paper no doubt gratefully, for he had been driven to a state of near dementia, so it was said, by the caprices of an old reporter named Tex Lane, who did not care for Elson's brand of high-powered journalism. One morning the staff arrived to find Elson applying steam to the major overnight stories. Lane had pasted them together, face to face. On another occasion Elson had, with a characteristic jerk, pulled open his desk drawer with disastrous results — Lane had urinated in it almost to the brim.

Now he had been hired as managing director of the *News-Herald* at the astronomical sum of six thousand dollars. That alone made Elson an immensely powerful figure in our minds — a journalistic God, or perhaps a journalistic Hitler, for he was a man of sudden, ungovernable rages. Not only did he eat copy paper but, it was said, he actually ate copy *pencils* when the mood was on him. Certainly, when Elson entered the cluttered editorial office one got the impression of a mad bull loose in a confined space. Desks seemed to topple, papers to fly, as he charged across the city room and flung himself onto the news desk, flipping through the news copy with wild abandon.

He came in one midnight while I was standing over the files trying to catch up on my continuing study of "Terry and the Pirates." If I recall rightly, that was the month in which Raven Sherman became the first comic strip figure to die in front of the readers, her face terribly lacerated as she expired in the arms of Pat Ryan in the lonely hills of China.

At any rate, it had been a long day, and I was particularly pleased with myself, for I had discovered a secret that the university always tried to keep for the afternoon papers. I knew and had reported the identity of the gold medallist that year. It hadn't been difficult. I simply got a list of all the top students and phoned each one asking if he knew who had won the honour. Finally one said that he knew.

"Who won?" I asked.

"I did," he replied.

"How do you know?" I asked.

"The *Vancouver Sun* just told me," he answered, to my considerable glee. And so my story lay in the basket on the city desk, and I was catching up on the comics before heading home.

Since Elson always talked in a loud voice it wasn't difficult to overhear his conversation with Reg Moir, the city editor who had replaced Everett Leslie.

"Who's that lounging over by the files?"

"A new man, Mr. Elson, name of Berton."

"What's he doing over there?"

"What're you doing?" shouted Reg.

"Reading the comics," I shouted back.

"He's reading the comics, Mr. Elson."

Elson turned a dark crimson. "Reading the comics?" he grunted. "*Reading the comics?* Why, he should be out gathering feature material for tomorrow's paper, not lounging about here. Fire that man!"

"Yes, Mr. Elson."

Elson began to riffle through the IN basket. At last he came to my story about the gold medallist.

"This is a damn good story," said Elson. "This is something those bastards at the university have tried to keep from the morning paper, and we've finally managed to get it. Who got this scoop?"

"Berton got it, Mr. Elson."

"Berton? The man I just fired?"

"The same, Mr. Elson."

"Well, hire him again."

Shortly after this, Reg became managing editor, and Jack Scott returned to the paper after a year's absence to become city editor, one of the best I've known. He was only twenty-six — a slender and attractive man with a great wit, a talent for an apt phrase, and a good deal of experience in spite of his youth. He did more than edit my copy; he taught me how to write it. The best advice he ever gave me — so simple, so pertinent — consisted of two sentences. "Always describe the places. Always describe the people." I've never forgotten that.

Scott was a sceptic, as a good city editor must be. Once he sent me off to interview a visiting seer, who received me wearing a turban in a curtained room complete with crystal ball. I was astonished at the man's accomplishments. He had, it appeared, predicted almost all the great events of the day well in advance and had the newspaper clippings to prove it.

"He's got the clippings to prove it," I told Scott.

"Hell," he replied. "Any cheap print shop can turn those out for you."

I was duly abashed. Of course we ran the story anyway, but I had lost some of my youthful naïveté.

I was lucky to receive this kind of training. Few newspaper editors today have time to tell a young reporter that his lead is way down in the third paragraph, or that something more can be made of a strong quote, or that certain phrases are libellous. I began to learn my craft under Scott, who seemed to take to me immediately. By the end of the summer we were the closest of friends and remained so until his death, some forty years later.

I had joined the paper at a dramatic and hectic moment. Bob Elson was about to turn it into the only English-language tabloid in Canada. That dreadful word "tabloid," with its connotations of sexy photographs, peephole columnists, and front page revelations of love nests, was never so much as whispered. "Buy the new, easier-to-read

News-Herald," the promotional ads shouted, and that was the euphemism we all used.

The night the paper changed over to the new size — June 22, 1940 — was memorable enough. Everyone was in a state of high tension. The emphasis, we were told, was to be on pictures. That was brave talk, because at that point the paper couldn't afford to hire a staff photographer. Free-lance cameramen were paid by the job.

I was assigned to cover a rose show in Burnaby, not the most exciting task for an eager young reporter. My story was to be four folios long, accompanied by a photograph of the prize-winning rose.

I wrote my four pages; Scott told me to cut it in half. "We're a picture paper now," he said. "We're going to make the rose bigger."

When I turned in my rewritten piece, Scott asked for another rewrite.

"Boil it down to one page," he said. "We're making the rose even bigger!"

I boiled it down; again Scott turned it back.

"We're not going to run any of your story," he said. "We've decided to run an enormous picture of the rose and only a caption to cover the show." And that's how it came out, looking very elegant and tabloidish in the first issue of the new, easier-to-read *News-Herald.*

Scott and the others used to shout across the city room in true Hollywood fashion, an effort that seemed unnecessary because the room couldn't have been much more than twenty feet wide. I can't recall that I ever had a desk of my own. I'd squeeze in most of my work on the society editor's typewriter while she was in the ladies' room.

All that summer I strove for by-lines and was rewarded with a few. I began to get a swelled head. I thought I was pretty good and bored my friends, boasting about my successes. I covered the Pacific National Exhibition in August, a wonderful assignment for a boy who loved fairs of all kinds. Here I got a scoop, thanks to Bert Galloway, an old carny hand, whose daughter I was squiring about town. Bert knew every trick of the carnival trade and told me exactly how to tell whether a game was crooked or not. I checked out the roll-downs, as they were called, and discovered that nobody could win a nickel at any of them. I watched the shills nudging the marks into more and more action, and I saw the operators pick up the lucky balls covering half the number sevens with their thumbs to make them look like number ones, just as Bert had said they would. And so I got another by-line. But covering speeches and exhibitions is relatively simple work. I had not been tested with a real assignment and wouldn't be.

Elson was totally unpredictable. One day, after I'd written a sentimental piece about the veterans of the First War parading again for the Second, he rushed into the city room, bumping against chairs and desks, to congratulate me.

"You've got a gift with words," he said. "Why go back to university? You can do better here. You've got a nice turn of phrase. We'll keep you on."

But I was determined to get my degree and told him so. He looked dejected. "You're making a big mistake," he insisted.

A few days later he rushed at me and literally bent me backwards as I sat in my chair.

"Do you realize you've called the *regent* of the IODE a *president*?" he shouted. "That's the kind of stupid, unforgivable error that puts newspapers in disrepute. I've been on the phone to her all morning. And look at these cut lines. How dare you start off with that cliché phrase 'Pictured above . . .'? *Pictured above!* Ye gods, can't you think of anything a little brighter and more imaginative than that? By God, I tell you if you weren't going back to university, I'd fire you."

I slunk away, chastened. I wasn't quite as good as I thought I was.

3 In the autumn of 1940, my parents sold their house in Victoria and moved to Vancouver. Lucy had finished her freshman year at Victoria College and enrolled at UBC as a sophomore. And so the family was reunited in a stucco house on Ninth Avenue, a block from the gates of the University Endowment Lands.

Lucy joined the staff of the *Ubyssey*, where I treated her with lordly condescension. As far as I was concerned, she was just another of the several bobby-soxers who hung around the Publications Board offices (or "Pub," as we called it) drinking Cokes and waiting hesitantly for an assignment — as I had done the previous year. Secretly, I was proud of her; to everyone's surprise, she *was* my sister, tall, animated, good looking.

By this time I had climbed to dizzier heights and was one of two senior editors on the paper. I put out the Tuesday edition; Janet Walker handled the Friday paper. I doubt that two more disparate personalities ever collaborated in college journalism. Janet was the most active woman on the campus, but no one would ever have known it, for she was easygoing, tolerant, relaxed, and unhurried. She had time for everybody, which meant that she was often late as she ambled around the campus, chatting with innumerable acquaintances. How she got through her courses I never knew, but the infuriating fact was that she got better marks than I.

She was a remarkably generous woman — and still is — and not only with her time. There is a recurring phrase that typifies the Janet of those days, which keeps coming back to me. "Would you like a bite of my sandwich?" she'd say. I see her now — the glowing face, the natural brown curls, the bright yellow sweater — leaning forward and proffering a half-eaten hot dog or a partly consumed banana or chocolate bar and offering a bite to whoever was close by. She once told me that as a child she had been given a magnificent treat — a large piece of candy of a kind she'd coveted for years. A stranger entered her father's store at that moment and Janet, in a kind of reflex action, offered it to him. To her horror and dismay, he accepted and ate it on the spot. The remarkable thing is that this traumatic experience did not in any way suppress her generous nature.

Janet and I worked under the paper's editor-in-chief, a quiet-spoken classics scholar named Jack Margeson, the direct antithesis of the God-like Garrett. Mild and self-effacing, he scarcely fitted the image of the iconoclastic campus editor, which is probably the reason he was chosen. The rest of us, I suspect, were considered far too radical and unruly to hold such high office in those wartime years when the university was doing its best to keep a low profile. These were serious times. Student pranks were frowned on. "Responsibility" was the order of the day.

Early in the year I wrote an official song entitled "The Illegitimate Children of the Publications Board," which is, I believe, still sung with different but equally scurrilous lyrics:

Refrain: There's a thriving kindergarten
In the depths of old Brock Hall;
They feed the kids on bottles
From the time that they are small.
They sleep on beer-soaked *Ubysseys,*
And Margeson is lord,
Of the illegitimate children
Of the Publications Board.

First verse: John Garrett was an editor
Drank whisky by the tub.
He's the guy who made the Georgia
An annex to the Pub.
Jack Margeson's of different stock,
Teetotalling's his boast;
So while we called John Garrett "God"
Jack's called "The Holy Ghost."

. . . And so on.

173

Fortunately, Margeson let us have our own way, and I took all the rope that was given me. I redesigned the paper, added big pictures, threw out column rules, slapped in bold dots and horizontal black lines, overturned the typeface, and persuaded Janet to go along with the revolution.

I wrote a front-page column in which I castigated the student council for a variety of sins I can no longer bring to mind. It must have been effective, for the president of the council, a sad-faced athlete named Harry Lumsden, called me into his office. "Why do you hate me?" he asked. I didn't hate anybody and tried to explain that it was the job of newspapers to attack authority. He shook his head and looked unhappy. I left feeling mischievous, like Peck's Bad Boy. Janet always claimed that she spent most of her time on Fridays apologizing for what I'd put in the Tuesday edition.

I engaged other columnists. Patrick Keatley, who was later to rise to dizzy heights on the *Guardian* in London's Fleet Street, and Lister Sinclair, who was to become jack-of-all-arts in Canada, were both persuaded to write columns. Sinclair, in fact, wrote two. He was only nineteen then, but he seemed like a patriarch to us — nineteen going on seventy — with his photographic memory and his encyclopedic knowledge of music and literature.

Actually, in those days, Lister seemed more knowledgeable than he really was. He had invented a ploy, which he continues to use to this day, designed to make anyone in his hearing feel like a clod. "Do you remember what Mozart said to Haydn on his birthday?" he'd ask. "Remember that?" Of course I didn't remember, never having known. But Lister always knew. The only way I could compete with him was to try to memorize some classical witticism and hurl it back at him. "You remember Van Gogh's celebrated remark to his brother on the occasion of his incarceration?" Lister would have to agree that he *didn't* remember.

The problem was that I didn't have the knowledge or the means or even the time or inclination to pore over the classics searching for epithets and anecdotes. Nor could I remember them when I did. Lister could. He had a mind like a filing cabinet and an ability to read at some two thousand words a minute. He burst upon the campus in my junior year at UBC and gained his first public recognition in a Players' Club presentation of Shakespearean selections. He insisted on playing Iago in Shakespeare's *Othello* with a Hitlerian moustache and forelock, an affectation that gave him instant notoriety. We became close friends and have remained so ever since.

But the real find was a handsome and extremely shy youth named Eric Nicol. At Victoria College I had been transfixed by a witty serial running in the *Ubyssey* called "Chang Suey," a spoof on Fu Manchu with a college background. The story was never signed, and it was with difficulty that I discovered that Nicol had been the author. I searched him out and he agreed, somewhat diffidently, to write, not Chang Suey, which had been ruined by lesser hands in the intervening year, but a weekly column to be called "The Mummery," under the *nom de plume* Jabez.

We saw very little of Eric. He would sidle into the Pub of a Tuesday morning, quickly drop his copy on the desk as if it were contaminated, and vanish. But everything he wrote was hilarious, and he was soon the talk not only of the campus but also of the downtown papers. Later I tried to persuade him to quit the academic life and become a journalist. He insisted he was going to continue his studies in French literature. In the end he succumbed, became a columnist for the *Province*, and, as I write this, continues to be. No one has captured more Leacock Awards for humour than he.

The paper's office was crowded with young would-be reporters who were treated with the same disdain I had received the previous year. I remember assigning a slight blonde girl named Helga Jarvi to cover a routine meeting in the auditorium. I asked for a couple of paragraphs; she gave me eight pages — a meticulous account of every single sentence spoken, over which she had sweated and laboured for hours. In a rage I threw her precious copy into the wastebasket. She burst into tears. It did not occur to me then, as it does now, that I was acting exactly like the terrible-tempered Bob Elson, and with as little reason.

As college journalists, our only interest was the university. Unlike today's college papers, the *Ubyssey* paid little attention to life off-campus. The great issues of our time did not concern us. Even the war was seen in terms of the university. We were turned in on ourselves, outside the main stream, partly, I think, because we were isolated at the tip of Point Grey, separate even from the city.

We could not escape, of course, the implications of what was happening in Europe. Although we were not anti-war, most of us were vaguely anti-military, an attitude solidified by our forced enlistment in the Canadian Officers' Training Corps, where those of our classmates who had had enough military training to be put in charge of raw recruits shouted and screamed at us. They certainly made the most of it.

Most of us were anxious to finish our university year before the war caught up with us. I don't recall much of the kind of patriotic talk that swept the country in 1914 when the youth of Canada were desperate to enlist. The effects of that dreadful conflict and the pacifist movement that followed it had dampened most men's enthusiasm for battle. It was acknowledged that Hitler was up to no good, but the horrifying implications of what he was really doing escaped most of us living in our own little world of campus politics and campus gossip.

I was now spending most of my time either in the offices of the Publications Board or at the Pub table in the cafeteria. I went to few lectures. On press days I didn't go at all. The paper's new publisher was a UBC graduate, Morris Belkin, who owned a small press in South Vancouver. Here we gathered on press nights to put the paper to bed, taking time off to grab a hamburger at the Jolly Roger Café and listen to an Artie Shaw record on the jukebox. Belkin went on to further triumphs, becoming the packaging king of Canada, his name on most of the milk cartons and cigarette boxes sold across the country.

Although I was skipping many lectures, no one chided me for it. At UBC you were on your own. *Tuum Est* was the varsity motto: it is up to you. I attended only one lecture in History 15, the history of the Renaissance. The professor was F.H. Soward, a highly respected historian and author of many textbooks, who enjoyed a towering reputation. I sat at the back of the lecture hall and watched as he marched in carrying a sheaf of ragged notes under one arm. As he began to read from these papers in a staccato voice, my fellow students would scribble furiously in their notebooks, trying to keep up with Soward's machine-gun delivery. *Ye Gods,* I thought, *I'm being turned into a stenographer!*

I decided not to return to Soward's class, mainly because his lecture schedule conflicted with my work on the *Ubyssey*. Instead I borrowed other people's notes and determined to take my chances on the so-called "objective" examinations by tossing a coin in those cases where I didn't know the answer. I ended up with exactly 50 per cent, a fact the professor commented on at the graduation tea.

"I did my best to flunk you, Berton," he said, "but you just squeaked through." I mentally thanked the gods of chance.

Another towering figure on the faculty was Henry F. Angus, one of the members of the Rowell-Sirois Royal Commission on Dominion-Provincial Relations. I felt that I, as a budding journalist, ought to learn something about this mysterious aspect of national life, so I signed up for Government 1, a course in dominion-provincial relations, right from the horse's mouth. Unfortunately this course too was given on press day, and I found myself giving it a miss. I got through by reading the actual report in the library.

I took Nineteenth-Century English Literature from Hunter Lewis, an odd, bearded little man with watery blue eyes, who handed us an impossibly long list of books to plough through. When examination time came, I panicked. The questions on the paper dealt with books I'd never *heard* of, much less read. I scribbled away in spite of this and was astonished to receive a passing grade, along with everybody else in the room. It turned out that Lewis, a typical absent-minded professor, had set the paper on the wrong subject. It was just as well; I hadn't read many of the right books either.

I slept through a good many lectures in those days, choosing a seat at the back of a crowded class where I wouldn't be noticed. I was not only editing the Tuesday *Ubyssey* and covering the campus for the *News-Herald* but I was also helping edit the *Point Grey News-Gazette,* which Morris Belkin now owned. I slept in buses and streetcars, in the cafeteria and the newspaper offices, but only rarely in my own bed. The Vancouver streetcars in those days did not run after midnight. Often enough I found myself downtown late in the evening, typing up copy for the morning edition, and faced with a seven-mile hike back home. Thus I learned to sleep in snatches, to quote an unfortunate remark made in class one day by my philosophy professor, John Irving. Too late, Irving looked down at the students, realized the sexual implications of what he'd just said, and went beet red. There followed one of those dreadful pauses, not unlike the one I remembered from my mother's dinner party when I'd used the F-word. Then somebody, a girl at that, tittered, and the entire class broke up. Irving was a remarkably sensitive man, and the remark haunted him for all his days on campus.

I never slept in Irving's classes for they were always challenging. Besides, he set me the one essay that I enjoyed and did well with — a dissertation on the freedom of the press. Medieval history was a different story. The course was given by a Professor Cooke, a kindly young man who lived with his mother and never once reproved me for snoring in the front row during his discussion of the feudal system. Since there were only seven students in the class, I couldn't hide. I felt sorry for Professor Cooke and did my best to keep awake, but his voice had a droning, hypnotic quality that put me into an immediate trance, especially after a late night.

For there were other exhausting diversions, not all of them journalistic. The gang from the Publications Board was as clannish as any Greek-letter society. It seems we were always in the Georgia Tavern, awash in sour draft beer — I once drank a dozen glasses in half an hour on a bet — or over at the Princess Elizabeth Tea Room on English Bay, playing big-band records, or tooling around in somebody's car listening to the D-X Prowl, a midnight program of records played in an era when the phrase "disc jockey" had yet to be invented.

The Princess Elizabeth Tea Room was better known as Greasy Alex's, after a large Greek who dispensed not tea but hamburgers, and who owned an impressive collection of swing and jazz records, any of which he would put on the jukebox on payment of a nickel. And so we listened to "Frenesi," "Tuxedo Junction," "Stompin' at the Savoy," "Big Noise from Winnetka," "Jivin' the Vibes," and "Caledonia" — all the great big-band numbers of those days that have since become classics.

When a big band came to town we stayed with it for the duration. We stood in front of the Duke's stand in the old Auditorium downtown, listening and swaying (but never dancing) to "Mood Indigo." We sat in the front row of the Beacon Theatre, desperate for the movie to end so we could watch Lionel Hampton do impossible things with drum-sticks. There we sat, munching egg sandwiches, for we had no intention of leaving until the lights went off and the band went home. The Hampton rhythm swelled as the leader jumped from drums to vibraphone, and the excitement welled up within us until Lionel Salt, the *Ubyssey*'s plump sports editor, could no longer contain himself and leaped to his feet, crying out, "Oh, butter me a slice-a that! Oh, butter me a slice!"

My parents, I think, were dismayed by the frantic pace I was pursuing and more than a little concerned that I seemed to be spending so little time on my studies. I was gaunt and hollow-cheeked. My eyes were red-rimmed, and I often looked as if I'd slept in my clothes, which I often had.

"What were you up to last night?" my father asked me once. "You didn't get in till all hours."

"Well, we hung around the White Spot for a while."

"The White *what*? What on earth is that?"

"Drive-in on South Granville. They have great hamburgers."

"Hamburgers? In the middle of the night?" He shook his head sadly. "You ought to be at your studies, boy."

Like almost everybody else in those days (and perhaps in these), he thought entirely in terms of marks. You got high marks, you got a good job; you got low marks, you had no future. But I didn't care about marks. Journalism and broadcasting were my goals, and I'd never seen anybody's scholastic record displayed in a newsroom or a radio studio.

For my other main extracurricular activity on campus was the Radio Society. Radio was still an obsession. In between the swing music and the variety shows and the soap operas we heard the more sober tones of the commentators — Kaltenborn, of course, and now Ed Murrow, Raymond Gram Swing, and Elmer Davis. Five nights a week, "The March of Time" performed the herculean task of actually dramatizing the events of the day using live actors. I tried to copy the doom-like voice of its announcer, Westbrook Van Voorhees, in a staged parody, which I titled "The March of Slime" and produced as part of a campus concert.

That winter I tried to copy the styles of all the major radio personalities, especially the announcers and commentators. I can remember standing in the family kitchen, late at night when everybody was in bed, reading aloud the main stories from the front page of the *News-Herald* in what I considered to be a suitably formal style.

At last the day came when I actually spoke on radio. Thanks to Dorwin Baird, the former *Ubyssey* editor who had been hired by CJOR, our club was given the opportunity to present news from the campus on the air. I was one of those to whom the task was assigned; the other, I believe, was the club president, Verna Mackenzie, who, appropriately enough, was later to marry Dorwin. We were an incestuous group in those days; I can recall at least six marriages that resulted from alliances within the Publications Board that year.

Radio was live; tape had yet to be invented. I sat at a small table in the studio, watching Dorwin behind the glass of the booth, waiting for the hand of the clock to reach the hour and Dorwin to point his finger. Microphones were much larger then. This one seemed overpowering. Dorwin pointed; I felt my throat go dry. As it constricted I thought I was about to strangle and realized I was suffering from mike fright, the most dreadful of all media diseases.

I kept thinking only of one thing: I was about to make a fool of myself in front of a million listeners. This was sheer arrogance, I doubt if anybody at that hour was actually choosing to listen to that particular program, with the possible exception of my mother. Who cared, really, about the inside workings of a distant campus?

Somehow I managed to speak, not with a croak as I had feared, but in the reasonable approximation of the silky tones I had learned to accept from the announcers of the day. The broadcast ended without incident, and I cannot recall that anybody, on campus or off, ever mentioned it to me in either praise or condemnation. But when it was finished, I felt a strange elation. I discovered that I liked broadcasting. It gave me a feeling of — what? Satisfaction? Accomplishment? Communication? Power? All four, no doubt. From that time on I seized every opportunity to become involved in radio.

The university year came to an end, and the paper published its final issue, known as the Goon Issue because all the stories published were spoofs. The lead article told how a group of Applied Science students had built a real monster who had escaped from the basement of the physics building.

"BEAST STALKS CAMPUS," the headline read. A photograph, ingeniously created by my friend Bill Grand, showed the actual monster climbing over the library, a fiendish expression on its face, a mass of hair covering its eyes. The monster, of course, was me.

Years later, when I was on the way to becoming a Well-Known Personality, my old college paper occasionally noted one of my triumphs with a paragraph or two, and invariably illustrated it with this photograph. Somehow the cut had been saved and lovingly cared for in the *Ubyssey* office. I believe they may have used it when I was given the Order of Canada — a piece of retrospective journalism that must have baffled the new crop of students on the campus who, I'm sure, had no idea of the photograph's history or my own background.

I had my degree, for what it was worth, but before I could return to the *News-Herald* I was required to spend two weeks at COTC camp on Vancouver Island. I was too young to take the actual training (I would not be twenty-one until July) but was allowed to go along as an orderly in the Officers' Mess. I have only one sharp memory of that fortnight: the dreadful moment when I stumbled and spilled soup on the commanding officer, Dr. Gordon Shrum, the most terrifying figure on the campus and also a lieutenant-colonel in the COTC. Shrum was a giant of a man, head of the Department of Applied Science at UBC, who seemed to have his finger in every campus pie. Now, as the soup spilled over him, he raised his hand to wipe off his shoulder, only to strike the bowl and knock the rest of its contents over his uniform. Thus ended my university career, not with a bang but a splash. I returned to Vancouver at the end of May, prepared to plunge into what we students had kiddingly called "the cruel, cold world."

4 Back on the *News-Herald,* my *Ubyssey* training began to pay off. I had learned how to write headlines and make up a page; I could tell a pica from an em; I knew the names of all the important typefaces — Kabel, Erbar, Bodoni; I knew how to crop photographs and read type backwards in its mirror image on the compositor's stone. At one point I was both religious editor and, in a sense, social editor. The social editor didn't understand newspaper make-up, so I was assigned to put her page together.

As religious editor I lost the final shreds of a tattered faith. I covered the major sermons of the day or at least procured transcripts or briefs, interviewed evangelists and priests, and came to the conclusion that religion was bunk. As Clem Davies, the local Bible thumper, told the press in a rare piece of off-the-record candour: "Boys, I found there was money in the God stuff."

The more conventional churches, it seemed to me, were out of touch with their dwindling congregations, droning on in their cavernous Gothic temples, repeating the same words and hollow phrases so often that they had lost all meaning, and communing with an establishment that went faithfully to church on Sunday morning only to abandon all Christian principles the following day. Thus was born an attitude that would, a quarter of a century later, find expression in a book called *The Comfortable Pew*.

I was reacting not only to the religious faith of my father but also to the political. I was no longer a Conservative. For years during the dreadful Depression, when the flower of the country had demanded a solution to the problems of hunger and unemployment, the political bosses, backed by the business and social establishments, had smugly insisted they couldn't provide one. The big phrase — we hear it again today — was that the country could not afford it: couldn't afford to feed the hungry, clothe the destitute, house the homeless, or put the nation to work. I came to realize that what the establishment really meant was that its own members did not intend to curtail their own comfortable existence in any way, to give up a single luxury in order to spread the wealth or give a boost to the wretched.

When the war came, it turned out that we *could* afford it. The political cry, echoed by the business world, that economic recovery was impossible, that the nation would be bankrupted if we tried to come to grips with the vast army of jobless men crisscrossing the land on freight cars, driven from town to town by railway bullies and local police — all this now stood revealed as a bald lie. Suddenly the government, when forced to, began to feed, clothe, house, and employ hundreds and thousands of the same men and women who had been told a short time before that they were on their own. The country could not only afford it: in fact, it could also prosper by it. But that lesson was not really learned, and today history repeats itself.

It was this realization, together with my coverage of labour and political meetings, that swung me to the left. Duff Pattullo's Liberal machine held the power in B.C. The Liberal rallies were grotesque caricatures of democracy. A small clique ruled the province. Labour was becoming increasingly militant, and I was on its side. No doubt my low pay in a profession that had no union had its effect. "I know you're going to ask for a raise," Reg Moir had once told me, "so I thought I'd better warn you as a friend that if you do you'll be fired."

I told my father I was a Communist. He listened indulgently, not believing a word of it, knowing that I was trying him on for size. The party was banned, but I covered several meetings of organizations that were clearly communist under a different name. I was offended more by the shrillness of their publications than the shrillness of their talk. I simply couldn't stand the jargon.

I was given a job on the news desk writing headlines along with Everett Leslie, my old city editor. (No job seemed to be permanent on that newspaper.) Soon I was putting out the *News-Herald*'s Final Edition, the front page printed on green paper to distinguish it from the Home. Thus my workday ended at two in the morning, when the streets were empty and the town shut tight save for a couple of all-night hamburger stands.

In partnership with Bill Grand, the *Ubyssey* photographer, who was now taking pictures for the *News-Herald,* I'd bought a 1929 Essex. The instalments were four dollars a week. I'd never driven a car before, so Bill would take it to work through the traffic and leave it for me to take home when the streets were empty and police surveillance at a minimum. He'd park it near the *News-Herald* office, pointed in the direction of Point Grey, and leave it for me.

I had no driver's licence, didn't know how to park a car, how to back it up, or even how to use the passing lane. I simply climbed in, pulled the starter (there was no ignition key in this ancient model), stepped on the gas, and rolled slowly through the deserted streets, trusting that nothing untoward would occur. Miraculously, nothing did. The car, which used more oil than gas, chugged along obediently, trailing dense clouds of blue smoke. To keep expenses down, Bill bought used crankcase oil. I'm afraid it added to the pollution.

Because I was now listed as "night editor," my pay had been raised from $50 to $85 a month — "the biggest raise in the history of journalism," according to Reg Moir. As the war made dents in the work force, the turnover began to quicken. Moir went off to join the *Province.* Jack Scott, who was also writing a daily column — the best Vancouver has ever known — moved up to managing editor. And I, who had just turned twenty-one, was promoted to city editor at the magnificent sum of $125 a month.

I had no business being city editor of anything at that age, but I wasn't going to argue; in fact, it never occurred to me that I wasn't really competent to do the job. As far as I was concerned, the *News-Herald* was simply an overblown version of the *Ubyssey.* And nobody seemed the least surprised that Everett Leslie, who had been my city editor a year or so before, was now back on the street as a reporter, taking assignments from me. Sudden demotions and promotions are all part of the newspaper game.

We all did double duty. Scott, besides being managing editor and columnist, would sometimes cover the bigger news stories. I also wrote news stories, picking up odd items from friends or former classmates. One day Janet Black, a girl I'd known well in the Yukon, walked into the office and showed me a bakery box containing a huge custard pie.

"For me?" I asked.

"No," said Janet, "for my boss . . ."

"How nice," said I. "What's the celebration?"

"I'm quitting," Janet said. "I can't stand it any more and I'm going over and push this pie right in his face." Which she did. It made a neat two-column box on the city page.

A few days before Christmas I ran into one of my *Ubyssey* cronies, Les Bewley, and asked him how he intended to spend the Yule season.

Bewley, who was an eccentric then and remains one now (he was perhaps the most controversial magistrate in the province until he retired to become a newspaper columnist), announced that he intended to forgo Christmas dinner entirely.

"I shall," he said, "drink a single glass of water as a personal protest against the gluttony inspired by the commercialism of the season."

The following morning *News-Herald* readers were treated to a picture of the suave Bewley solemnly raising his spartan glass and railing against Yuletide gourmands.

I doubt if my old political philosophy professor, John Irving, ever forgave me for one news story, which I dug up as the result of another encounter with an old campus friend. A provincial election was in full swing in British Columbia; Dufferin Pattullo's Liberal machine was tangling with the upstart CCF; and Irving had assigned his class to attend the meetings and report on them — a class composed very largely of the sons and daughters of prominent Liberals including Shirley Wismer, whose father was the attorney general. I got on the phone, asked the students for comments, and was handsomely rewarded. They had all been appalled by the low quality of the oratory, the sleaziness of the meetings, and the general odour of ward-heeling cronyism that pervaded politics in the province in those years. This was democracy? Several scions of prominent establishment families declared they preferred the CCF, which that year for the first time made impressive gains and forced the two major parties into a coalition that under a different name still holds power in the province.

On more than one occasion I saved a reporter's bacon by *squashing* a news story. It was always the same news story. Somebody would rush into the office announcing that Hedy Lamarr was in town incognito.

"Get a photographer fast! Hedy Lamarr's in town!"

"No she's not."

"She *is*. I spotted her in the Devon Café, eating grilled mushrooms with bacon."

"No, you didn't. That was my sister, Lucy."

"*Your* sister. Come *on!*"

"Why would Hedy Lamarr be sitting in the Devon Café eating mushrooms and bacon? It's my sister. She works at the White Lunch but she eats at the Devon."

For Lucy, at nineteen, *did* look like a movie star, with her mother's lustrous brown eyes and her mane of jet-black hair. She worked only that summer at the White Lunch, a cafeteria distinguished by a frieze of signs encircling the walls, all reading: WATCH YOUR HAT AND COAT. She hated it, and often came home far more exhausted than I; but it was a paying job.

In addition to ferreting out news stories from my friends, I also began to draw a weekly cartoon strip based on the news and entitled "I See by the Papers." I worked Thursday nights, often all night, drawing and laying it out. There were times when I completed it just in time to reach the office by noon.

187

It didn't occur to me to ask for an extra cheque; I did it because I wanted to.

My mother thought I was killing myself, but actually I was having a wonderful time. The paper had become my life. We worked a six-day week but were allowed one free day every month. I didn't know what to do with my day off and usually ended up back at the newspaper office, hanging around, waiting for my friends to finish so we could go out and eat Chinese food and drink rye whisky.

We indulged in crazy campaigns, which at the time we believed represented the acme of journalism. The most grotesque was the *News-Herald's* Rat Campaign. It was our fancy that the city was on the verge of an attack of bubonic plague, carried by the rats that lived in the city dump. We ran story after story doing our best to panic the town into some kind of action, but the town remained remarkably serene. We thought of ourselves as Cassandras who would one day be honoured for our perception when half the populace was carried off in the dead carts to a communal grave. But the Black Death never came.

No grisly tale escaped our notice. One day Scott came to the office and called a halt. "Jesus Christ," he said, "I could hardly get my breakfast down this morning."

On the front page of the paper that day we had carried an enormous photograph of the city dump, steaming in the sunlight. Inside, the reader was rewarded by a ghastly photograph of the corpse of a gargantuan rat, held at arm's length by its killer. At least we called it a rat; it turned out to be a nutria and it wasn't found anywhere near the dump. To complete this gruesome gallery, we had printed another photograph of an armless man drinking coffee from a cup, the handle of which he held between his bare toes. A remarkable feat, certainly, but not one calculated to go with bacon and eggs.

Elson had brought in a new editor in the person of Barry Mather to handle the front page and the foreign news. He was a tall, lugubrious figure with a pocked face and a deadpan sense of humour that would eventually launch him into a popular column on the front page of the post-war *Sun*. He had come from the staff of the CCF's weekly newspaper, which meant that he was officially a radical. In fact, he turned out to be the most conservative desk man I ever worked with. He wanted only serious news on page one — no rats, no movie stars, no accident victims, no murderers. Scott and I struggled with him night after night. Our one small victory was that he agreed we should have a human interest story on the front page every day.

This victory went unnoticed. The co-owner of the paper was a Vancouver broker named Duncan Hamilton, a small, rotund business man who knew little about newspapers but was impressed by the glamour of being a newspaper proprietor. In his office were little motivational signs, such as " 'Get Your Paper Talked About' — Colonel Robert McCormick." One day he encountered Scott and me on the stairs, and he seized upon us like a limpet. "I've got a great idea for you fellows," he said. "And I want you to put it into effect at once." Scott looked at me and I looked at Scott. What mad proposal was Dunc Hamilton about to foist upon us?

"What we need in this paper," he said, "is a human interest story on page 1 every day. That's what I want. Got it? A human interest story on page 1 every day!"

Since he had no idea what a human interest story was, we simply nodded and mumbled agreement and let him go his way. He kept an office, well furnished, in one corner of the city room. On his desk was a handsome vacuum jug, which he never used. At nights, when he was gone, we sat in his easy chairs, Scott and I, and filled the vacuum jug with rye whisky and ice for our personal enjoyment.

About this time, Bob Elson departed, lured to the States by Henry Luce. Subsequently he became a major figure in the Time-Life organization, eventually writing the official biography of his benefactor. He was replaced by J.L. Burton

Lewis, the brother of the Hunter Lewis who had set the wrong examination paper during my university days. With his arrival, the *News-Herald* entered a new and even more eccentric phase.

Lewis was a short, wiry man with a neatly clipped moustache and a pair of pale blue eyes that popped but never seemed to blink. He wore a black slouch hat and carried a worn leather briefcase which, I discovered, contained nothing more important than half a dozen partially consumed bottles of Canadian Club. I liked him, for he was a member of that fading coterie of itinerant newsmen who had once shifted from town to town and paper to paper as their inclination and the fates determined. He had come to us from the *Province* but had worked on most of the papers in Canada and several south of the border. He was a fund of newspaper lore, a restless little man whose arms and hands moved ceaselessly, massaging his shoulders, scratching his neck, twisting about his body like eels in conflict. He had an odd habit of speech. His sentences never really seemed to end but were joined onto others by conjunctive couplings like so many rail cars.

He was a good newspaperman and a good drinking companion. Often he would call Scott and me down to his office on the floor below. "Got a minute?" Burt would ask, and down we'd come, pencils at the ready, copy paper neatly folded, expecting to receive some editorial dictum. "I thought we all might enjoy a little shot," Burt would say, much to our relief. We'd all enjoy a little shot and return to our respective tasks until Burt called us down again.

The war had accelerated. The Russians were now on the Allied side and the papers were running maps of Eastern Europe showing pincer movements, troop envelopments, flank attacks, routs, retreats, advances, and stalemates. Lewis invented the Instant Map that fall. He had several basic maps drawn and had ordered a series of little symbols on gummed cellophane: tiny cutouts of German and Russian soldiers, cannons, arrows, little swastika and hammer-and-sickle emblems. Just before deadline, he'd tear a strip off the news wire, work out the strategic and tactical situation of the opposing armies, and start to stick dotted lines, arrows, swastikas, and soldier figures at appropriate places on his map. There was no proper spot for Lewis to toy with his new creation, so he used the city desk. He actually *squatted* on it — sometimes on top of an important feature story — working away with his basic map, while the sticky little symbols flew about attaching themselves to whatever they settled on.

By deadline time the desk and the copy were crawling with them. Sober tales of city council meetings would go to the composing room plastered with swastikas. Tiny Germans in coal-scuttle helmets could be seen gummed to a photograph of the new president of the Board of Trade. Shots of a Liberty Ship being launched would bear the emblem of the hammer and sickle. But Lewis persevered. He was nothing if not a man of imagination. During one dark moment in that grim war winter of 1941-42 he gazed out of the window and saw fresh snow powdering the North Shore mountains. He ordered a panoramic photograph of the setting and spread it across the front page to replace one from the Russian front. It was his signal that some things are eternal.

The *News-Herald* took on a unique quality during Burton Lewis's tenure. One day some red ink got mixed in with the black and the social page came out in sepia. Lewis liked it so much he wanted to print all future photographs in sepia. Unhappily he was never again able to achieve that accidental mixture of inks, and the paper appeared in harlequin hues.

Then, on December 7, the war took its most ominous turn. I had been invited to breakfast that Sunday morning with two women from the art department when the phone rang in their West End apartment. It was Al Williamson who was, I think, news editor at the time.

"I didn't want to disturb you until you were finished breakfast," he said, "but you'd better get down here now. The Japs have bombed Pearl Harbor and we're putting out an extra."

In fact, we put out two extras on that grim, exciting, bewildering day. When I reached the office I could hear the bells on the teletype clanging — the signal that another major story was coming over the wire. The newsroom was already a whirl of activity. I felt lost, swamped by the immensity of the news. Nominally I was city editor, doing a multiplicity of the routine tasks required on a small, understaffed daily — handing out assignments, thinking up feature stories, editing copy, writing headlines, making up pages. But now, with a big story breaking, I realized my limitations. A score of questions had to be asked and answered. What about the Japanese Canadians? What about the Army? What about the Mounties? What about spies in our midst? Was there a local angle on Hawaii? It was, after all, Vancouver's holiday playground. Was there going to be a blackout? If so, how would we cover that?

I was not exactly pushed aside; every hand was needed. But I was glad to have Jack Scott's support and Al Williamson's, for I realized that under this kind of pressure I could not run the city desk alone. And yet, when the long night was over and our extras were both on the streets, I had a sense of solid satisfaction. We'd had the story to ourselves, for the other papers didn't work on Sunday. But there was something more than that. For me, journalism had come alive; I'd been involved with the real world and real news, something far more pertinent than the puffed-up threats of plague-carrying rats infesting the city dump. A real plague was raging in the world. It had touched Vancouver. Soon it would divide the city.

These were the *News-Herald*'s finest hours. We took a strong editorial position opposing the racist feeling that had been simmering below the surface in town all season, sparked by veterans' groups and newly formed white citizens' organizations, and fuelled by the bigotry of the *Vancouver Sun*.

I had covered one rally in which the speakers had

demanded that all jobs be withheld from anyone who couldn't prove his British ancestry back for seven generations. I was acquainted with several Nisei, as the Canadian Japanese were called, and was appalled to see what was happening. But the *News-Herald* had little effect on public opinion.

Vancouver was blacked out that month, and the gloom was increased by the presence of fog. I crept through Stygian streets, hearing ghostly footsteps behind me, beside me, in front of me, but unable to identify the passersby. Cars slid slowly past with slitted headlights. Shades or blackened curtains were pulled over office windows. Even the lights in the harbour were extinguished. It was whispered that the Japanese were planning to attack the west coast of North America. Vancouver itself stood in danger of being bombed. For the first time the war became a reality, something more than a front page headline competing for space with our local human interest. Every jukebox that month was pounding out "Tonight We Love," Freddy Martin's version of a Tchaikovsky piano concerto. There was a sense of doom in those opening chords. I felt as if the world had suddenly gone topsy-turvy. Nothing was certain any more. My own career, which had taken off like a rocket, was quite likely to fizzle out, obliterated by events over which I had no control.

Early one morning, with the final edition in bed, Burt Lewis and I were sitting in Dunc Hamilton's office, finishing off the last of one of his innumerable bottles of rye. Everyone else had gone home. Suddenly, on the little balcony above the city room, the bulletin bell of the British United Press teletype started to clang — that electrifying clarion that sets every newsman's nerves tingling.

I raced up and tore the strip from the chattering machine. There it was: the British battleship *Prince of Wales* and cruiser *Repulse* had been sunk in the South Pacific by Japanese aircraft. The details were still pouring in.

"This means an extra," said Burt. "Get the printers back, call Blackie the wholesaler, and try to find a couple of cuts of ships in the morgue, ones that look reasonably like the two that have gone down. Meanwhile I shall write an editorial."

It was typical of J.L. Burton Lewis that he would proceed to do what was never done — to grind out an editorial for a hot extra. There he sat, with the news pouring off the teletype, methodically having his say, fortified by the contents of another of the bottles in his briefcase.

Just as he started to write, the doors swung open and two members of the Vancouver Chamber of Commerce, wearing steel helmets and air-raid warden armbands, marched in and began turning off the lights.

"What's this?" Lewis asked wearily, turning on the light above his desk.

"Blackout," said one of the Chamber of Commerce men, turning it off again. "Don't you know there's a war on?"

"I know," said Lewis, turning the light back on. "I mean, that's what I'm trying to say here in this editorial."

"Gee," said the amateur air-raid warden, "are you actually writing an editorial? Here? Now?"

"I'm trying to," said Lewis, turning on the light that had again been switched off. "Here — help yourself to some cheap rye."

The Chamber of Commerce man sat down with his companion and poured himself a couple of fingers. Lewis continued to tap out his editorial. I pasted up the yellow sheets from the teletype onto copy paper, wrote headlines and picture captions. Blackie Black, the wholesale distributor, who stood to make a tidy sum from the results of our work, brought in a bottle of Scotch for us editorial men who stood to gain nothing but memories. For of all the memories I have of those halcyon days, that scene stands out most vividly in my mind. It has a certain symbolism: the sprawling city, black as the tomb save for the pinpoint of light in the newspaper office; the two newsmen and the two air-raid wardens drinking Blackie's Scotch and Burton Lewis's rye, as the presses were being oiled to tell the waking world it was on the edge of crumbling.

Lewis pulled the final copy from his typewriter and handed it to me.

"Here," he said, "set this in twenty-em banks across the top of page 1 and see if you can get red ink for the line."

"What did you write?" one of the air-raid wardens asked.

"I wrote that the world as we have known it has come to some sort of end," said Burt. "I wrote that because of what happened this night, we know at last what we are up against. And because of that, nothing will ever be quite the same again."

He was right, of course. In a few more months Scott and I and Bill Grand, the photographer, and Reg Moir and all the others would be in uniform. Burt Lewis would be an army auditor. The *News-Herald* would return to its original form, the ads trumpeting that it was "easier to read." Strange men would take over the little paper, and other strangers would eventually kill it.

And nothing would ever be the same again.

Chapter Five

Marching As to War
1942-1945

1 I didn't want to become a soldier any more than I wanted to become a steam fitter or a shoe salesman. I had found my niche in life and I was supremely happy. I wasn't even ambitious; if I could just stay as city editor for the rest of my career I would be more than satisfied — or so I thought. My whole life revolved around the *News-Herald*. My family at home saw little of me. After work, around midnight, a bunch of us would leave the office for a late-night supper at the Empire Café on Hastings Street or the W.K. Gardens in Chinatown and carouse until three or four. I'd sleep until noon, then turn up at the office to hand out the day's assignments. On Saturday nights the newspaper gang would go to the Palomar, the Cave, the Panorama Roof, or the Commodore, usually on passes from the social department, which in those days listed the names of the prominent and not-so-prominent who danced to the "Jersey Bounce" and kept bottles of rye in brown bags under the tiny tables. On Sundays, I'd go over to Jack Scott's in West Vancouver and we'd sit on his verandah overlooking the inlet and talk about the newspaper and how to improve it.

A tiny, blonde girl named Thelma Wyles joined the staff. When she wasn't working, she stood behind the city desk watching me edit copy. It was some time before I realized that she had a crush on me. I didn't have a crush on her; I was in love with the paper. It was my only obsession. I did weird things with type and make-up, driving the composing room half crazy with oddly shaped cuts — arms poking out of pictures into the next column, for instance.

I remember showing one of these wonderful intricate pages to my parents at breakfast with a great deal of pride. They looked baffled. My mother stared at the page and then handed it without comment to my father, who put down his coffee, donned his glasses, and inspected it carefully.

"I don't quite understand what it is you're trying to show us," he said.

I started to explain that I'd had three reporters cover three stories all from the point of view of one of the participants and that I'd given each story an identical type and photo treatment. Symmetry and perfection! Flair! Pizazz! Human interest!

My father shook his head. "I'm afraid I don't follow you," he said. "These are quite ordinary stories."

And they were. It was years before I learned that what really counts in a newspaper is the content, not the package.

All this was about to end. No one was more eligible for compulsory military service than I. I was just twenty-one, healthy, and without dependants. Others in the same category were rushing to volunteer for the air force or the navy — anything to keep out of the army. I didn't. That first flight into the Yukon in the Ford tri-motor had unnerved me. I hadn't been able to keep anything on my stomach for days. I saw myself being constantly sick or an object of derision during a bomber flight over Berlin or on the deck of a heaving battleship, and so I opted for the army, spent thirty-four months in uniform, and ended up having a pretty good time.

I didn't join the army; the army joined me in February, 1942. On my last night on the paper I sat with Burton Lewis in his office. He'd been in the previous war, and now as he squirmed nervously in his chair, his left hand twisted around the back of his neck, his right pawing the opposite elbow, he began to talk about my future.

I've forgotten a lot about those last days on the paper, but that scene stands out sharp and clear in my mind, as in a movie: the skinny youngster, nervous and insecure about what lay ahead, and the weathered journeyman, both of us pouring ice water out of Duncan Hamilton's vacuum bottle into paper cups full of rye whisky as Lewis talked about the experience of war in one of those long, convoluted sentences that I find difficult to recreate in print:

"I mean in terms of the experience you're going to have you shouldn't regard this as anything but an adventure, because, you know, in terms I mean of the friendships you'll make — and many of these will be enduring friendships — you are going to have a pretty marvellous time, because, you see, war does that, I mean in terms of comradeship and that sort of thing so that when it's over you are going to find you've made the kind of lifelong associations that might not ordinarily occur in civilian life, I mean in terms of real friendship . . ."

As usual, I didn't believe him. As usual, he turned out to be right.

Bill Grand and I still had the old Essex that was always running out of oil or running out of water. I seem to remember that we once poured Coca-Cola into the radiator to keep it going for an extra mile. Now Bill, who was joining the air force, disposed of it in a summary fashion, simply leaving it parked on a side street. Many months later, returning from a bombing mission, he was ecstatic to receive a letter from home. Alas, it came from a Vancouver garage, which had found the abandoned vehicle and now revealed that the storage costs came to the exact amount of its value. Neither of us ever saw the car again.

On the day of my departure, a large contingent trooped down to the Canadian Pacific station to see me off. It was not a tearful farewell, for I was only going to the Basic Training Centre at Vernon, in the Okanagan Valley of British Columbia. The war still seemed a long way away, and no Canadian troops were yet in action. There I stood, trying to look like a military figure and failing abysmally — a beanpole of a youth, my hands dangling below the cuffs of my jacket.

My parents were there, of course — my mother concerned, my father proud, my sister looking arch and telling me to beware of strange girls. There were some brittle jokes ("Give my regards to Mr. Hitler") and some repartee on my part ("You guys will be next"). Janet Walker arrived, slightly late, pressed a small package into my hands, and said she'd see my parents home. She'd held a going-away party for me on New Year's Eve at which I'd got gloriously drunk and very sick. I was a little surprised to realize how glad I was she'd made the leave-taking. And then I was on the train and the train was moving and they were all gone and I was seated in a car full of strange young men glancing uneasily about them.

I knew at once that this was a turning point in my life and determined to make the best of it. I tried to think of it, in Burt Lewis's term, as an adventure, but that didn't prevent a certain queasiness — the same kind of feeling I'd had when I first took the truck to Middle Dominion or the first time I'd timidly entered the offices of the newspaper. But then all of us on that train were in the same situation.

There we sat on the green plush seats — truck drivers and clerks, security guards and farmers, policemen and bootleggers — wearing our civilian clothes for the last time, watching each other sideways, grunting a few words of greeting, but generally lost in our own thoughts. I think I was the only university graduate on that train and therefore the only one with a slight knowledge of what was to come because of my training in the COTC. There I had seen my classmates transformed into screaming martinets as they tried to teach us the rudiments of close order drill. I remember how startled I was the first time when an Honours English student stared straight into my face from a distance of only a few inches and bellowed at me to smarten up. So I had a fair idea of what we were in for.

199

The journey to Vernon took all night. It was several hours before we began to talk to one another. We could not know it then, and wouldn't have believed it anyway, but before our two-month period of training was over we would become the closest of comrades. In fact, when we broke up at last in April, some of these men, now staring glumly out of the window or looking nervously about at the other strangers in the car, would actually weep at parting. Yet few, if any, would ever see each other again. The music of those days brings it back: "Elmer's Tune," "Deep in the Heart of Texas," Dinah Shore singing "Blues in the Night."

Our train roared through the blue night as we tried to sleep or made wry little jokes to one another about the future. This was not a trainload of eager volunteers rushing to the colours, determined to fight for King and country. These were all men like myself who had been reluctantly wrenched from the even tenor of civilian life and wanted to get back to it as quickly as possible.

Two faces stand out from that experience: the faces of two strangers who sat down with me in the dining car and because of that propinquity became intimates until they cracked under the pressure of military life. One was a big gregarious truck driver in a tweed jacket whose first name was Harry; his last escapes me. The other was a slender blond youth named Wilson, whose first name I've also forgotten, if indeed I ever knew it. Both seemed to me to be normal, cheerful young men, but the strange, foreign world into which they were thrust would eventually unnerve both.

I have a confused impression of that first morning, when we discarded our civilian clothes forever and were herded, shambling and bleating, onto the parade square in the heart of that grey and sombre camp in the rolling Okanagan hills. There we stood, with the fuzzy new battledress hanging slackly on our frames, the service caps sitting uneasily on our heads like fezzes, the gaiters buckled backward, the webbing hopelessly tangled, and the freshly greased rifles carried like truncheons. Our betters — the ones with stripes on their arms — looking at us sadly as NCOs have done from time immemorial, shaking their heads and making it clear that we were quite simply the worst bunch of soldiers they had ever seen — "poor sad bastards," in the army phrase, unteachable and untrainable. They knew better, of course, but we didn't.

We were known as Zombies — conscripts who had not signed up for overseas service. Most had no intention of doing so. The Zombies hated the army and made no bones about it. They had none of the Larger Loyalties the officers used to talk about. A decade of Canadian isolationism, anti-militarism, and black Depression had done its work. There were few patriots in that barrack room of seventy-five new recruits. Their real loyalties were to home towns, families, and girl friends. When the pressures of military life became too great they simply took off but were quickly apprehended and then confined to barracks for a week or so. For some that became a way of life.

But from the start I had decided to Go Active, to use the phrase of the day. If I was going to be in it, I wanted to be in it all the way. What was the use of learning to fight if you knew you were never going into battle? That seemed silly. I didn't even think about being killed; I don't think anybody did, at that distance. But I didn't want to be half a soldier like almost everyone else in our barrack room. Two others joined me to sign up for the active army and to put on our shoulders the CANADA flashes that indicated we were real soldiers, ready to do battle for our country.

Thus I became a reinforcement for the Seaforth Highlanders, a unit I never actually joined. But I was now allowed to wear either the Balmoral or the Glengarry rather than the despised field service cap, thus adding a touch of flair to my otherwise drab battledress. The defection of the three of us from the ranks of the Zombies did not sit well with our comrades. We returned to the barrack room to be greeted by a chorus of sardonic jests. "Suckers!" they cried. "Suckers!" We took the gibes manfully. It was some time before the official policy of hazing and shaming the Zombies came into practice.

It took all of us a while to get used to army life. Some never got used to it. We were no longer free: we needed a pass to leave camp, another to go home to Vancouver. During our waking hours we were yelled at hour after hour by our instructors. We were told when to go to sleep, when to rise. This was foreign to the experience of most, although my own summers in the mining camp had prepared me for a similar routine.

We were taught to do weird things. The weirdest of all was to hurl ourselves at a sack of straw, thrust into it with a bayonet while shouting "Kill! Kill! Kill!" and then jump on it while clobbering it with the butt of a rifle.

"Remember," our instructors would shout, "the German hates cold steel!" Why anybody would *love* cold steel while being skewered with a bayonet was beyond all of us.

All the same, there was a certain exhilaration involved in bayonet practice. I much preferred being out in the field, clambering over the obstacle course (or trying to) or learning the intricacies of the Bren gun, to performing army "fatigues," which were not only fatiguing but also boring. I hated peeling potatoes more than anything else in the world, and there always seemed to be mountains of potatoes to peel. When one mountain disappeared, a new one turned up. I hated scrubbing out the barrack room, or acting as night fireman to keep the stoves stoked, or going on all-night picket duty.

On those chill February nights we pickets would patrol the camp, shivering in our greatcoats, ordered to guard the premises against any Nazi interloper or spy but, in reality, to prevent any fellow soldiers from sneaking in after lights out. Of course they did sneak in and of course we let them.

One scene from those stints as a picket or a night fireman has never left me. Each barrack room, with its double row of two-tiered bunks, was like a cave hermetically sealed from intruders. When we entered, slapping our hands together to get rid of the chill of the night, a wall of suffocating heat almost drove us back. The scene was Dantesque: the stove, glowing red hot in the centre of the hut, causing our shadows to leap against the walls, and the blanketed figures, squirming, snoring, and groaning on their sheetless cots. In that dense atmosphere, as thick as soup, it was difficult to breathe; and the stench, compounded of rifle oil, sweat, Lysol, unwashed clothing, steaming greatcoats, old socks, boot polish, coal smoke, body odours, stale bedding, and even staler tobacco, was overpowering.

The only way to escape fatigues was to become a noncommissioned officer — no potato peeling for them; but this was beyond my abilities, or so I believed. To me, our platoon sergeant was an awesome figure. How he had managed to master all the bewildering army techniques to the point where he could teach them to others astounded me. He seemed to know everything — how to strip a Bren gun in three seconds, then put it back together in a twinkling; how to handle complicated drill movements; how to set a compound fracture using only a bayonet scabbard and standard webbing; how to achieve a perfect group on the rifle range; how to estimate distance in the field and explain the principle behind an anti-tank rifle.

This man was more than a simple soldier and marksman; he was a better teacher than any I'd known in university! I tried to figure out what he'd been in civilian life: president, no doubt, of some vast business enterprise, or perhaps the head of a large technical institute. Finally, I decided to ask him outright. To my astonishment, he told me that only the year before he'd been a clerk in a Nanaimo hardware store. I pondered that remarkable revelation and next day applied for an NCO's course. At least, I thought, I ought to be able to make lance-corporal.

Each man handled the culture-shock of military life in a different way. In the bunk above me, a thin-faced, sharp-nosed boy named Codweed lay scribbling letters to his girl friend. Codweed didn't look like the sort to have a girl, for he was gaunt and hollow chested, with little or no personality. But he wrote her a letter every night and received one every morning. By letter I don't mean a cursory note or a couple of scribbled pages. I mean a tome, a White Paper, an immense pamphlet containing dozens of sheets inscribed in his tiny, cramped hand. It astonished me that any man would have so much to say, especially a man like Codweed, who among the group of us said almost nothing.

It is clear to me now that those letters were Codweed's real life. Everything else, the everlasting close order drill, the fatigue duty, the sham hate of the bayonet practices — these were a mock life for Codweed. He lived vicariously in his letters; the rest of the time he simply went through the motions, a Zombie in more ways than one.

There were others who beat the new system as they had once beaten the civilian system. I knew one bootlegger in the army who, in those days of liquor rationing, simply continued to bootleg. He had all the equipment — special pens, ink, stamps, and ink remover with which to forge or alter liquor permits, supplying his fellow soldiers (not to mention officers) with all the booze they could handle.

Others were determined to get out of the service one way or another. We had in our hut a stubby little man called Hayward who announced he had no intention of staying in uniform. And he didn't. He used to sing a crazy song at night: "I never knew what misery was till I started herding sheep." It summed up his attitude to the army. To our amazement, Hayward managed somehow to get a discharge, perhaps for medical reasons, real or spurious. At any rate, there he was one day, back in his civilian clothes, surrounded by his barrack mates all wishing him well and most wishing they were in his shoes.

There were a few who never came to terms with military life and a couple who cracked under it. I had an odd experience in those early weeks with my friend Harry, the big truck driver with whom I'd sat on the train. All that morning we'd been taking close order drill, accustoming ourselves to the staccato tongues of the instructors as they assailed us with the curious jargon of command: "Atten-CHAP! Slow-ap HIPE! Pick it up, that man! Abow-at CHAP! Quee-ak MATCH! Take that man's name! On your feet — MOVE! Wipe the smile off your face, that man! Stan-at HAIZE! Stan HAIZAY!"

At five minutes before the hour we were given a smoke break. Harry didn't smoke nor did I, so we sauntered over to the edge of the parade square and stood on the grass. I made one of my wry jokes: "Hey — waddya say we make a break for it?"

But Harry did not laugh. An odd look came over his face. "They'd cut us down before we reached the fence," he said. "We'd never make it alive."

I saw, to my astonishment, that he was deadly serious.

A few days later when I was on duty as night fireman, I opened the door of our hut to replenish the stove, seeing once again those sleeping forms and hearing the grating sound of more than seventy men all snoring. But one man wasn't snoring. There, seated on the edge of his bed, fully clothed, was Harry, sombrely sharpening his bayonet.

At the same time, something was happening to Wilson, the curly-haired youth whom I'd also got to know on the train. We had become closer friends, wandering into town of an evening and playing chess together. But now Wilson had stopped playing chess and no longer wanted to go into town. More and more he seemed to withdraw into himself. One payday I suggested we go down to a local restaurant for a decent meal. At first he didn't answer, just lay there on

205

his bunk, staring at the ceiling. Finally, without moving, he responded in a voice devoid of expression. He didn't feel like it, he said.

Harry had taken to prowling up and down the length of the bunkhouse late at night, his bayonet in his hand. He said "they" were out to get him. Some thought it was a gag, others that he was bucking for a discharge; but it was more than that. One morning, as our platoon was trudging up a hill in a column of threes, a bulky figure detached itself from the line of march and charged straight into the path of an approaching Coca-Cola truck. It was Harry.

By a miracle he wasn't killed. The truck stopped with a jerk as our sergeant, moving like a cat, pulled him out from under the front wheels. And that was the last we ever saw of Harry.

As for Wilson, he had simply stopped speaking. I mean he didn't speak at all except on parade. The rest of the time he lay rigid on his bunk; if you spoke to him, he wouldn't answer. I don't think he really heard. It was as if his mind had left his body and was drifting freely, far from the parade square's asphalt, far from the canine barking of the instructors. The loudest noise could not disturb him; he didn't flinch or even blink.

Yet he went faithfully on parade, going through the motions without a murmur. He seemed to be the perfect soldier, marching in step, swinging his arms, clicking his heels, standing stiffly at attention, until one day at noon on battalion parade — the entire camp drawn up on the big square — there came a truly appalling sound, that of a rifle clattering to the ground. A figure drifted out from the ranks and began to wander aimlessly without any real direction. It was Wilson. A cluster of Military Police quickly surrounded him, and Wilson was taken away. We never saw him again, either.

These were the first war casualties I encountered. Perhaps they might have been casualties anyway, army or no army. Certainly the cold shock of military life triggered something inside them. But then, it did that for each of us. The man least affected by the experience of basic training slept in the bunk opposite me and was the butt of many jokes and not a few pranks. He was mentally retarded and known universally as Jesus, a nickname he accepted, as he accepted everything, with great good humour. No matter what was said to or about Jesus, he always grinned happily. He was totally army-proof. The instructors could scream their heads off at him; it didn't faze him. He followed orders, a little slowly perhaps, but he gave no trouble. In some ways he was the perfect soldier.

The man who had our sympathy was Codweed, my bunkmate, the inveterate letter writer. Something was seriously wrong with Codweed's back, and the callous army command was doing nothing about it. It wrung our hearts to hear Codweed groaning in his bunk and to see him trying to stand upright. As the days went by he walked about bent almost double, and yet he couldn't get treatment.

He reported sick often enough — a feat that took some doing in the army. A man could be shaking with ague or burning with fever, but he still had to get fully dressed, put on his greatcoat, shoulder his pack, and march off in step to the Medical Inspection Room. There, the air was blue with invalids cursing, coughing, and spitting. The chances were that if you weren't sick when you arrived you certainly were when you left. I reported sick just once — that was enough; but Codweed kept it up day after day.

The corporal, the sergeant, and especially the Medical Officer seemed to us to be unfeeling brutes when it came to Codweed's infirmity. They refused to have his back fixed and kept sending him out onto the parade square where he was usually to be seen limping along several paces behind the rest of us.

In the evenings we would sit around Codweed's bed, shaking our head in sympathy as he described his symptoms — the terrible pain that racked him, the nausea he felt when he was forced to march. We would clench our fists and grit our teeth and curse the army, which cared not a whit for human suffering. Codweed was our martyr, and we took turns helping him onto the parade square.

Meanwhile a camaraderie was developing among the men of the platoon. A sudden quarantining of the camp for measles threw us upon our own resources, for we could no longer go into town on Saturdays. Instead a group of us would wander over the hills bordering Kalamalka Lake and talk about life, religion, politics, and sex — topics allegedly banned in all officers' messes but matters of intense interest to private soldiers.

We shared a common hatred of church parade, which some of us managed to skip. It was offensive to me to be forced to take part in any religious service against my will — especially as these parades had nothing to do with turning me into an efficient soldier. In this instance the chore was especially demeaning because the padre was a confirmed British Israelite. This insufferable man did his best to convince us that the lost tribes of Israel had somehow made their way to the British Isles — a piece of fantasy no more difficult to swallow than the burning bush or the parting of the Red Sea but so patently spurious that it caused our gorges to rise, whether we had any religion or not. The hatred of church parade was one of the elements that united us, slowly transforming us from a rabble into the beginnings of a disciplined military formation.

The other element was the platoon competition in close order drill. At first nobody cared about the competition, but as the days wore on and our drill improved we began to grow a little cocky, shouting taunts at other platoons as they marched across the square. By the sixth week of training, it was clear that something was happening to us. It no longer mattered that all but three of us had no intention of shedding blood for our country. What suddenly seemed to be important was that our platoon should be proclaimed the best — that we should be presented with a plaque before the entire camp, that we should all have our photographs taken holding the trophy, with a copy to each man to send home or to cherish.

The problem was poor Codweed. It was apparent that he was holding us back. He missed training because he was forever going off on sick parade. As a result, we were denied our break periods because the instructors were always helping him catch up. We were getting weary of hearing the sergeant continually telling Codweed to keep in step.

Gradually Codweed found himself a liability. We could scarcely win the platoon competition with him limping along behind us. The little knot of sympathizers around his bunk dwindled and evaporated. Now when Codweed complained about his back he got angry looks. On parade, when he missed a step, the man behind would kick him. From martyrdom, Codweed had become a pariah.

And then, one day something remarkable happened: Codweed's back began to improve. He stopped reporting sick. He came out on parade and began to keep in step. It was, as a few of us remarked acidly, a miracle rivalling those of Lourdes.

From that point on, there was no holding us. Perfection in close order drill became an obsession. It is hard to believe, looking back on it now, that we actually gave up our precious evenings and practised at night in our own time. Of course we won the competition and were photographed with the coveted trophy on our last day together, and celebrated and swore eternal loyalty to one another — promising to write faithfully and get together for a grand reunion after the war. The following day we broke up forever — an emotional leave-taking that saw tears in the eyes of several of us. In just ten weeks the army had taken seventy-five strangers from all walks of life and turned them, for a little while at least, into the closest of comrades.

Yet few of us were to see any of the others again. Did Codweed ever marry the girl he wrote to so often? I have no way of knowing. All I remember is that as the training intensified and his back improved, he wrote fewer and fewer letters. As for the others, a face occasionally peers out of a crowd at an airport or on a city street, a face without a name and sometimes without a place. Was it at Vernon that I knew him, or at Calgary or Brockville or Aldershot? Sometimes we indulge in a kind of stilted conversation, this stranger and I, who were once close buddies. We grope for some common ground and only rarely find it. We announce that we must get together soon but never do. And then we go our separate ways, often unsure of exactly where it was we met and what it was we did together in those bizarre war years when comradeship was transitory and valediction as ephemeral as gunsmoke.

2 Suddenly I was a leader of men — sort of. I had been accepted for the NCO's training course and passed it. Now I had a lance-corporal's stripe on my arm to go with the CANADA badge on my shoulder. Somewhat to my surprise I discovered that I could do most of the things the sergeant could do. By shouting a command I could cause a platoon of more than seventy soldiers to halt in their tracks or turn as a body to the right or to the left or even to reverse their movement. It gave me a giddy sense of power to move these phalanxes around the parade square like chess pieces. When the others left for advanced training, I was kept behind as an instructor to teach others what I'd learned.

This was not my first choice. In the course of the mandatory interview with the army psychologist I had expressed a desire to join the Intelligence Corps. He looked at me owlishly. "There is no intelligence in the army," he said and laughed at his own feeble joke — a young man, just out of university like myself, going through the motions without any great enthusiasm.

So here I was, a seasoned hand after only ten weeks, placed in charge of the newest batch of recruits, detailed to round them up, help them untangle the mysteries of web equipment, and bully them onto the parade ground. Now it was I who shouted the well-worn phrases — "Smarten up, that man!" (*What* man? We never knew.) "Slo-ap HIPE! In! Out! On Guard!" It was I who revealed the morale-building secret that the German hates cold steel, I who taught them how to practise the butt stroke with the Lee-Enfield rifle, designed to mash in a man's head after the first bayonet thrust. I doubt that the butt stroke was ever used in actual warfare. As for the bayonet, it was useful, no doubt, for opening tins of Spam but not very practical as a weapon in a war where close combat was a rarity. It belonged to earlier times, when men formed hollow squares to beat off spirited attacks by a splendidly costumed cavalry. Nonetheless, the new men were taught to rush at sacks of straw screaming imprecations, while we instructors shouted, "Kill! Kill! Kill!"

Now that I was a lance-corporal I was beginning to enjoy army life. I was no longer yelled at, and I didn't have to peel potatoes. I felt the need to express myself — the same need I'd felt in my mining camp days when I started the *Pipeline*. A concert party was being organized to entertain the camp on Saturday nights in the drill hall. I resurrected "The March of Slime" from my university days with new jokes, as corny as the old ones. Doug Watt, a UBC buddy of mine on a two-week training course at Vernon with the COTC, winced perceptibly when he read the script. "I can't *believe* they'll laugh at that," he said. But laugh they did, for I had learned what Bob Hope already knew: the feeblest local reference always produces a guffaw. Kid the establishment and you can't lose. When I lampooned the army's venereal disease parades, euphemistically known as short arm inspections (I called them "long arm inspections"), the troops went crazy. For the first time I heard the sweet music of applause. Something I had written and performed had produced an instant reaction!

But it wasn't enough. I needed other outlets. I found myself writing long letters home to my parents, to Jack Scott, to Janet Walker, and to others, describing army life. I was a frustrated writer, seeking an audience. The letters weren't really letters; they were magazine articles. It didn't occur to me, of course, that this was for me as much a release from army routine as it had been for the wretched Codweed. I was practising my journalism, reporting my discoveries, but like Codweed I was also living vicariously in the pages of my prose.

My large pack was heavier than anyone else's because I insisted on trundling about an eight-pound Hermes Baby typewriter, one of the most maddening machines ever invented. Its only asset was its small size. My two-finger style invariably caused the keys to jam. The margins were uncertain. The space-bar kept jumping. The upper-case letters popped up halfway above each line, like small nervous insects. Nonetheless I persisted, churning out page after page at night and sometimes writing letters for those of my fellow soldiers who found it difficult to put their sentiments on paper. I wooed one girl by proxy, like Cyrano but with poorer results. She wrote to her boy friend that he was becoming far too flowery. She much preferred his earlier, simpler prose.

And it *still* wasn't enough. At last I determined to start a camp newspaper, but not the bulletin-board variety. This one would be a real newspaper, printed on a real press with real type and real photographs taken by the official camp photographer. I had a name for it that seemed to fit a basic training centre. It would be called simply *Rookie*. I slaved over the first cover photo, showing a newly arrived recruit changing from civilian clothes into spanking new battledress. I designed the masthead, chose the type, and began to churn out stories on my Hermes Baby.

In the midst of all this I got a welcome message. Burton Lewis had arrived in Vernon and was anxious to see me. I could scarcely contain myself. I hadn't realized how much I'd missed those halcyon days in Vancouver. Now, at last, my old friend and editor had turned up. It would be like old times.

I couldn't wait to get down to the hotel. Fortunately, we were at that point between courses, and I had a free afternoon. Burt met me at the door with a glass of rye in his hand; there were several army people in the room with him, and I learned that he was now attached to the military as some sort of financial adviser or expert. I never did find out what his job was because Burton Lewis was so drunk he could scarcely speak.

He explained, thickly, that he had been engaged to speak to the Women's Canadian Club at lunch the following day. He proposed to dictate the speech to me while I typed it up, a sensible idea since he was too far gone to type anything. His plan was to speak to the ladies on the subject of Pierre Laval, the French traitor who was the puppet dictator of Vichy France. Lewis had interviewed Laval years before and hadn't liked him.

"I well recall Pierre Laval, with his greasy tie and his greasy white shirt," Burt began as I typed away.

"Got that?" Burt asked, pouring each of us another slug of rye. I'd got it; now I waited.

"Well recall Pierre Laval," said Burt. "Greasy greasy tie."

He sat down. "Got that?" he asked.

I told him I'd already got it.

"Greasy man," said Lewis. "Distasteful. Knew it then. Proven now. I well recall interviewing Pierre Laval . . ."

At this point my old friend and mentor became totally incomprehensible. There he sat, staring into space with his round blue eyes, his hands creeping over his neck and

213

shoulders, trying to remember his interview with Pierre Laval.

He looked at me and I could see the bewilderment on his face.

"You write it," he said.

I shook my head. I hadn't interviewed Pierre Laval.

"Well, have a drink," said Burton Lewis.

We had several drinks; but we did not talk about the old days, for Burton Lewis had trouble communicating. It was years before I saw him again, a reformed alcoholic by that time who took nothing stronger than orange juice. But he was never able to give that talk on Pierre Laval to the club-women of Vernon.

Meanwhile the first edition of *Rookie* was almost ready to go to press. Dorwin Baird, the former *Ubyssey* editor and CJOR announcer, had arrived with a new bunch of recruits and was helping me put the paper together. I never saw the finished product. Before the paper could be published I was gone, and Dorwin took over the editorship.

This was in early summer of 1942. The war was growing hotter and the army was expanding. New camps were being built as the recruiting drives accelerated. In June I was dispatched to help open another Basic Training Centre at Vedder Crossing, near Chilliwack in the Fraser Valley. Vancouver was only an hour and a half away by electric tram.

For the next several weeks I was a member of a work party digging latrines, putting up bell tents, and building outdoor washstands, while carpenters constructed more permanent barracks. I remember hammering in tent pegs one morning beside a mild young officer named Bonelli — a small, blond man with soft blue eyes and a wispy moustache. Bonelli didn't look like the kind of man who would so much as kick a dog in anger, but now, as we hammered away and talked about the future, he suddenly turned to me and said, fiercely, "All I want to do is kill Germans!

"I want to kill Germans!" Bonelli repeated, hammering

away viciously, as if the tent peg were a member of the Waffen SS. Coming from him it could only sound incongruous. He had adopted what he thought was a stern and even vicious look, but on that innocent face it didn't work. I had no idea what Lieutenant Bonelli had done in civilian life — perhaps some quiet office job. Now here was this mild-mannered man with the shy smile doing his best to gnash his teeth, announcing that he wanted to murder people. He kept saying it over and over again. "All I want to do is kill Germans!" History, I thought, is turning all of us into savages. Not long before I'd read a piece by Alan Morley in the *Sun* on how necessary it was for everyone to hate — *really* hate — the enemy, if we were to win the war. Poor Bonelli had two years of life left in which to hate the Germans, but he never did come face to face with one. His death was impersonal, mechanical, and swift. He was scarcely in action before he stepped on an enemy land-mine and was blown to bits.

With the tents up, the new recruits shambled in. I was promoted to corporal and given inhuman powers over the newcomers.

We lived under canvas all that summer; in the fall we would move into a new barracks. I turned twenty-two in July, sun-burned, hard-muscled, with energy to burn. On most nights I'd sneak out of camp without a pass to visit the fleshpots of Cultus Lake. Actually there was only one fleshpot, a roller rink, where to the sounds of "Sleepy Lagoon" and the "Johnson Rag" we whirled about eyeing the girls.

Sometimes on the weekends friends would come up from Vancouver: Jack Scott and his wife, Grace, and, on more than one occasion, Janet Walker accompanied by one or two friends from university days. Janet always brought me something, or tried to. One day she baked a batch of chocolate cupcakes for me — a real delicacy, after camp food. Alas, having missed her lunch in a mad dash to make the interurban tram, she ate them all before she arrived.

On one of those Saturday nights I lured her away from the others and into a rented canoe. And there, for the first time, I kissed her. What was it, I wonder now, that prompted this first embrace? Was it the moon, dappling the waves, and the wind sighing in the frieze of conifers beyond? Was it the music of the "Anniversary Waltz," wafting across the lake from the roller rink? Perhaps. I think it more likely that it was the canoe itself. One cannot lunge at a woman in a canoe: caveman tactics won't work and a gentler, softer, more romantic approach is required to avoid capsizing. *Colombo's Canadian Quotations* includes my definition of a Canadian as one who knows how to make love in a canoe. It is not original with me, but all the same I learned the technique in that healthy, comradely necking session at Cultus Lake, B.C., in the summer of '42.

I took my platoon on route marches by day and repeated the process on my own at night, for the lake was several miles from camp. I'd hike back at midnight, half asleep, so groggy that I actually saw visions in the gloom, ghostly troops tramping toward me round the bend in the roadway, and heard phantom footsteps treading beside me as I stumbled on. Shades of the Walker of the Snows!

At one or two in the morning I'd tumble into bed; at six I'd be up, rousing my troops. Once I found a man still slumbering when the others were up and shaving. "It's all right, Corporal," he said. "I'm dressed." And so he was, right down to his leggings and boots. He'd gone to bed that way in order to grab a few minutes' extra sleep. Off he went, stripped, to the showers.

Whenever I got a weekend pass I'd head for Vancouver to visit my parents, to lie on the beach, or to spend a Saturday night at the Scotts', listening to Jack play his Mary Lou Williams records.

At midnight on Sunday I'd race for the B.C. Electric terminal to grab the last interurban tram for Chilliwack. One night I fell asleep or perhaps passed out on the streetcar. I overshot the terminal and woke up on the outskirts of Vancouver at the end of the streetcar line. *My God,* I thought, *I'll never make camp by reveille. They'll take away my stripes and I'll be back to peeling potatoes with the rest.* I got off blearily and began to wander in what I thought was the general direction of the Fraser Valley. Suddenly I heard the jangle of a bell, looked back, and to my astonishment and relief saw the tram rattling toward me, with my friends waving me aboard. Everybody is blessed with a little luck, but I have had more than my share.

Sometimes I'd drop into the *News-Herald* office to say hello to the old gang, but it wasn't the same. The old gang was dwindling, especially the men. Strange women now occupied the majority of the desks, making me feel like an interloper, for it seemed to me that they looked on me with irritation if not hostility. Ralph Daly, among others, had joined the air force. By summer's end Jack Scott, too, had gone — to army public relations.

On these visits home my father urged me to apply for a commission. He'd risen to lieutenant in the First War and seemed surprised when I said I didn't expect to get much higher than corporal. "The pay is better and you'd be much more comfortable," he said more than once. He still had his Sam Browne belt from the old days and obviously treasured this symbol of commissioned rank.

He wasn't well that year; his circulation had always been poor, and he'd already had one operation for varicose veins. He'd taken up weaving, which required less energy but a good deal of brains. He'd actually built himself a loom with some refinements of his own design and was busily weaving not only table runners and scarves but cloth for a tweed suit for Lucy, now in her senior year at UBC and writing the "Mary Anne" advertising and gossip column, which she had inherited from Janet Walker. He even carved the buttons himself.

But I shrugged off the idea of a commission, partly

because I felt — or thought I felt — that there was something noble about being in the ranks, partly because I didn't believe I could ever attain the necessary skills to reach commissioned status.

My best friend was the camp barber, Jack Arding, a man of considerable wit and intelligence. It was well known that on the army's compulsory intelligence test Arding had received the highest score of anybody in camp, including the commanding officer himself. In fact, the Colonel had barely scraped through, with a score of 160, the minimum requirement for an officer, while Jack was given a whopping 210, a figure that put him in the genius category.

"This is ridiculous, Arding," I told him. "Here you are, a mere private, and yet your M-Test shows you're smarter than the Colonel. *You* ought to be Colonel!"

"Not me," said Arding reasonably. "I'm making more money than the Colonel and don't have any of the responsibility."

It was true. Arding was not only the smartest man in camp but also the richest. For a quarter he'd give you the standard army haircut — or "pigshave," as we called it. For seventy-five cents he'd do a proper job. Everybody, including the Colonel, paid the higher price.

It has always been my fancy that by the end of the war I was the best-trained soldier in the Canadian army. Millions of dollars must have been spent sending me on course after course until so much was invested in me that it would have been fiscally irresponsible to waste me in action. I was sent off to Nanaimo to take a six-week weapons training course designed to make me an expert in infantry small arms. Later I was given a course in marksmanship and was able to achieve a perfect group on the rifle range — but only with a .22, which had no kick. Even more startling was the physical training course that turned me, a totally unathletic twenty-two-year-old who'd never been inside a gymnasium, into a PT instructor.

218

The troops I was to train were in terrible physical shape; indeed, their general condition gave me a new insight into the human wreckage left by the Depression. One man in ten couldn't read, and only a handful knew the name of the prime minister, although Mackenzie King had been in office for the better part of two decades. Now I found myself trying to give lectures on such subjects as "Why We Fight" and, on alternate days, taking charge of a physical training class and shouting things like "standing astride, arms swinging forward, sideways and upward by numbers."

"I guess you'll go back to your old job after this is over, eh corporal?" one of my class remarked during a break. I said I certainly would, meaning the newspaper business. "What gym?" he asked, and I realized that he thought I'd been doing physical jerks all my life. I didn't enlighten him. Army instruction was always part bluff.

Late that fall I determined to start another newspaper in my spare time. It would be called the *Torch*, a title that reflected the camp's symbol. My friend Les Barbour, the editor of the Chilliwack *Progress*, provided the presses. I got together a staff, including a photographer, wrote most of the copy myself, drew the cartoons, and launched it with as much fanfare as I could muster. It was a hit with the officers, but not with all the men. One of them put his finger on its chief flaw when he told me that the *Torch* "was just too much like a real newspaper." My face fell, for that, of course, was my whole purpose. Those earlier bulletin-board papers in the Scouts, in college, and in the mining camp had been little more than scandal sheets. But now I was a real journalist, trained to put out a "real" paper. It never really hit home to me that the troops didn't want a carbon copy of a professional newspaper; they wanted something racier and kookier. They wanted gossip and irreverence. They wanted outrageous, iconoclastic stories that poked fun at the officers and sergeants. They wanted half-truths and scandal. They wanted laughs. They did not want a sober journal covering the official events of camp life. It occurs to me now that if I'd had less professional experience, if I'd put out a paper more like the *Pipeline,* the *Torch* would have been far more popular. For me it was an outlet; for the private soldier, I fear, it was a bit of a bore.

At this juncture — the midwinter of 1942-43, at the time of Stalingrad and El Alamein, when we were all trying to whistle "As Time Goes By," from the movie *Casablanca* — a strange thing happened that changed my military career.

I was Orderly Corporal that day, but I cannot remember what it was that an Orderly Corporal did. All I recall is that a runner came out to me on the training field with a message that the Regimental Sergeant Major wanted to see me on the double.

On the double! A chill ran through me. The RSM was the most awesome figure in camp, far more to be feared than the Colonel, a remote creature of frightening power who *never* sent for a junior NCO on the double unless there was trouble. What had I done? I had sneaked out of camp without a pass after Lights Out, that's what I'd done, and I'd sneaked back in over the obstacle course — the easiest way into the enclosure with the pickets looking the other way, although it did require a certain amount of agility. It was surprising how so many men who couldn't master the obstacle course by day during training had no difficulty negotiating its walls, hurdles, and hoops late at night.

I trotted across the parade square, bracing myself for what I knew was coming. I'd be out of the corporal's mess by nightfall, reduced to a private's pay of $1.30 a day. Well, I might was well swallow it, and so I marched into the RSM's office prepared to take my medicine.

He gave me a queer look.

"Colonel wants to see you."

The Colonel! It was worse than I thought.

In I marched, halted, clicked my heels, saluted.

To my astonishment, the C.O. leaned across his desk and shook hands with me.

"Congratulations, Mr. Berton," he said.

Mister? It was passing strange to be called Mister after a year in which I'd been called everything else. It left me bewildered.

"Here," said the C.O., reaching into his desk. "These are a couple of spare ones I've had kicking around. Get your batman to sew them on right away."

They were the pips of a second lieutenant. At last it dawned on me that they were making me an officer, although the reasons were never properly explained. The prospect was dizzying. I was to be a provisional second lieutenant with all the privileges and perks of an officer. At a later date I would have to take officer's training. Meanwhile, for a few months I would actually be in command of a platoon.

I was one of three who were given provisional commissions that day. My own sergeant, John David, was another. He, at least, was perfect officer material. He loved the army — loved it with a passion that was almost past belief. Too young for the First War — or "show" as he insisted on calling it — he was too old to go overseas in the second. He made up for this frustration by turning himself into a caricature of a spit-and-polish NCO. Unfortunately he didn't look like a soldier. He looked exactly like Mahatma Gandhi and was called that behind his back. Like my father, he believed in the King, the Empire, the Army, and the Conservative party, and when eventually he met my father, he clicked his heels so hard and saluted with such force that he almost fell over. (In fact, on another occasion, he *did* fall over — backwards — such was the energy of his salute.) He saluted everybody, civilians as well as superiors, and, of course, he addressed my father as "Sir."

"Missed the last show, Sir. Bad piece of luck that. Hope to get across the pond for this show, though."

He talked that way, his sentences crisp and forthright as befitted command. With his English accent and his imperial posture he might have come straight out of Victorian England, but he was actually a Canadian from the Okanagan Valley. Neville Chamberlain was his hero, a loyalty that got him into more than one argument during the lectures he conducted on "Why We Fight." His students thought that Neville Chamberlain was a jerk, but John David knew better.

He'd always been scrupulously correct with me. I was invariably "Corporal Berton." He never used my last name without the rank. Now suddenly I was "Pierre" and he was "John." I found that abrupt transformation unnerving.

John David was clearly the perfect choice for a provisional commission. But why me? Obviously I'd achieved a passing mark in my M-Test, but I couldn't believe it was spectacular. I recalled one of my egregious blunders on the test. I was supposed to put a handle on the drawing of a receptacle I took for a teapot. I gave it a cuplike handle and only realized later that it was a tea-*kettle*. Anybody who couldn't tell a teapot from a tea-kettle was scarcely officer material.

I walked out of the office in a daze, as the Regimental Sergeant Major sprang to attention, saluted, and in an overly loud voice shouted: "Sir!" I really didn't know what to do. Suddenly, by the addition of a single bit of cloth to each shoulder, I had been turned into a different kind of person. It was the strangest thing that had ever happened to me: no warning, no preparation, no build-up. It was also an experience I would not care to repeat in spite of its many obvious advantages. But at least my father would be pleased, and I would be able to wear his Sam Browne belt from the Great War.

My change of status was unreal. I had risen that morning from an iron cot with two blankets, in a hut with some fifty men, many of them close friends. My breakfast had been thrown at me, cafeteria style; after wolfing it down I had washed my own dishes and folded my own blankets. But I lunched that day in the Officers' Mess, where the food was excellent and the tables clothed in linen. I slept that night in a bed with real sheets. I had a servant who made my bed, shined my boots, and polished my brass. Before supper I crowded around the bar with men who had been my superiors that morning and sipped a dry martini. My pay increased fourfold.

I was told quite explicitly by the Colonel that I must no longer associate with my friends of the previous day. My new buddies would be lieutenants, captains, and majors. They all greeted me genially, partly, I think, because I was editor of the camp paper, a position that had made me a minor celebrity in their eyes — in short, a local Personality.

But now I was given to understand that the price of my new position was the abandonment of such lowly types as Jack Arding. I decided to ignore the dictum. On my first night as an officer I went as usual to Arding's quarters. He and my other close comrade, Corporal Henry Ricci, the camp tailor, sprang to attention and called me "Sir" with big grins on their faces. We all laughed and went off to the movies, but it wasn't quite the same.

Indeed, nothing was ever the same again. The gap between enlisted men and officers was as deep as Miles Canyon on the Yukon. The following morning I found myself in command of a new platoon. The sergeant saluted me with a straight face. In the space of twenty-four hours our positions had reversed, and I have no doubt he resented it. He'd been in the army for more than two years and had served a tour of duty in England. Now here was this pipsqueak of a kid with only a year behind him, taking his salute and giving him instructions. It was too much for both of us. I didn't even know how to act as an officer. I hadn't learned how to delegate. I was still marching beside the platoon, shouting orders like a corporal instead of letting my NCOs handle the job. Our relations were correct but distant.

In the Officers' Mess, subalterns who had once told me what to do now slapped me on the back, called me by my first name, and bought me drinks. On the other hand, the Quartermaster Sergeant, whom I disliked because of his officiousness, became positively obsequious — and all because of one small pip on my shoulder.

I did not consciously drop my old friends, nor did they consciously drop me. We simply began to see less and less of each other. It had not been necessary for the C.O. to order me to shun them. The army situation was such that continued association became more and more difficult.

I cannot say that I felt comfortable during this odd period in my military career. I felt first like a renegade and second like a fraud. I got over it, of course; indeed, I was surprised to discover how really easy it was to be an officer. At last, in March the army let me off the hook and shipped me off to a proper officers' training course, where I was reduced in a twinkling to the status of cadet, a rank slightly lower than that of worm. Here I was again subjected to all the abuse, humiliation, and travail that the army lavishes on its trainees. But when I put the pips back on my shoulders three months later, I felt at last that I had earned them.

3 I was quickly discovering that army life was a constantly changing kaleidoscope of intense intimacies and sudden farewells. The man in the next bunk could for a couple of months be your closest crony, your most intimate confidant, your bosom companion. If you were late getting back from leave, he cleaned your rifle for you and made your bed; you did the same for him. If you were broke, he shared his funds; if you were in love, he shared your heartaches. He knew more about you than your own mother; he was father confessor to you as you were to him.

Then suddenly it ended; you said goodbye, not without emotion, swore you would never forget each other, went your separate ways, and, more often than not, never saw each other again. Burton Lewis had told me that I would make lifelong friends in the army, but when I left Chilliwack and arrived at Gordon Head, outside Victoria, for officer's training, it still hadn't happened.

Then one day, while I was shaving, a burly cadet on the opposite side of the wash bench looked over at me and made an extraordinary remark.

"I'm getting married on Saturday," he said, in a kind of low grunt. "Do you think I should?"

His name was Harry Francis Xavier Filion, a big man (six feet, two hundred pounds) with a quizzical expression. I didn't know what to say; the question seemed rhetorical.

"I have noticed that you read *The New Yorker*," Filion said, not bothering to wait for an answer. "I personally consider that to be a very fine magazine."

Thus was begun an enduring friendship that lasted until he died of a heart attack forty years later.

We hit it off immediately, for we had more than *The New Yorker* in common: a love of good literature, a fascination with the nineteenth century, an irreverent and often jaundiced attitude to the world, especially in its more pompous moments, a passion for food (everything from *haute cuisine* to Cantonese cooking), and an abiding belief in the healing properties of rye whisky.

Filion was the wittiest man I have ever met, even when he was morose, which was fairly often. He had a dry, offbeat wit and could do more with a raised eyebrow or a sideways glance than many a rubber-faced comedian. He spoke in a series of grunts, emphasizing odd words, giving sentences twists that were funny only when he worked on them. Whenever I listen to Vicki Gabereau on the radio, I hear faint echoes of the Filion style, which isn't surprising, since Vicki is his daughter.

The clichés of the time delighted him; he recognized them for what they were and used them gleefully. Sometimes, when we'd sit around glumly staring at our thumbs, Filion would cock an eye, raise a brow, and grunt, "Let's all go out and have a million laughs." Once at a staid society party in Vancouver when the conversation flagged and boredom fell across that glittering company like a shroud, Filion looked up and broke the silence. "Let's all engage in group sex activities," said he. Often, in moments of desperation, he'd turn to me and say, "I don't suppose you have a dry martini about your person?" He was good company even when he *wasn't* good company.

He peppered his conversation with droll figures of speech that he'd either picked up somewhere and remembered or had invented himself. The weather was either "colder than a well-digger's ass" or "hotter than a bandit's pistol." He remarked of one woman who gave her favours loosely that "she had stopped more rubber than Turk Broda." He referred to another as "having a figure like a sack of horns." In spite of his immense size, or perhaps because of it, he was attractive to women. One attempted, vainly, to seduce him on the Victoria boat. "She was all over me like a short overcoat," Filion declared.

In spite of his bulk, which grew greater over the years — he would eventually tip the scales at three hundred pounds — he was light on his feet and the master of any game that involved a ball. He was a superb golfer, a champion ping-pong player, and a tough man to beat at snooker. In his teens he'd been a Yo-Yo champion. One day his father, a sober businessman, was walking down Granville Street in Vancouver when he noticed a youth in the window of the Owl Drug Store demonstrating a new brand of Yo-Yo. To his horror, the elder Filion realized the Yo-Yo salesman was his son. He hauled him out by the ear.

The Filions at that time were well off. When his father bought a new Cadillac, Harry took it out for a trial spin and wrapped it around a tree. His father bought a new one the next day and turned it over to his son. "Don't want you to lose your nerve," he told the boy.

Alas, he lost his fortune and died, leaving his son with a private school education but few skills. Harry worked on the periphery of the newspaper business until war was declared in 1939, promptly joined the army, and was sent overseas to become a Corps photographer with the 1st Division. Now he was back home, learning how to become an officer.

The other officer cadet with whom I enjoyed a lifetime association was Lloyd East, a tall, skinny minister's son from Regina. At six feet five, Lloyd towered over me by two inches. His height was the main reason why he was chosen to be right marker for our graduation ceremonies in June. The right marker stands at the extreme right of the first three rows of an infantry platoon.

When the platoon wheels or dresses by the right, he is the pivot man and therefore slightly more equal than all the others. In fact, the success or failure of any parade ground manoeuvre depends to a considerable extent on the right marker. That explains why nobody in the ranks ever wanted the job.

The graduation ceremonies at Gordon Head were the culmination of three months of hard training, in which we'd been taught everything from map reading to Methods of Instruction. It was here that I learned to think on my feet and to hold an audience. The army technique was to hand you a subject, give you five minutes to prepare a lecture, and then have you deliver it verbally to your peers. The subjects could range all the way from the stoppages in the Bren gun to the significance of China on the international scene. It was under these conditions that I learned something of the art of communication — perhaps the most valuable lesson the army taught me.

None of this was as important, in the eyes of the top

brass, as our behaviour on the graduation parade. It was as if our training had been devised entirely to teach us how to march in step rather than to lead men into battle. We must move across the parade square as one man in a knife-sharp line, wheeling and reversing, sloping and ordering arms so smartly that the butts of all the rifles striking the ground would be heard as a single slap.

It seems to me that we were on that parade ground day in and day out, hundreds of us, learning to march in such perfect order that the wives, mothers, sweethearts, and cousins who came to see us receive our commissions would be stunned and dumbfounded by the beauty and precision of it all, secure at last in the knowledge that we were the most efficient fighting formation in the world.

Our drill master was a Major Faulkner. Everyone who passed through Gordon Head remembers him — a ramrod-straight, craggy-faced drill instructor, obsessed with perfection. The slightest hesitation on the march, the tiniest wobble in the ranks brought down a scalding torrent of condemnation on the offender. As the great day approached, Faulkner's mania increased. Did we want to disgrace ourselves in front of our loved ones? Bring shame upon the Corps? We must present arms with a single slap — scores of palms whacking the rifle butts in the space of a split second. Try it again, and wipe the smile off your face, that man! (*What man? Me? Was I smiling?* I knew the army game, for I'd played it myself in my days as a corporal and a provisional one-pip wonder. "That man" could be any man or no man, and I knew it; but I fell for the hoax and pursed my lips just in case I had been smiling unconsciously and the terrible major had caught me at it.)

At last the great day came. My father came over from Vancouver, proud of his officer son. My sister came too, and a girl friend (mine, not my sister's). Off across the parade ground we marched, men who would some day be majors or colonels and one or two who might even end up as generals and a good many more who would shortly be dead or blind or, like Harry Filion, wounded and out of action.

We were peacock proud, strutting across the square, keeping our ranks as straight as the creases in our dress trousers. We halted as one: a single echoing thump on the asphalt of the square. We ordered arms as one—another thump, as several score of rifles hit the ground. The perfection of it! I could almost see Major Faulkner's chest swell with pride.

And then, a dreadful clatter... *Crash!* Somebody had not only dropped his rifle but had also toppled face forward onto the parade square. It was our right marker, Lloyd East, the most prominent man in that whole assembly, occupying the most prominent position in the corps, stretched out — all six feet five inches — marring the perfection of Major Faulkner's military geometry.

A moment of dreadful silence followed. Nobody budged or even breathed. I stole a glance at the Major and thought he was about to burst from apoplexy. He looked directly at me and in a hoarse whisper rapped out a command: "Get him *off!*" he hissed. "Get him off! Get him off! Get him *off!*"

It took two of us to drag Lloyd East feet first across the square and conceal him behind a large sign. Nobody, I noticed, had inquired about his condition. Had he suffered a heart attack? A brain tumor? A sudden paralytic stroke? Nobody cared, least of all Major Faulkner, who took the salute as the ranks closed and we all marched past. I doubt that the Major was ever quite the same again. As for Lloyd East, he quickly recovered from what had been a hangover, brought to a kind of boil by having to stand rigidly in the June sun. The affair gave him a moment or two of minor celebrity. That night we all celebrated and the following day, nursing East-like hangovers, left Gordon Head forever and headed off for the various Advanced Training Centres scattered across the country.

4 Filion, East, and I were among the contingent of infantry officers dispatched to Currie Barracks to endure the month-long course of advanced infantry training that would gain us our second pip and turn us into first lieutenants. The barracks lay on the bald prairie, beyond the outskirts of Calgary; today, of course, the camp has been all but swallowed by subdivisions. It was then the headquarters of the Lord Strathcona's Horse, a venerable regiment whose battle honours went back to the Boer War when it had been commanded by the legendary former Mounted Policeman Sam Steele.

The Officers' Mess resembled a large residential hotel, with its magnificent drawing rooms, sumptuous bar, big dining room, stuffed moose heads, long glass-covered verandah, and huge billiard room. Some of the older inmates seemed contemporary with the stuffed trophies. These were the veteran officers of the regiment, no longer fit for battle. To us they were fossils from another age, old sweats from an old war, unfamiliar with the new army manuals and unwilling to learn — Saturday-night militiamen who had stayed on in the reserve army for social reasons, only barely competent to handle the complicated training required for the new conflict. To them, of course, we "reinforcement officers" were a temporary nuisance who invaded the sanctity of their mess, disturbed the even tenor of their ways, but could be suffered because our stay would be brief — or so they thought.

Among that number there was a Major Finnegan, a one-time floorwalker in an Edmonton department store who fancied himself a champion ping-pong player. It was the Major's habit to inveigle young subalterns into a game and proceed to beat them hollow, often for considerable sums. Few dared to turn him down because of his superior rank.

Filion and I watched the Major play night after night, carefully applauding his prowess as he humbled each of our friends; but Harry declined to play.

"Come on, young Filion," the Major would say. "I'm told you're pretty good. How about trying your hand against me?"

Filion would demur, pleading fatigue. The insufferable major continued to insist. At last Filion allowed himself to be talked into a set. The stakes, I remember, were substantial.

The Major served. The ball crossed the net and bounced off the edge of the table in Filion's court. I have forgotten a great deal about my days at Currie Barracks but not that game, which seems to me now to resemble a spectacular scene from an old and well-loved movie.

Filion strode back to the wall, faced the bouncing ball, swung his arm back and slammed it at the Major. *Wham!* The ball rifled across the net, struck the edge of the Major's court, and sizzled past his face like a bullet. Finnegan looked startled, even frightened. Yet this was only the beginning. On and on it went, point after point to Filion, who continued to serve like a marksman, humbling the Major twenty-one to zero, three games in a row. I do not recall that Major Finnegan ever played ping-pong again.

During that first month, however, we saw very little of Major Finnegan or the other permanent inhabitants of the Currie Mess. We spent most of our time under canvas on the Sarcee Indian Reserve, a portion of which the army had leased from the tribe. Here we sweated and groaned, crawled on our bellies through ice-cold streams, while live bullets cracked over us, or trotted at the double with full packs up impossible slopes, until finally we set a vast chunk of the reserve on fire with mortar bombs.

This took place under the tutelage of two of the toughest instructors in the business. It was widely assumed that both these superman would come to a glorious end, probably winning the Victoria Cross, no doubt posthumously. But no man can tell how anyone else will react in battle. One instructor died gallantly rushing forward ahead of his men during the Italian campaign, falling with a full burst of machine-gun bullets in his chest. The other, whom we all thought of as godlike was stricken by a blue funk and sent home with shaking hands and an ashen face.

We took our training seriously, for we all knew that our lives might be at stake. A member of the Ottawa general staff arrived to warn us that we must soak up all available knowledge because this was the last training we'd get before going into action. The Canadians had landed in Sicily the month before; we all expected to be sent to Africa in a few weeks.

But nothing happened. We gained our second pips and were sent off on leave. Back I went to Vancouver, proudly displaying my new summer uniform of tropical worsted, complete with my father's Sam Browne belt. It wasn't as fancy as my winter barathea, which I'd bought before austerity clothing came in; unlike the uniforms of my fellow officers, it had real bellows pockets and pleats. But by the summer of 1943 no one, soldier or civilian, could have a pleat in his trousers, let alone in his vest pocket.

The war had brought other changes. The newspaper offices were full of women. Lucy now held a summer job at the *News-Herald*; Janet Walker was on the *Province,* writing the Tillicum column for youngsters under the pseudonym of Diana Gray. In this position she found herself in charge of the Junior Commandos, a fledgling group spawned by the Little Orphan Annie comic strip and touted by the newspaper's promotion department. One of the tasks of the Junior Commandos was to collect old rubber, presumably to be recycled for the war effort. As a result, Janet's desk was half hidden by mounds of old tires and some not so old, which I strongly suspect had been stolen by the little Commandos in the interests of patriotism.

I had broken up with my most recent girl friend that summer — actually *she* had broken up with me — and was squiring Janet about in the interim. To my horror, she insisted that I help her keep the Junior Commandos in line during one of the innumerable Victory parades being held to sell war bonds. There was I in my new uniform, helping to hold up a gigantic banner reading "JUNIOR COMMANDOS," with Janet, decked out in a steel helmet, on the other end and a ragtag band of tots, all in fake steel helmets, trailing along behind us while bands played and people cheered. Was it for this, I asked myself, that I had signed up to do battle for my country?

"I'm not supposed to be doing this," I told Janet. "An officer isn't supposed to carry anything."

"Oh, come on," she told me. "Don't forget you're helping me move tonight."

She was always moving, from one boarding house to another, from one crowded flat — a jungle of clothes lines, packing boxes, and nameless roommates drying their hair — to another. It was difficult to find suitable housing in those wartime years. One landlady turned out to be a bootlegger. Janet moved. Another was running a house of ill fame on the side, which meant that the hallways were crowded with strange men knocking on the wrong doors. Janet moved again. This explains why I, First Lieutenant P.F. Berton, was to be seen on the Number 1 streetcar, carrying a suitcase and two pieces of pie on a plate, accompanied by three dishevelled girls loaded down with shopping bags.

"An officer isn't supposed to carry anything," I kept saying.

"It's only a short ride. Then we transfer and we take the Number 9," Janet replied. "The general will never notice. Generals never ride streetcars."

Nor, fortunately, did any of my fellow officers.

The following day we all took the train back to Calgary, where we were put in charge of training platoons, waiting for the call to arms. Weeks went by, but there was no call. More graduates arrived from Gordon Head, and they too gained the extra pip and were put in charge of training platoons. Soon there seemed to be as many officers as men, wandering about the parade square with very little to do.

The army, it was said, had created too many officers. There was a rumor that some incompetent clerk in some bureaucratic office had mistakenly added an extra zero to the number needed. Certainly there were far too many at Currie. What had really happened? Had the authorities blundered, as we believed? Certainly they were capable of blundering. Every time I moved from one camp to another the army lost my papers, often for several weeks. But I no longer believe the tale of the extra zero. What the army did not want to tell us was that infantry platoon commanders, more than anybody else, are expendable in battle. Only one of Canada's five divisions was in action at the time, in the Italian campaign. The day was coming when junior officers would be knocked over like wooden rabbits in a shooting gallery. The army was merely facing hard truths, getting ready for the day when thousands of trained leaders would be needed to replace the dead.

To me at the time, the situation seemed ridiculous. There were so many officers at Currie that extra barrack rooms had to be found to house them. The newspapers were filled with stories of the Italian campaign and the part the Canadian 1st Division was playing in it. Training had become boring. I wanted to try out what I'd been learning and teaching. After a year and a half in the army, I felt a growing sense of frustration. I'd offered to fight for my country; now it didn't look as if the country wanted me.

And then in early October the news came. A draft of officers was ordered overseas for the twelfth (my sister's birthday). My name was on it! I rushed out and bought myself a trench coat and a watch. If I was going to lead men into action I'd need something to synchronize! Since I had assigned part of my pay to my parents I had little spare cash for a going-away party, but as it turned out there was no going-away party. The draft was cancelled suddenly at the last moment, without any reason or explanation given.

It is hard now for me to understand the disappointment I felt — that we all felt. Why were we plunged into the depths of gloom because the army had postponed what might very well have been a rendezvous with death or, at the least, dismemberment? But the army system was designed to key men up, to bring us to the point where the desire to get overseas and have a go at the faceless enemy would become an obsession.

I'm not sure that patriotism was involved, although there was a lot of patriotic talk. Some of us, in fact — I was one — had come into the army reluctantly. But now, after months of indoctrination, we had been transformed into the keenest of fighting men. Part of it, I'm sure, was peer group pressure. It was fashionable to say you were dying to get overseas (an unconsciously grisly remark). Before you knew it, you *were* dying to get overseas. Part of it was army brainwashing, to use a current term; the whole point of our training programs, especially those for young officers, was to prepare us for and to make us look forward to the ultimate moment when that training would be tested and justified. And, finally, there was the feeling that this war, unlike so many that had come before (and several that came after) was a just war; that the enemy was truly evil; that we were fighting for a principle; that there was a purpose to our sacrifice.

At the time, all I wanted to do was to get moving. But as the months went by my chances of getting overseas grew dimmer. The army had decided that officers with previous overseas experience as NCOs would be given priority on the drafts — that meant that Harry Filion would leave long before me. But, in fact, no one left. It was as if the army were playing a cat and mouse game with us all. Drafts were ordered, then cancelled. More officers poured in. We stayed put.

My class was the twenty-third to be graduated from Gordon Head and the first to be held back at Calgary for that whole winter of 1943-44. We shared the same barrack room — two long rows of beds facing each other, not unlike a similar bunkhouse in the Dominion Creek mining camp, and we developed an *esprit* sparked by numerous blowouts. Booze was hard to get in those days. The Alberta government allowed us one gallon of wine, one case of beer, and one mickey of hard liquor a month. Bootleg rye was bringing twenty dollars a bottle, the better part of a week's pay for a junior officer. Mothers, aunts, even grandmothers who'd never seen the inside of a government liquor store now became wearily familiar with the bureaucratic routine of permits and order pads as their boys nudged them toward the counter to boost their meagre supplies. Some officers singled out the teetotalers in their platoons and actually paraded them downtown to the vendors.

We all drank too much, drowning our frustrations with gin mixed with Logana — a dreadful wine made from B.C. loganberries — and washed down with Calgary stock ale, the most potent if not the most palatable malt beverage available in those lean days. This dreadful concoction once caused Lloyd East to pass out after he had locked himself in a lavatory cubicle. It took half the night before we were able to hoist him, six feet five inches of dead weight, back over the partition. We paid a great deal of attention to our apparel, attempting, each in his own way, to bring some individuality to the almost shapeless khaki battledress issued by the quartermaster stores. Like many others I took mine to the regimental tailor and paid him a handsome sum to face the canvas lapels with serge and reorganize the pleats at the back of the blouse. I twisted the wire in my hat until it had a suitably battered look. I filled two shoelaces with live forty-five-calibre ammunition, tied them in circles, and dropped them down around my legs inside my battle-dress trousers; the weights kept the pants from pulling up over the half puttees that, against all regulations, I wore in place of the more awkward-looking gaiters. Fortunately, I didn't suffer the fate of another officer who tripped on the mess hall steps, detonating two such cartridges and thus shooting himself in the ankle. Filion went me one better. Instead of gaiters he had a special pair of high boots made for him, into which he tucked his pants. He was proud of the effect and announced he would wear the boots into battle.

Thus pressed, polished, booted, and tailored we wandered out of an evening down Calgary's Eighth Avenue. One night, to my public embarrassment and private gratification, two girls actually whistled at me.

By now, Harry and I were inseparable. In fact, because of the static situation, a curious kind of male bonding was taking place among many members of the twenty-third class at Currie. At least half our number formed themselves into partnerships that were often as binding as marriages. Some men remained loners without any single close buddy, but the pair bonding dominated. Many of these partnerships continued long after the war. In one case, when a man married, his buddy actually went along on the honeymoon. In another dramatic instance, Tommy Tompkins of the Loyal Edmonton Regiment saved the life of his buddy, Bob Spencer, at Arnhem. They had formed an inseparable alliance at Currie; forty years later they were still visiting one another, though Spencer lived in California and Tompkins in Alberta.

I don't think that any of us noticed this phenomenon. Harry and I were similarly bonded, but neither he nor I nor anybody else discussed or even thought of these male marriages. It only occurs to me now as I look back on that strange, frustrating, and oddly nostalgic period, when of a Saturday I sat in the Filions' tiny apartment, eating Veryl Filion's eggs, Harry and I almost insensible from bootleg whisky, wondering aloud when we would be allowed to have a go at "the beastly Hun" as Filion, the cliché collector, insisted on calling the enemy.

Veryl Filion was one of the most sensible women I'd ever met, firm-minded when she needed to be, indulgent when she didn't. She spoiled Harry as a mother spoils a small, well-loved, but errant child; but she also kept him on a tight leash, rescuing him from his own improvidence, for he had been born to money and was an incurable impulse shopper. They were opposites in every way. He drank; she didn't. He loved Chinese food; she couldn't stand it (though later she learned to like it). He was a gambler; she watched every penny. He loved sports; she couldn't have cared less, which was strange because she was a member of the famous Patrick sporting family: her uncle, Lester, ran the New York Rangers. In short, they fitted together like pieces of a Chinese puzzle, each complementing the other, each supplying strengths to match the other's failings.

They bickered constantly — for them it was a stimulating form of communication — and loved each other to excess. They had known one another from childhood and were clearly meant for each other. "You're dead a long time," Harry said to me once, "but you're married forever." (Where did he get these aphorisms?)

In Calgary they became my closest friends. I'd often spend Saturday night in their cramped apartment, sleeping on the floor and occasionally rising to hammer a few last notes on the piano. I had actually learned to stumble through the opening bars of the "Moonlight Sonata," and late one bibulous night, after much gaiety, insisted on attempting it.

"For God's sake," cried Veryl in a panic, "do you want to get us thrown out?"

Even as she spoke, a knock came at the door.

"See what you've done?" she said. "I hope you're both satisfied. The two of you will have us thrown out into the street, drinking and singing away like a couple of half-wits."

She opened the door gingerly. There stood one of her neighbours in his dressing gown.

"Oh, please!" he cried, "please, play it again! It's so beautiful . . . so beautiful."

There are certain small triumphs in life that can never be duplicated. As the saying has it, you had to be there. Veryl closed the door, unable to suppress a giggle that quickly became a hoot.

"All I can say," she said, as the tears ran down her cheeks, "all I can say is that he must have been as drunk as you two."

"Let's have a round or two for Glen Worple," said Harry brightly.

"No!" cried Veryl, stamping her foot. "Let's not tempt fate." And that was that.

We all sang in those days, usually around the piano in the mess — bawdy verses that I've never forgotten and that still bring back the comradeship of that otherwise frustrating wartime winter of 1943-44 — "A Man Went into a Chandler Shop" . . . "I used to Work in Chicago" . . . "I Don't Want to Join the Army" . . . "The Whore of Jerusalem." Having little else to do I decided to harness some of this talent. I produced and appeared in a series of radio variety programs before an audience in the drill hall, broadcast live from a Calgary radio station. The announcer was a plump, curly-headed young man named Don McNeil, who after the war became mayor of Calgary, only to be ousted from office on conflict-of-interest charges.

For all of that winter the army continued to train me in all manner of useful techniques — from the mysteries of the Harley-Davidson motorcycle to the proper way to cut up a hind quarter of beef. There were courses on every imaginable subject. I took a driving and maintenance course, learning how to handle and disassemble motorcycles, jeeps, field-artillery tractors, thirty-ton trucks, and Bren gun carriers. Since I have little mechanical ability I found it difficult; in those days I didn't even have a civilian driver's licence. On a convoy to the Turner Valley during a

September blizzard, I threw both the tracks on my carrier and subsequently failed the course.

I didn't do much better when Harry Filion and I were sent off in January of 1944 to Camp Borden to take a Health and Sanitation Course. Here we were taught the correct method of digging an army latrine, how to tell one vitamin from another, how to butcher meat, and how to treat a case of VD in the field. Neither of us took it seriously. Our main purpose was to spend the weekend in the fleshpots of Toronto, a city that turned out to have no fleshpots at all. I couldn't believe it! Toronto, which had been a fairyland to me thirteen years earlier, now seemed to be a community of stupefying dullness. We engaged in various thrilling escapades, such as visiting the *Globe and Mail's* new art deco headquarters on King Street and wandering through the lobby of the Royal York — "largest hotel in the British Empire." There wasn't much else to do.

I remember nothing else about the Health and Sanitation Course except for the spectacle — strangely satisfying — of all the tough paratroopers in the front row collapsing during the showing of a film depicting the horrors of syphilis.

On our return from Camp Borden to Currie we found ourselves roundly reprimanded. We had barely squeaked through the course. The army had five categories by which it judged its students: D for Distinguished; Q-1 and the Q-2 for Qualified (Class 1 or 2); Pass; and Fail. We had been given a mere Pass, and that wasn't considered good enough. We were made to understand it must not happen again.

As more and more officers poured into the barracks that winter, the army realized it had a morale problem on its hands. It did its best to solve it by inventing a "refresher" course at Brockville, Ontario, to which hundreds were dispatched. Thus we leaders of men were once again transformed into sheep, with the usual gaggle of corporals and sergeants barking orders at us as we made a pretense of re-learning that which we already knew by heart. The chief purpose was not to train us, only to keep us occupied until the bloody day when we would be needed.

Those two months at Brockville are pretty much of a blur. I remember more about the mess bar than I do about the training. Whenever I hear that old Mills Brothers record, "Paper Doll," my mind goes back to a certain Sunday morning when Filion and I, desperate for a pick-me-up, proceeded downtown to a neat, two-storey brick house, identified as a blind pig. We were met at the door by a man and his wife decked out for church. They welcomed us in, invited us to take a seat in the neat little living room, and announced they'd be back in a few moments with the required medicine. As we sat there thirstily, I became aware of a framed sampler on the wall with this inscription:

CHRIST IS THE HEAD OF THIS HOUSE
THE UNSEEN GUEST AT EVERY MEAL
THE SILENT LISTENER TO EVERY CONVERSATION

Filion cocked an eye at it, frowned, looked hesitantly over his shoulder for any Unseen Guest, and rose unsteadily to his feet.

"This is not a fit place for man nor beast," he said, and we beat a hasty retreat.

By this time I had decided to write a book about my life in the army. It was to be a serious work — nothing like *See Here, Private Hargrove*, then a raging best seller about a rookie's comic career in the American forces. It would end, of course, with a thrilling account of battle — a fitting climax to a long build-up. To make it work, though, it was necessary for me to get into battle. There was, as yet, no hint of that.

Hemingway was the young writer's hero in those days, but I was influenced more by John Dos Passos, whose monumental trilogy, *USA*, was, I felt, underrated. I wrote to Jack Scott, who was now in Ottawa with army public relations, explaining how I was borrowing the Dos Passos technique of short, staccato passages, newsreel interludes, and stream-of-consciousness sections to enliven my work. Scott urged me to show a little humility before linking my name with that of one of the great novelists of my time. I was duly chastened.

Meanwhile I seized the chance of writing articles and drawing cartoons for the *Blitz*, the Brockville camp magazine. I also managed to write a periodical column for the *News-Herald* under the pseudonym "Joe Fraser" and one funny article about army life for the Montreal *Standard.* The refresher course remains in my memory, not for the training, but for the writing. It ended after two months with a party so raucous that we did not know until the following day that one of the worst earthquakes in the history of the area had taken place overnight.

5 I returned to Currie Barracks in April 1944. *Surely*, I thought, *I'll be on my way at any moment.* There was a great deal of talk about a second front — a landing in Europe. But nothing happened. I was back at the old stand, giving the same training to private soldiers that I'd been given on the refresher course. I did not feel refreshed. Then, suddenly, a week or so after our return, all the members of my class who'd had overseas experience — but *only* those with overseas experience — were placed on a draft. Harry Filion was among them. I went down to the train with Veryl to say goodbye.

The platform was crowded with Calgary girls, all saying farewell to the husbands they'd married during the winter. Almost every member of my class except me seemed to have been wedded during our long hiatus. The most recent wedding had taken place only a few days before, and at least one baby had been born since we'd first arrived ten months previously. There was Paul Lougheed's new wife, Betty, trying to hold back the tears. They'd been married for just two months and now it was over, though they had no way of knowing that. He was killed by a sniper shortly after going into action.

Veryl and I said our goodbyes to Harry. I watched him board the train, wishing with all my heart that I was going with him, and so, I'm sure, did he. I think Veryl and I were both overcome by that sense of finality that so many others were feeling but never voicing. Would we ever see him again? It was a question we asked ourselves but never asked each other.

Veryl returned to Vancouver, I to the training routine at Currie. Those of us who were left were given to understand that our prospects of going overseas were small. In spite of the casualties in Italy, the army was said to have enough officers to fill the gaps until the following January. Indeed, it seemed at its wits' end as to what to do with us. Time and again an overseas draft was announced and then cancelled. Meanwhile we'd all go off on the mandatory embarkation leave. As these leaves mounted up it began to be embarrassing. Friends no longer crowded to the station to press gifts and bottles upon me and make strained remarks about giving their regards to Mr. Hitler. Acquaintances meeting me on the street couldn't believe I was *again* on embarkation leave. One said dryly that he hadn't realized embarkation leave lasted for a year.

Each time I said goodbye to my family — believing that *this* time I was really heading off across the water — there was a painful leave-taking with my father. He was convinced that he was about to die and would remark, sadly, that he probably wouldn't be around when I returned. The spirit was going out of him. Although he still kept up his weaving and regularly attended meetings of the Royal Astronomical Society, he had stopped reading the classics and was contenting himself with cheap detective novels. He was ob-sessed with the idea of death, convinced that his angina would kill him at any moment. I didn't know how to respond to this. I'd mutter that he looked in great shape and then try to change the subject, but he returned to it again and again. "You're fine," I'd say, but he'd shake his head. The doctor in Dawson had told him he had serious heart trouble, and my father believed as implicity in doctors as he believed in science, royalty, and the Conservative party.

"That damned doctor," my mother said. It had not been the same doctor who'd given him the overdose — no doctor stayed long in the Yukon — but they were all damned doctors to her. "Why did he have to scare him that way? He's lost all his old interests."

"And what are we going to do about Lucy?" my mother said. "She wants to join the service. The CWACs."

I put my foot down. There was no way my innocent little sister was going to join the Canadian Women's Army Corps! God only knew what trouble she'd get into with these tough, hard-bitten lady soldiers. The odd thing is that I knew several CWACs, and none of them was tough or hard-bitten; I had, in fact, dated one or two in Calgary. But I still thought of Lucy as a fragile, sheltered child in spite of the fact that she was a university graduate who had worked as a waitress in a rough cafeteria, as a factory worker at American Can, and as a reporter on a daily newspaper. In short, I was still trying to cling to my role as the big protec-tive brother. I even disapproved of some of her boy friends, as if that were any of my business. Lucy didn't join the CWACs. Instead she got a wartime job in the weather office. She might easily have had more fun and a greater range of experience in the women's army.

More and more on these leaves I found myself phoning Janet Walker for a date — often, I fear, at the last minute.

"I'm just an old shoe," she said to me once after accept-ing my tardy invitation to a movie. No doubt she was right.

Certainly I found her comfortable to be with, and she wore well. Still, she didn't have to accept these last-minute invitations; there were plenty of men dying to date her. What was it she saw in me?

Years later, I asked her. She thought for a minute; then she said, "Well, I'll say this for you: You weren't dull. You were never boring." I accepted the accolade with proper humility.

D-Day came and went, but I went nowhere. That June, at Currie, we were told that we would all have to take a seven-week course at Vernon and another four-week course at Wainwright, Alberta, to qualify for overseas service. I signed up for the Vernon course, but nothing came of it. In fact, I signed up for everything that was going, in the hope that sooner or later the luck of the draw would get me moving. I even signed up for an army intelligence course (in spite of the old joke about there being no intelligence in the army).

To my amazement, it worked. I was out in the foothills of the Rockies near a place called Bragg Creek, in charge of all field training for my company, when the news came. I had exactly half a day to get back to Currie, pack my kit, and take the night train back to Ontario for the Royal Military College in Kingston. There I would take a tough, eight-week course in military intelligence. If I passed I would qualify either for the Intelligence Corps overseas or as the Intelligence Officer of a battalion in Europe. I was elated. By September I ought to be on my way to France.

Lloyd East had also been accepted for the course, and we arrived together at that curious blockhouse of a building known as the Stone Frigate, built as a ship by the former naval command in the nineteenth century.

I knew better than to fool around at RMC. If I was going to get anywhere, I'd have to swot. The Health and Sanitation Course had been a one-week romp, impossible to take seriously. This was different: I faced a gruelling two months

245

of hard study. Nonetheless, at last I was being tested for the very corps I had tried to join at the beginning of my service!

My fellow students were no dummies. Two I recognized from the University of British Columbia; both had been medal winners — scientists of awesome intelligence and capability. I determined to measure myself against them, to see if, when the marks were issued at the end of the course, I could do as well as they.

The army didn't dawdle. In peacetime we were told a similar course had occupied two years. We would cram it all into one-tenth the time. And so we did, in our chilly cells in that historic building. We studied from seven in the morning until long after midnight, learning the make-up of the German army; the profiles of enemy generals, enemy tanks, and enemy aircraft; the complexities of map reading and signal jargon; the staff structure of opposing armies; tactics, strategy, administration.

There was little time for carousing. Our nights were spent at our desks, our days in lecture halls or in the open country on military exercises. One night I remember I worked until four in the morning, drawing profiles of German tanks and aircraft in my field notebook. Four hours later I was out in a jeep, drawing contour maps of the Shield country near Kingston. We got little sleep, but then we were all, as they say, fighting fit. In those days I could sleep anywhere at any time — hanging onto the strap of a streetcar or bus, on the hard ground for five minutes during a break, on the seats of a transcontinental train, even on a night march with a pack on my back and one foot in the rut of the road to steer me along as I snored. This ability has never left me. I can sleep on my feet and I can also talk on my feet, thanks to hours of waffling during the seminars at the Royal Military College at Kingston.

A month went by before I was able to take any leave. Indeed, in all that time I left the confines of the college on only one occasion. Early in August I went to Ottawa to visit my father's relatives, whom I'd first met in 1931. My Uncle Jack was dead of a heart attack and my Aunt Maude looked considerably older. The place was full of cousins, many of them men in uniform, all of whom seemed to know a good deal about me because of their obsession with family history. I was embarrassed because I could scarcely tell one cousin from another and even more embarrassed when I was asked to act as umpire at what appeared to have been a heated discussion of several days' duration over whether the original Bertons had landed at Rhode Island or elsewhere on the American coast. It was apparent that both sides considered me an expert on this early trivia and had full confidence in my making a decision on the subject, of which I was lamentably ignorant. I escaped by claiming that the original records had been destroyed and so the hallowed spot had never been definitely established. That was untrue; it was, I learned later, Rhode Island. But my judgement was immediately accepted.

There followed a lively round-table seminar on Berton history during which I caused some consternation by contributing the only fact I could remember — that we Bertons were descended also from German stock. My cousin Audrey was particularly discomfited. Her husband was an officer serving overseas, and she had for some time been proudly and vehemently declaring that there wasn't a drop of German blood in her body. I didn't know that, of course. I knew very little about my Ottawa relatives and even less about the Berton family history. My ignorance, I think, was a reaction against my father's obsession with his ancestors. He talked so much about them that I tended to turn him off, like a radio, when he got onto the subject. Besides, I'd not quite forgiven him for calling me Pierre de Marigny.

I was more interested that month in the German army, or at least in its structure. The grindstone was never far from our noses as we crammed and swotted. In our last exercise we were required to go for thirty-six hours without sleep as we fought a paper war complete with signals, messages, and situation maps while a recording device played the sounds of battle in our ears. At one point I discovered the room where the records were being played, and to the relief of my colleagues, if not my teachers, substituted, briefly, a jazz record to replace the screeching of bombs and the whine of howitzers.

The course ended on September 9. To my astonishment I did better than I expected; in fact, I led my class with the only "D" (for Distinguished) awarded that year. I suspect the waffling helped; the ability to jabber at top speed during a seminar came easily to me.

Surely, I thought, *now that I've proved myself, I'll get a posting overseas.* Indeed, all my prospects had suddenly become exciting. The C.O. in a final interview congratulated me and told me he'd recommended me for a job as Brigade Intelligence Officer with an active unit, as soon as such a job came open. A staff job at Brigade level! Right up there among all the red tabs, practically dictating the course of battle — or, at least, explaining what the enemy planned to do (or what I figured they planned to do). Then another staff officer, a GSO 2 at that, called me in and said how very much he would have liked to have me on his staff at Corps in London. *Corps!* That was even higher than Brigade; I was dizzy with anticipation, but had to remember that he was no longer with Corps in London. I cursed the Psychology Officer at Vernon for making fun of my aspirations back in February 1942.

This was all very well, a boost to my ego — as were the congratulations I received when I returned to Currie Barracks in late September. But now I found myself following the same old training curriculum. The men were dispatched overseas immediately after they had finished their four-month course and went into battle a week after reaching England. But there were still too many officers.

And then, in mid-October, a telegram arrived from

National Defence Headquarters ordering me to report to the staff at Military Intelligence Wing, Royal Military College, Kingston. I had no idea what that appointment held, but at least it was something tangible and different. "I'm pretty sure," I wrote to my mother, "that it will send me overseas quicker than if I stayed here."

It didn't turn out that way. When I reached Kingston I learned that I'd be teaching again the same intelligence course I'd just finished taking. I'd led the class; this was my reward. I wasn't grateful. Several who'd got mere Q-2s were already heading overseas to become intelligence officers with active units. Others were given glamorous jobs or adventurous assignments in North America. The two UBC brains whom I'd beaten out were dispatched to Washington, D.C., then the most exciting city on the continent. Lloyd East went off as I.O, on Exercise Muskox, the vast and ambitious army manoeuvre in the Arctic. And I was banished to Kingston, a city of such insufferable dullness that it made Toronto seem like Sodom. For this I had slaved and swotted into the dark hours of the morning.

There were certain perks. I was now an Acting Captain, GSO 3, a staff rank that paid me twenty-five cents a day more than a major received. The quarters were comfortable, my fellow staff members companionable, and the food in the mess excellent. But the work was demanding. I was teaching courses in everything from photo interpretation and prisoner interrogation to Japanese army tactics. In addition I was conducting seminars, setting field exercises, collating the great mass of information pouring in on the Japanese situation, and marking exercise and examination papers. In short, I was working as hard as any student. There were vague promises of an overseas posting, but nothing definite.

My only contacts with the real war were the secret situation maps in the information room, which were also my responsibility. These charted the progress of the war from the enemy's point of view, and this was the most interesting part of my job. Messages marked MOST SECRET poured in daily directly from Europe assessing the position of all enemy formations. Each morning I pored over them and made the necessary changes on the maps with a grease pencil. One day the flow of messages accelerated, and the changes began to come thick and fast. Suddenly, the German units that had been in retreat were reported moving forward through the Ardennes forest. The newspapers were still silent on this desperate enemy push, but my maps told me the story of the Battle of the Bulge before the world knew of it.

A series of letters, meanwhile, began to arrive from Harry Filion. He had run into Jack Scott in England, and the two had become fast friends, thanks to our mutual acquaintance. They had embarked for the continent together not once but several times, the convoy being forced back on each occasion by bad weather. Filion wrote a hilarious account of how he and Scott, climbing down the gangplank after one of these abortive sallies, had been mistaken for returning veterans, hailed as heroes, and greeted with cheers, embraces, even flowers.

In Normandy at last, the two had demolished a bottle of Calvados, the local apple brandy, in a French graveyard while composing a long and maudlin letter to me. I never received it, Filion explained, because the Calvados had acted as a laxative, and the missive was put to a more immediate purpose. Meanwhile, he reported, he had saved Scott's life, or so he believed. Through some army bungling, Scott, a public relations officer with no infantry training, was about to be sent to the front in command of a fighting platoon. It took all of Filion's powers of persuasion to convince the C.O. that this would be sheer suicide — not only for Scott but also for his men. Jack didn't even know how to put on his web equipment, let alone fire a Lee-Enfield.

Then in December another letter arrived, the handwriting shaky, the address a base hospital in France. Harry had been in action somewhere near Antwerp. A German fighting patrol had come out of nowhere and decimated his platoon. He himself had been shot in the right forearm — his golfing arm — but not before he'd actually killed a man. He told me, not without pride, how he'd got him in his sights and, in spite of the chaos all around him, had remembered his training on the rifle ranges and had followed the manual to the letter — stilling his breath and squeezing the trigger ("like an orange," the instructors used to say) — not pulling it. To his amazement, the German soldier toppled at his feet from the dike where he was standing. Shortly thereafter, Filion himself was wounded. At the Regimental Aid Post a Roman Catholic padre examined his dog tags and tried to give him the last rites. "Bugger off," said Filion. "I'm not bloody dying." Whereupon the padre pulled off Filion's prized pair of boots and vanished with them. This loss, it appeared, bothered him more than the wound in the arm.

Filion's letter made me feel like a slacker. Here I was, eating lobster thermidor in the mess each Sunday while my best friend was groaning in pain somewhere in Europe. Worse, my chances of getting overseas had diminished. No more intelligence officers were needed. The course, it was announced, would be shut down when the present student body graduated just before Christmas.

My final lecture dealt with the Japanese. There had been a farewell party the night before, and no one was in very good shape. In the front row I noticed that a red-headed subaltern named Hilliker had fallen fast asleep. I didn't have the heart to wake him, remembering perhaps my own experiences with the hypnotic Professor Cooke at UBC. Thus Hilliker missed the entire lecture. As fate would have it, he was the only member of that class who actually faced the Japanese. He was landed secretly at night on an enemy island in the Pacific and badly shot up. I doubt, however, that my lecture at RMC would have helped him.

I wasn't sent overseas, as I'd expected. I lost my acting rank and I was shipped right back to Currie Barracks as an instructor once again in advanced infantry training — the same job I'd been doing on and off since the summer of 1943. I took Christmas leave, spent a few days with my family, and tried to reply brightly to those of my friends who accosted me with the maddening phrase "You still here?" Others, to my embarrassment, thought I'd *been* overseas and insisted on treating me like a hero until I blurted out the truth.

Back at Currie Barracks, I discovered to my chagrin that while I was at RMC, the other members of my class had at last been sent overseas. These men, who had been my closest friends for the best part of two years had gone off to war without me. I felt betrayed and lost with all those familiar faces gone. New officers continued to arrive, including some who'd actually been overseas, seen action, and had now returned to Canada. One had been blinded in action, another wore the white-and-purple ribbon of the Military Cross. We swarmed around him, awed: a man we knew intimately, whom we'd drunk beer with in the mess, and who'd shared the same barrack room — a hero!

Finally, in late February, my name came up again on a draft for England. I took the usual embarkation leave to Vancouver. It seemed to me my father was fading away. He'd been to the hospital for tests — no one appeared to know what they were for — and the results, I gathered, were inconclusive. He was seventy-two years old and seemed less and less interested in life. When I told him that I was going overseas at last, he replied again that he didn't expect to be there when I returned.

It had become a fixation with him, this idea that his death was imminent. Each time I'd come home he had told me he didn't expect to see me again; each time I'd return to find him alive. It was as if he was willing life to ebb away.

"I wish he'd stop talking about it," I said to my mother.

"I know," she said. "All he does now is read detective stories. He just doesn't seem to care."

She was also concerned about me, certain that I would be killed in action. "Couldn't you join something else?" she asked. "Something, well — safer?"

I shook my head. I was equally concerned about her. She not only had the worry over my father but she was also worried about Lucy, as mothers of twenty-two-year-old women usually are. Boy friends came and went. There were tears and clashes. Would Lucy ever marry? She had only recently reached voting age, but in those days girls were expected to wed early and, in the phrase, "settle down." And what if Lucy married somebody totally unsuitable? My mother wasn't specific, but it was clear she felt that some of the young men who turned up on the doorstep weren't good enough for her daughter.

On the second day of my leave I called Veryl Filion to see if she'd had word from Harry. To my astonishment, she told me that he was on the way home — in fact, he was due to arrive in Vancouver in a couple of days. Ye gods! My best friend had been overseas, in action, shot and almost killed, and I hadn't gone anywhere!

He got off the train, resplendent in an Essex Scottish kilt and Glengarry and carrying an immense shepherd's crook. His mother, an ardent church-goer, rushed to embrace him. Filion gazed gloomily at her and grunted out a single sentence of greeting that summed up all the frustrations of that single hour in combat. "The RC padre stole my boots!" he told her. One could forgive her for looking more than a little bewildered.

I was fed up with embarkation leave, especially with my best friend home from the wars, reliving his adventures before a horde of admirers. For Filion, this was the most glorious moment of his life. He had done his bit and he'd survived. For me, it was understandably frustrating.

When I returned to Currie, I learned with relief that there

would be no more embarkation leaves. The army, throwing monetary caution to the winds, had decided to risk me in battle after all. I was actually going overseas. To my astonishment, I discovered that there were one or two on the same draft who didn't share my elation.

"My God, Berton, it's dangerous over there," Jack Simms said to me when his name appeared on the draft. Simms was not his name. I've long since forgotten everything about him except his face — worried blue eyes, lean jaw, and a mouth that quivered slightly. The scene has stayed with me — one brief moment caught as in a lightning flash. There we were, standing on the steps of the barrack room, with Jack Simms clutching my battledress. "It's dangerous over there," he repeated, and I thought at first he was joking. But then I heard the quaver in his voice and realized that he meant it.

"People shoot at you," Jack Simms said. "Honest to God, Berton, I'm just not cut out for that sort of thing." *A little late,* I thought, *to discover that.* Off he went in a blue funk; I never did discover what happened to him.

Another, whose name I've also forgotten — I'll call him Johnson — suddenly developed back trouble the day before he was to be dispatched overseas. This officer had been the most vociferous of the hawks; now he pretended to be bitterly disappointed.

"Goddam it!" he cried in the mess that night. "Goddam it! What a lousy break. I was raring to go — and now this. You guys know that, don't you? I was raring to go. How unlucky can a guy get?"

Johnson fooled nobody and was shunned in the mess. He had been the epitome of the swaggering junior officer, stomping about in specially made high boots, talking big. I ran into him on the UBC campus after the war. He'd taken advantage of the veterans' student program and was a leading light in the campus Legion branch — and still talking as big as ever.

I left Currie Barracks for good during the first week in March, in charge of a car full of private soldiers on a troop train heading for Debert, Nova Scotia. As the officer in charge I was given a compartment of my own. I left the troops to their own devices and used this privacy to continue work on my great opus, which I had decided to call "Marching As to War." In those days I was better at writing titles than I was at writing prose. I carried a small black notebook full of brilliant titles. "Brief Candle," for instance, would make a wonderful title, I thought, for the biography of a young Shakespearean actor struck down in early life by debauchery. "Snowball in Hell" would be the stirring tale of an adventurer flirting with death. Alas, "Marching As to War" marched nowhere, I never finished the manuscript, which has long since vanished.

We crossed the Atlantic in the *Aquitania*. It had been a troop carrier in the First War and was due for the scrap-heap when the new war began. With only two meals a day, each twelve hours apart, we found time hanging heavy on our hands and hunger gnawing at our bellies. I'd stolen a copy of Romain Rolland's *Jean-Christophe* from the camp library at Debert, figuring (rightly) that it was long enough to occupy the entire voyage.

It was a boring as well as a hungry crossing. We had nothing to do but read or wander round the decks, wondering what our fate would be. Germany was at last under siege; the ship's bulletins were predicting the end of the war. Would we arrive in time to see any of it? My memory of those days aboard ship is confused. It seems to me that several of us, having nothing better to do, spent a great deal of time waxing our moustaches. These had now reached enormous proportions, a bit like the one sported by Lord Kitchener on the First World War recruiting posters.

Alas, this subconscious attempt at nonconformity in a khaki world failed miserably. Since we each had a moustache, we looked even more alike; it became as much a part of our uniform as our battledress, and so we stepped off the boat looking like a bunch of clones. My own moustache, by dint of much waxing, was drawn into two points, rather like the whiskers on a cartoon rabbit. That did not pass unnoticed. By the time I reached Liverpool I was known to all as Bugs Bunny Berton — not the best kind of nickname for an eager young subaltern intent on setting an example to his men. By the time I reached Canadian Infantry Training Centre No. 6 at Petworth in Sussex, I had trimmed my moustache to a reasonably accurate facsimile of Clark Gable's. Now, at last, I was ready to face the foe.

Chapter Six
Over There
March 1945–October 1945

1 I could not help feeling a pang of sympathy for Lord Leconfield, the British peer whose immaculate estate we were proceeding to rip apart as we trained for the final assault on Germany. Here, on the outskirts of the cosy village of Petworth, against a background of exquisite little Greek temples and herds of small, nervous deer, I found myself in charge of an infantry platoon waiting to leave for the continent. The grounds were a mess. Lawns that had been rolled for generations now bore the imprint of thousands of army boots and the ugly scars of dozens of slit trenches.

It was bitterly cold in England that March of 1945. In fact, I had never before been so cold, not even in the North. The Yukon was cold, of course, but it was a dry, exhilarating cold, not this insidious damp chill that crept into my bones and stayed there. And in the Yukon, where the rooms were rendered tropical by red-hot stoves, there was always escape from the climate. Here there was none. According to the calendar it was officially spring; an inflexible officialdom had followed the rule book and turned off the heat. It was actually chillier inside the barracks than out. Only the cinemas were heated, and so to keep warm in the evenings I watched the same movie over and over again. *Hollywood Canteen* tended to pall after the first couple of rounds.

London was my goal. Jack Scott was there, working on the Canadian army paper, the *Maple Leaf*. I had, at his written request, hoarded two mickeys of Canadian rye — something unknown in wartime England — and we were both pledged to down them when we were reunited. But even more I was captivated by the idea of seeing at last a city that had figured so much in my reading. I thought of Dick Whittington and his cat, walking the high road to the city. I thought of Dickens's London. I thought of all the Gothic, Romanesque, and Classical buildings that I had been learning about in *The Arts,* a book by that great popularizer, Hendrik Willem van Loon. Having skipped Professor Soward's classes on the Renaissance I was determined to make amends and soak up as much culture as possible. I would go to the National Gallery and study the paintings! I would go to the Albert Hall and listen to a real symphony orchestra! I would go to the theatre and the opera! But first, of course, I would consume two mickeys of rye with my friend Jack Scott.

And so, with a weekend pass in my pocket at last and the rye wrapped in an extra shirt in my small pack, I stepped off the train at Waterloo Station and set off into the Unknown on a voyage of discovery. I have been to London many times since — it remains my favourite city. But I can never recapture the thrill of that first encounter, any more than I can bring back the flavour of that first bottle of Coca-Cola.

To me, it was like entering fairyland, reminiscent, in fact, of my first encounter with Toronto after coming out of the Yukon. I was headed for the Canadian Legion Officers' Club, halfway across the city, but I had no intention of taking a taxi or the underground to reach it. I had made up my mind to walk, soaking up the spectacle, not really knowing or caring which way I was going.

The station was crowded with servicemen from every Allied nation — Yanks and Sikhs, South Africans and Aussies, Free French and Poles. RAF pilots with battered hats and vast moustaches jostled stiff-backed British staff officers with red lapel tabs; others in strange headgear — fezzes, turbans, slouch hats — squeezed past pretty WAAF secretaries with their hair in buns or teenage sailors hauling seabags. All of London was like that. A whirlpool of uniformed humanity eddied around every street corner, every public park, every hotel lobby, every railway station — men and women who had seen death or would soon see death, all descending on London for one glorious weekend of fast, fast, fast relief, not knowing whether it might be their last.

In that company, I felt an outcast. Men with wound stripes on their tunics and ribbons on their chests hailed taxis. Fighter pilots with battered caps and DFCs hugged good-looking girls. Private soldiers in worn uniforms carrying greasy packs, looking as if they'd just come in from the continent, walked arm in arm toward the NAAFI counter seeking tea and sausage rolls. I was the new boy on the block, surrounded by veterans who had fought for their country.

I pushed my way through Waterloo Station and came to Westminster Bridge across the Thames. I knew of two bridges only: Waterloo Bridge, because of the movie of the same name, and, of course, the famous London Bridge. I could see that not far away — or thought I could, making the same mistake so many other newcomers make. It was, of course, the Tower Bridge that I saw.

But now, as I was crossing over, I found myself gazing on familiar territory. There, looming up on the far embankment, was the Gothic pile of Westminster, familiar from a dozen cinematic establishing shots. I trotted across the bridge and shortly found myself in the shadow of the great abbey. To see it like this — suddenly, unexpectedly — hit me with the force of an electric shock. I kept on up Whitehall, my stomach churning with excitement. Every building seemed to leap from a picture postcard or from the pages of an illustrated book.

There, on my left, a small sign identified Downing Street (I could see a knot of people clustered outside Number 10); on my right was Scotland Yard; and directly ahead, looming out of Trafalgar Square, Nelson's Column with its guardian lions secure in their bombproof covering. I followed my nose, turning right past a curious monument at Charing Cross Station and then on down the Strand, past broken walls and ancient public houses, past the shattered little Wren church, and on and on, not knowing where I was and not caring until, on the corner of a building, I spied a small plaque with the head of a man in bas relief. It was Edgar Wallace, the crime writer, whose novels I had once devoured. The plaque told me that he had once worked in this very street. A little thrill ran through me as I realized I had stumbled upon newspaper row. I had been walking down Fleet Street, the journalist's mecca! I felt a bit like Stanley trekking through the jungle and coming suddenly upon Dr. Livingstone.

Later that day, when I had soaked up enough of the city and was ready to soak up two bottles of Canadian rye, I arrived at the Canadian Legion Officers' Club, where Jack Scott met me. I left him in my room and went down to the front desk for two glasses, a bottle of ginger ale, and some ice.

"And what would you be wanting that for, Lieutenant?" the girl behind the desk asked, a little archly.

I told her about the rye.

"Why, Lieutenant," she said, as she produced the ice and mixer, "you've got pure gold there." She was tall, dark, and pretty. I invited her to join us, and she said she'd be happy to come up in half an hour when her shift ended. Her name, she said, was Frances. To this day, I don't know if that was her first name or her last.

The three of us drank most of the rye, and then Scott and I invited Frances to dinner. After dinner, we crawled from pub to pub, watching in amazement as she downed double shots of Scotch. I had never seen a woman put away so much booze and with so little effect.

When the pubs closed, Scott headed home to his flat and I told Frances that I would be delighted to take her home.

"Ah, but you can't do that," she said. "I live in the country, don't you see? Scads of miles away. There's no train back."

I told her, with as much gallantry as I could muster, that that was no problem. "Don't worry about me," I said. "I'll find my own way back." I had a vision of myself wandering about in the moonlit countryside for hours, but, warmed by nips of pub Scotch and Frances's dark and elegant presence, I put it out of my mind.

"No, no, no," she said. "I can't have you doing that."

She thought for a minute.

"I tell you what," she said. "I have a friend who's getting married today — *has* got married, in fact. They've reserved a room at the Russell Square Hotel. Actually, I don't expect they'll be using it, so perhaps I could stop there for the night."

She looked at me. "Would you see me to the door? I'd be awfully obliged."

We took a taxi to the Russell Square Hotel. I kept the taxi running, shook her hand, and told her how much I'd enjoyed her company.

"I say," she said. "Would you mind awfully coming to the desk and asking for the room key? It's in the name of Captain Harding, and I doubt they'd give it to a woman."

I paid off the taxi, and together we walked into the lobby.

I can still scarcely give credence to the scene that followed. The lobby was vibrating with American GIs, all trying to reach the desk, some pleading and shouting for rooms, others waving banknotes at the harassed clerks. Frances propelled me through the struggling mob. I could see one of the desk clerks look up, almost hidden by the mass of soldiers. somehow I managed to catch his eye.

"Captain Harding's room," I said, feeling a little silly because I was no longer a captain.

Instantly, like a magician pulling a rabbit from a hat, he produced a key. I could scarcely believe it. I pushed my way

261

through the crowd, seized it, and made my way back to Frances.

"I wonder if you'd mind seeing me up to my room," she said. "I'm a bit afraid of all these chaps."

Of course. Up we went. Paused at the door of the room. Again I stretched out my hand to say goodbye.

"I was wondering," she said, "if you happened to have any more of that rye."

I had the heel of a mickey in my back pocket.

"Why don't we have a night cap?" said Frances. Why not, indeed?

In we went. The door closed behind us. She turned to me.

"I don't really want your rye," she said. "I want you."

I stared at her.

"My boy friend was killed six months ago," she told me. "I haven't been with anybody since then, and I can't stand it any longer."

I left the Russell Square Hotel about noon the next day, having extracted a half-promise from Frances to meet Jack and me at a pub that afternoon at five. I didn't really expect her to turn up and she didn't. When I left her she had called me a "crazy Canadian." Now, as Jack and I sipped our mild and bitter, it occurred to me that I still didn't know her full name.

To this day the circumstances surrounding that odd wartime evening remain a mystery to me. Who was this Captain Harding whose magical name, muttered by a Canadian lieutenant in a crowded lobby, instantly caused that most precious of objects, a hotel room key, to be produced without a question? Why had he not used this room on the day of his nuptials? How was it that Frances (*a*) knew he had a room and (*b*) knew he wouldn't be using it? For me, these unanswerable questions served to heighten the romance and mystery of my first day in London.

But these were bizarre times. We all lived recklessly, for we half expected that every moment might be close to our last. I welcomed the prospect of getting into action — anything to escape the same old routine of training. Like everybody else I engaged in a kind of double-think about my chances of survival. On the one hand we all believed it *couldn't* happen to us. It could happen to the next guy, and it often did. Several of my friends from Currie Barracks who'd been sent overseas while I was at RMC were already dead. Yet each of us was consoled by the belief that somehow he would survive when others fell about him. Every soldier in every war, I think, has felt this way; it is what gives him the guts to keep going.

On the other hand, there was the incontestable fact that infantry platoon commanders had the highest casualty rate of anybody in the army. And so, just in case, most of us spent every cent we had on good living in the belief that we mightn't survive to enjoy our savings, such as they were. The British banks were remarkably free about extending overdrafts to army officers. Many built up huge debts in the half-belief that they might never have to pay the money back. As for sex — everybody sought it.

Off we went from Petworth on our free Saturday nights to the nearby cathedral city of Chichester — officers and men all looking for fun and trouble. An army truck picked us up after dinner, plunked us down in the Chichester town square about eight, and picked us all up, slightly the worse for wear, at midnight. We had four hours in which to get drunk, get in a fight, find a girl, see the sights, or enjoy a combination of all four.

On one such Saturday night I found a girl riding the Moon Rocket in the local carnival. I cannot remember her name or even much about her except that she was plain and rangy and worked in a shop. After the Moon Rocket we took a whirl on the ferris wheel, tried out the shooting gallery, and drank a gin and orange in the local pub. Arm in arm we crossed a small park on the way to the town square. The grass was as soft as any mattress. It was inevitable on that dark, mysterious, romantic, wartime night that we should seize the moment. But even as we coupled, the clock on the town hall began to chime. I felt a sudden panic: My God — was it midnight already? I *had* to be back at camp that night, for I was tabbed as Orderly Officer the next day. If I wasn't on hand at dawn to raise the flag I'd be facing a court martial. It all seems inconsequential now. What, in the long run, did it really matter? But to me then it meant disgrace and, worse, delay. By the time I got to the continent (as a private, and not as an officer, thanks to my crimes) the war would be over!

It is not easy to make love while counting the chimes of a clock. Somehow I managed. *Twelve!* I sprang to my feet, streaking for the town square. She followed, crying out, over and over again, "It's cruel! It's cruel!" And so it was, but all I could see in my mind's eye as I raced for that departing truck was the dreadful spectacle of my pips being ripped off my shoulders before the eyes of the entire camp.

Hands reached for me and hauled me aboard as I waved a weak goodbye to my companion. I toppled gasping to the floor as the truck gathered speed. A close call, I thought; oh, the wages of sin!

I looked about. Oddly, I couldn't recognize anybody in the truck.

"This *is* the truck for Petworth?" I finally said.

One of the strangers shook his head.

"Midhurst," he said.

"My God, what time is it?"

"It's a bit past eleven."

Eleven! Damn; I'd counted wrong. Not surprising under the circumstances, I thought ruefully. The echoes of the girl's voice began to haunt me. Somehow I'd have to make it up to her.

"Stop the truck," I shouted. "Let me off!"

After what seemed like an age, the driver heard my plea and I found myself standing in the pitch dark in the woods that bordered the road to Midhurst. I had no real idea of where I was. I didn't even know where Midhurst was in relation to Chichester and Petworth. Disgrace seemed certain unless my luck held. I thought of two similar occasions — the time in the Yukon when I'd been stranded miles from camp after our accident with Joe Fournier's truck, and that other time when I'd overslept and missed the last tram to Chilliwack. In each instance my luck had been with me. But it would need a miracle to get me back to Petworth on this Stygian night, on a road that seemed to have no directional signs.

I wandered about for an hour, turning at crossroads, not really knowing which way I was supposed to go. Southern England in the spring of 1945 was fairly buzzing with men and machines, but here all was desolation. No car or lorry passed by me. No light appeared on the roadway. I was totally alone.

And then the extraordinary took place once again. An army truck loomed out of the night, identifiable only by its slitted headlight. I waved. It stopped. Familiar voices hailed me; friendly hands hauled me aboard. By one o'clock I was back in my own barrack room.

I phoned her the next day to apologize. She said she understood. I promised her that I'd meet her the following weekend without fail. She promised me she'd find us a room. We would spend an idyllic weekend together.

And then on Friday the orders went up on the board, and I learned to my chagrin that I was to be Orderly Officer for the entire weekend. I phoned and broke the news to her as gently as possible. There was a pause on the other end of the line. Then, in a firm, determined voice, "I'm coming to Petworth," she said.

I tried to tell her it was insanity. I couldn't meet her until after Lights Out. Worse, there was nowhere for her to stay. The only hotel in town was booked for weeks in advance. Every room was taken. "I don't care," she said. "I'm coming anyway. We'll find something." I protested in vain and ended up promising to meet her at the railway station once I'd finished my duties.

I find it difficult now to believe that we actually traipsed from house to house, knocking on doors, trying to maintain the obvious fiction that we were a newly married couple seeking a room for the night. We didn't *look* like a newly married couple. Even in wartime brides managed a new outfit; I hadn't even been able to give her so much as a corsage to wear on her old tweed suit. Nor had we any luggage. No wonder we encountered frozen faces and slammed doors.

Midnight was fast approaching. What were we to do?

"We'll sleep out in the woods," she said brightly.

The woods were five miles away, but we were both young and in good shape. After all, I'd once trudged forty miles across the Sarcee Reserve in the middle of the night with a pack on my back and no sleep. So off we went, hand in hand, past pubs and shops, out onto the winding roadway, past stone walls guarding stone mansions, past football fields and cricket pitches, past hedgerows and farmers' fields and small neat cottages until, at last, we reached a copse of trees that seemed suitably private.

It was a bitterly cold night. During the first hour or so that was a minor problem. But the time came when I lost interest in anything but sleep. The April moon set; the ground suddenly grew hard; romance vanished with the dew. Somewhere in the trees a cuckoo called and called. The memory still haunts me; I can never listen to those same calls in Beethoven's Sixth without a shiver. We slept fitfully and woke before dawn, covered in leaves and twigs, our clothing damp and rumpled.

I had to make haste to return to camp and resume my duties. It was a long hike. I left her at the station, still brushing the grass from her skirt. She seized me impulsively, with a look approaching panic. "For God's sake," she whispered, "take me back to Canada!"

I felt a chill and then a rush of compassion, mingled with guilt. There she was, a prisoner of her class, her only route of escape through one or other of the soldiers from overseas — Canadians, Australians, Yanks — who had invaded her island and who represented a freedom and, presumably, riches she could never know in England. In that moment I felt for her more strongly than I had in those earlier hours of transport. But I did not see her again. I can only hope she found someone else to deliver her from the shackles of a segregated society.

Shortly after this incident I was ordered to report to Canadian Military Headquarters in London for an interview. I felt a ripple of excitement. A headquarters interview! I had a feeling I was going to be seconded to a fighting unit as an intelligence officer.

At CMHQ a red-tabbed officer looked up from a folder containing my papers and all but confirmed my expectations.

"You didn't tell us you'd been an instructor in army intelligence at staff college in Canada," he said.

"You didn't ask," I responded. "Besides, it's in my documents."

"Just so," he said. "Well, we'd better get you off to Aldershot."

Aldershot?

"Right. You'll be taking the Intelligence Course there."

I couldn't believe my ears.

"I've taken it," I told him. "I took it in Canada. I not only took it, I *taught* it. It's all there in my papers."

"Not the same thing at all, I'm afraid. That's Canada." His voice took on a patronizing tone. "Over here you'll find we do things a bit differently."

I couldn't move him. I was a trained infantry officer — no doubt the best-trained infantry subaltern in the army. I was also a trained intelligence officer. That wasn't good enough. The army, which had been training me for years, now wanted to train me some more. The infantry was hungry for replacements. Platoon leaders were being scythed down in Germany. But I was condemned to sit in a stuffy classroom in Aldershot to learn what I already knew. It was true that they did do things differently at the Intelligence School at Aldershot. The course was badly planned and badly taught. But the army could never rid itself of the belief that anything done in Britain was superior to anything done in Canada. Here, too, the Canadian inferiority complex was showing.

The Intelligence School was close to the Western Infantry Training Regiment, where several of my friends were stationed. Glancing at the day's orders in the Officers' Mess there, I wasn't surprised to find that Jamaica Jim Harper was again under close arrest. I'd known him at Brockville and at Currie where, it seemed to me, he was always in some kind of trouble. Drunken Duncan had got himself posted as mess secretary, which meant there would be plenty of good stuff at the bar. He'd been sent off to Devon to bring back two barrels of hard cider and had actually returned, tardily, with one, having consumed the other en route. And Lloyd East was also on hand. We sampled the cider, which tasted like watery apple juice. And then we sampled some more. Our brains remained clear; it was only our legs that were paralysed.

The war was moving swiftly now. Roosevelt was dead. The Russians were at the gates of Berlin. My friends were dying in battle. Word came that Pete Hepburn, with whom I'd shared a tent on the Sarcee Reserve, had been killed — and here was I, still studying the make-up of the German army, which I already knew by heart. Anyway, in that last week of the war, the German army was crumbling away. I thought of Pete Hepburn, short and cocky, a man who hated Mackenzie King more than anyone else in the world. No day went by without Hepburn delivering a tirade against the Prime Minister for what he considered to be a lengthy catalogue of monstrous sins and imbecilities. Now, he lay dead, somewhere in Germany. He was a member of the twenty-third class at Currie — my class. I would have gone over on the same draft if I hadn't been called back to RMC as an instructor. In short, if I hadn't swotted so hard and tried to outdo all the others I wouldn't be here in Aldershot, drawing pictures of Panther tanks at a time when every Panther tank in Germany had been gutted. I'd be in Germany with Pete Hepburn. What would my children say, years hence, when they heard the answer to the embarrassing question that was on every recruiting poster: "Daddy, what did you do in the war?" (How could I know that by the mid-sixties, with the Vietnam struggle at its height, they'd ask me why I hadn't had the guts to be a draft dodger?)

I talked to Lloyd East about all this. We had all started together at Gordon Head and with about the same abilities. Why was it that East and I were still in England, alive, and Pete Hepburn was a corpse in Germany?

"Maybe we're being saved for a higher purpose," said Lloyd, the minister's son.

2 On the morning of May 8 — VE Day — I was still studying the make-up of the German army, but not with any sense of dedication. Because there had already been a false armistice, the actual Day of Victory was something of an anticlimax. The whole of England had been celebrating for the past twenty-four hours, expecting the official word that finally came. London was technically out of bounds, but few cared about that. I took an early train to the city, already crammed with celebrants. The crowds at each station were dense; the cheering never seemed to stop; people danced by wearing fancy hats and waving flags or bits of bunting in every shape and colour. The city itself seemed to have gone

insane. Soldiers, sailors, and airmen climbed pillars or made love on benches. Madmen rushed hither and thither waving open bottles. Girls rode on the backs of sailors and kissed everybody in sight. Lines of dancing Yanks snaked through the mob. A great line of intoxicated Russians marched abreast across Piccadilly Circus. Everybody sang "Rule Britannia" and "There'll Always Be an England." Every uniform in the world — from Sikh to Senegalese — waltzed by.

With my friend Wayne Ems I made my way to the Canadian Legion Officers' Club where, shortly, we found ourselves seated at a long table of celebrants enjoying a victory luncheon. I felt badly out of it; most of these men had been in action and faced death. I had never had the chance to test myself. How would I have behaved in the face of enemy gunfire? To this day I have no way of knowing.

I looked around for Frances and found her serving platters of food. I finally caught her eye; she looked at me coolly. No doubt, I thought, she is ashamed of me, a fledgling with no battle experience. When the luncheon ended I managed to get a word in her ear: "Let's go to a pub and celebrate." She hesitated for a long moment and then she said: "Oh, very well."

The pubs were as crowded as the streets. Every bar had brought out the bottles of Scotch that had been hoarded in expectation of this moment. We fought our way through the mob and found a small table. Here France gave me a strange look.

"I want you to go over to the bar and bring back two very large Scotches," she said. I was happy to oblige.

I pushed through the crowd and struggled back, drinks in hand.

"Drink it up," she said. "Drink it all." It was an order.

I gulped down my Scotch. She sipped hers.

The noise around us was deafening. People coming and going, singing, dancing, shouting for more drinks.

She leaned forward so I could hear. "I've got something to tell you," she said. "And I don't quite know how."

"What's up?" I cupped my ear.

"Well," she said, and paused. Then, all in a rush, "This is the first time I've ever had to tell a man he's about to become a father."

It hit me like a blow in the solar plexus. I couldn't even gulp. I started to speak, but she put up a hand to stop me. In the background a group of GIs were singing "Bless 'em All."

"Look," she said. "It's not your concern, is it? You didn't seduce me. I seduced you. You're not responsible."

"But . . ."

"*No!*" She looked at me fiercely. "It's nothing to do with you. There's a nice man wants to marry me. He's an old friend. I'm comfortable with him, and I intend to go through with it. He knows all about it, incidentally."

"Yes, but . . ."

"I don't want you to get involved. Can you understand that?"

I felt numb. In later years I sometimes wondered whether she was telling me the truth. Or was this merely her way of brushing me off? But I don't really think so.

"Listen to me, now," she said. She had an upper-class accent, but I remember that she had told me on that earlier occasion that she had been born in the United States and was still an American citizen. "Listen to me, now. I want you to get up from this table and leave. Now. And that's that."

And that was that. My memories of the rest of that remarkable day are understandably muddled. History was being made. Not far away, the Royal Family stood on the balcony of Buckingham Palace with Winston Churchill, waving at the crowd and making V-signs; but I didn't see them. When I pushed my way aboard the train that night I was still stunned. All around me, the lights of England were coming on again after almost six years of blackout. The sky was bright with searchlights, rockets, and fireworks. Most buildings were floodlit. There were even a few old neon signs glowing redly. We passed bonfire after bonfire, with people leaping about and cheering hoarsely. "You're awfully silent," Wayne Ems said, looking up at me. (We made a strange pair: he was not much more than five feet tall.) I didn't answer. I still didn't know her full name and I don't know it to this day.

Meanwhile it was business as usual at Aldershot. For a few days the army refused to concede that the armistice was permanent. I had no idea of how my future would be affected, nor did anybody else. There was a hint I might be sent to the continent to do intelligence work with the army of occupation or, as I wrote to my father, "I may be able to volunteer for the Pacific." Service in the Far East was not mandatory, but almost every officer I knew who had missed action in Europe was eager to be in on the coming invasion of Japan.

Having nothing better to do with us, the army gave us a leave. I had hardly returned when we all received an offer to sign up for the Pacific War. I signed immediately and was dispatched to a Repatriation Depot on the coast where I was given *more* time off — another embarkation leave, in fact. My whole army career, I thought a little ruefully, has been spent on embarkation leaves.

By now I had decided to make the most of my brief period in England and to see as much of it as possible. I wrote home that I had given up girls and hard liquor. Actually, I couldn't afford the pleasures both of the flesh and of the soul since so much of my army pay had been assigned to my parents.

I remember sketching the animals in London's Regent's Park Zoo one afternoon and watching, out of the corner of my eye, a pretty blonde girl in a WRCNS uniform. I sketched; she sat and stared at the sky. I stole glances; she cast down her eyes. I struggled with myself, for I knew I had two choices: I could ask her out for the evening or I could go to the Haymarket Theatre and watch John Gielgud in his own production of *Hamlet*. I certainly didn't have funds for both. In the end Gielgud won out.

In England I felt like a hick from a small town, uneducated and uncultured. Here I was, a university graduate with a sheepskin, and I hadn't even heard of Impressionism until my Aunt Florrie sent me a book on Claude Monet. I had cheerfully skipped all of Professor Soward's lectures in order to put out the *Ubyssey*, and as a result I couldn't tell Baroque from Rococo. My friend Lister Sinclair had tried to get me to listen to Beethoven and Mozart at university, but I was more interested in the Duke and the Count. Fortunately, Walt Disney saved me; I saw *Fantasia* five times, and now I couldn't get enough of *The Nutcracker Suite*.

To use a phrase not yet in the language, I OD'd on culture in those last few weeks in England. It became, for me, an obsession — almost a drug. No museum was too small, no art gallery too obscure, no church too insignificant for me. I rushed up to York to prowl around the huge minster and make sketches of its Gothic arches and then pushed on to Aberdeen and after that to Edinburgh, with its castle. I felt a surge of urgency, almost of panic. I was like a child in a cake shop. I wanted to gobble as much as I could before the plate was snatched from me; I knew my time in England was limited, and I determined to make the most of it. There was so much to see and so much to learn in this great museum of a country.

I had no set program. I simply took whatever chance laid before me. Back in London, I happened to come upon the bookstores in Charing Cross Road. I still have some of the strange titles I devoured there: Gilbert Murray's *Five Stages of Greek Religion* was one. I soaked it up as I soaked up everything: the all-Beethoven Concert in the Albert Hall, the noonday piano recitals in the National Gallery, the art shops in Bond Street.

I had very little money, but the theatres, fortunately, were not expensive. I don't believe I bothered with a single movie in this last hectic scramble for education. I bought shilling seats for *A Midsummer Night's Dream* (Gielgud again), *The Skin of Our Teeth* (Vivien Leigh), and *Jacobowsky and the Colonel* (Michael Redgrave). I was enchanted. I had not seen a professional performance in the theatre since those childhood days in Toronto. Now I realized what I'd been missing.

I decided to take in an opera. *Rigoletto* was playing at the Sadler's Wells theatre. Again, I was knocked out. The familiar strains of *La Donna e Mobile* took me back to the Sunday evening in Victoria when I'd heard Bobby Breen sing it on the Eddie Cantor show. Even in a foreign language, I thought, the story isn't too difficult to follow. And then, in the second or third act, I heard the hunchback cry out: "The Curse! The Curse!" and realized that all this time they'd actually been singing in English. I felt vaguely cheated.

To save money I roomed at the Chelsea flat of Jack Scott, who published some of my cartoons in the *Maple Leaf*. Scott writhed under the fact that he, a top Vancouver newspaperman, was a mere lieutenant while his colleague on the *Maple Leaf*, Pat Slattery, was a captain. Slattery, after all, had been a minor sportswriter in Vancouver. Now he was Scott's superior. The idea of actually having to salute Slattery grated until the day Scott found himself promoted.

"I'm a captain!" cried the delighted Scott. "Now, at last I'm equal to that son of a bitch Slattery."

At that point Slattery walked into the *Maple Leaf* office.

"Congratulate me, guys," he said. "I've just been moved up. They've made me a major."

When I returned from leave to No. 3 Repat Depot a cable and two letters were waiting for me from my mother. My father's condition, which had been growing worse, was now critical, and he'd been taken to hospital. As I wrote to her at the end of June, the "kindest thing to hope is that it will be all over soon."

"Poor Daddy," I wrote, "the greatest tragedy of all, I think, is his inability to read."

A few days after this I found myself with fifteen thousand other troops aboard the *Queen Mary* heading for New York. The men slept in eight-hour shifts on the decks. The officers were given staterooms. There were triple-tiered bunks for twelve in the cabin to which I was assigned. I was the thirteenth and so slept on the floor.

Crowds greeted our New York arrival with cheers and horn blasts. More crowds met us at every station across Canada — women with cigarettes, chocolate bars, and doughnuts, crying out that we were heroes. I felt like a fraud and remembered Harry's story about his reception when the troopship had been forced back from France.

I arrived in Vancouver in mid-July, less than five months after I'd left, and was immediately given thirty days' leave. On Granville Street I ran into a group of old friends. "You still here?" said one. "Not *another* embarkation leave?" asked another. I tried to explain that I'd actually been overseas in the intervening period, but they refused to believe that, and I cannot say I blamed them.

Our house in Point Grey had become a hospital. My mother had brought my father home and since he was too weak to climb the stairs had turned our dining room into a bedroom. She and Lucy were distraught and exhausted from caring for him. There he lay, haggard and skeletal, staring at the ceiling, clinging to life. He needed constant, twenty-four-hour care, which meant that we worked in shifts, bathing him, feeding him, changing him, keeping him company. I sat beside him, telling him something of my time in England; he did not have the strength to respond or even to show interest. He had moments of delirium in the night, and these were the hardest to bear. He had lost so much weight that his legs, once so sturdy and muscled, had been reduced to matchsticks, and he knew it. One night, as I sat beside him, he looked at those wasted limbs and, in his semiconscious state, uttered a terrible cry. "Matchsticks!" he moaned. "Matchsticks!" The memory of it haunts me to this day.

My mother, too, had lost weight, her face drawn from the strain of seeing him waste away. She took me aside in the kitchen late in the evening, the tears streaming down her cheeks. "Oh, my God," she whispered, "I want him to die! Isn't that dreadful? I wish he would die! Oh, Lord, it's so awful to want him to die."

But he too wanted to die. He had no specific ailment — no heart disease or cancer — just a general deterioration brought on by advanced senility. Ironically, his heart, which had caused him so much concern, was holding out long after the rest of his body had given up the struggle. It was heartbreaking for us all to see this big strapping man, who had once thought nothing of hiking forty miles through the snow, drifting with maddening slowness toward the grave. There were nights when he was convinced he would never see morning and so called us together for a deathbed scene — the kind that was common in the nineteenth-century novels he read. But still he clung to life.

I had no close male friends in Vancouver except for those who had gone on leave with me: Jack Scott was still overseas; Harry Filion was at an army base in the East. On those evenings when I was not attending my father I wandered down to the officers' leave centre in the West End. It had two attractions for me. The slot machines, which, in the interests of the war effort, had been rigged so that we could actually win, were one. The second was the presence of Janet Walker, who had by now become my closest woman friend and confidante.

Janet was doing her bit as one of the club's hostesses, and

she was bursting with news for me. She had, for the first time in her life, fallen head over heels in love. He was a young New Zealand airman who had come through Vancouver and swept her off her feet. It was a joy to see her face aglow and her eyes sparkling as she talked of the man she called "her beautiful love." The courtship had been brief; he had already left for the Far East and was flying supplies over Burma. She showed me a funny cartoon he'd sent her about two airmen, crouching in a jungle, congratulating themselves that the war was over as Japanese bombs dropped all around them.

As Janet herself found out, the war was by no means over. Two of our closest friends from the *Ubyssey* days were about to be married — Marg Reid and Lionel Salt, the ex-sports editor and Lionel Hampton fan, now a Flying Officer in the RCAF. On the day of the wedding — July 20 — Janet learned that her beautiful love, Bill Hamilton, had been killed over Burma.

Of course she went to the wedding, at which I was an usher. She had no intention of casting a pall over that day. It must have been a trying experience — it could have been she in a white wedding gown standing at the altar — but never by as much as an eyelash flicker did she betray her inner turmoil. She hugged the bride, kissed the groom, and seemed to be her usual cheerful self.

There was to be a lively party later — a reunion of all those who had worked together on the campus paper, several of them now married to former classmates, like Marg and Lionel.

"You don't really want to go, do you?" I said to her.

She shook her head.

And so, as our friends whooped it up, the two of us went down to Stanley Park, walked around the seawall in the dusk, and then sat on a bench overlooking Lost Lagoon, throwing breadcrumbs at the ducks.

We didn't say much, just sat there. She didn't cry. Once

she turned to me, her eyes bright, like the waters of the lagoon. "Thank you," she said. That was all.

I thought: *I've underestimated her. She does know how to love. She's capable of passion. It's just that her standards are higher than most.*

3 On August 6, a few days before my leave ended, I picked up a copy of the *Sun* on Granville Street and learned that the Americans had dropped an atomic bomb on a Japanese city. Not everybody understood the significance immediately. Janet did. She was now a full-fledged reporter and had the good sense to phone Dr. Gordon Shrum, the Dean of Applied Science at the university (on whose uniform I had once spilled soup), and he explained what was going on exclusively for readers of the *Province*. I knew too, for I had as a boy read a prescient novel about nuclear devastation written shortly after the turn of the century by H.G. Wells, and I still recall his description of bombed cities glowing red like open sores for decades after the attack — a close approximation of the lingering effects of radiation. I knew then that the war was virtually over. A few days later Japan surrendered, and Vancouver went almost as crazy as London had on VE Day. Coincidentally, it was the last day of my leave.

The war was over! I had spent forty-two months in the army and had accomplished very little for my country. I consoled myself with the thought that perhaps something I'd taught in those infantry training days had helped save somebody's life, but that I would never know. Now, however, I could get back to my old job on the city desk of the *News-Herald.* And so, as whistles blew and guns fired and thousands cheered, I made my way up to the Little Mountain Barracks to sign my discharge papers, pick up my clothing allowance, and say goodbye to the army forever.

How naïve I was! The adjutant looked at me as if I'd taken leave of my senses. The war, he explained, was by no means over. The peace treaty had not been signed. The army had no official word of any cessation of hostilities. Would I care to look at a long order on the bulletin board? There it was: a full draft was leaving that night by troop train for Brandon, Manitoba, to study — I couldn't believe my eyes — jungle warfare. And lo, my name, starting as it did with *B,* led all the rest.

Brandon, Manitoba? *Jungle warfare?* Surely this was a ghastly error or an equally ghastly joke. Others were clustered around the bulletin, assuring each other that it was all a mistake, probably the nuttiest mistake the army had ever made. It was nutty, no doubt, but it was no mistake. That night, with the sirens still howling and the bells ringing and half the populace snake dancing through the streets, a group of us with full packs and rolled groundsheets climbed aboard the train and headed for the jungles of Brandon.

When I boarded the train, my friend Harold Bell, whom I'd palled around with on the *Queen Mary,* was already seated in the Men's Smoking Room. A large can of grapefruit juice was on the bench beside him.

"The war is over," said Harold. "Have some grapefruit juice."

The first swig warmed my stomach; the second brought on a desire to laugh and sing.

"My brother has an interesting job," said Harold. "He works in the railway yards here."

He took a big swig of the grapefruit juice.

"One of his jobs is to clean out the empty tank cars. This week he found several that had contained ethyl alcohol."

He passed me the tin.

"I was visiting my brother this afternoon," said Bell in his mocking deadpan style. "He was kind enough to share his discovery with me. The estimable chef has supplied the grapefruit juice in return for a portion of the alcohol. He has also provided us with this entire turkey. The war is over. Let us celebrate and be thankful."

And so we sat up all night celebrating VJ Day, tearing pieces off the turkey and mixing Harold Bell's brother's alcohol with grapefruit juice.

Two days later a conductor came along announcing that Brandon was next.

"You know what's going to happen, don't you?" said Harold Bell. "The old army stuff. A lance-corporal is going to meet us at the station and he is going to say, 'Gentlemen, will you please form up in columns of three, march to the quartermaster stores, and draw your blankets?' "

I nodded.

"The war is over," said Harold Bell. "I suggest that when the lance-jack utters those words, we two step down off the station platform and holler 'Taxi!' "

Which we did. The taxi dropped us at the door of the Officers' Mess while the rest of the draft was still toiling up the hill to the quartermaster stores.

"What's the preferred drink in these parts?" Harold Bell asked the mess sergeant.

The sergeant avowed that it was a Red Eye — a mixture of beer and tomato juice.

"Keep them coming," said Harold Bell.

Periodically, another NCO would arrive to remind us that we hadn't yet drawn our blankets from the quartermaster stores. We ignored him. The bar was filling up with friends of mine who had vowed to fight the Japanese. At midnight, when the bar closed, we still hadn't drawn our blankets.

"Well," said Harold Bell, "It is a warm and salubrious night. We will sleep out under the stars."

We stumbled out of the mess, found a grassy spot near the parade ground, and were soon insensible. The next thing I knew the sun was shining in my face and I could hear the shrill barking of NCOs. Entire platoons were marching past us — at one point almost *over* us. With the army it was business as usual. Harold Bell and I drew our blankets and began to study jungle warfare, which, if I remember rightly, was pretty similar to other kinds of warfare the way they taught it at Brandon.

A certain lassitude developed. It was difficult to show a man how to stick a bayonet into a Japanese when the Japanese were signing an armistice with General MacArthur on that battleship. Our hearts were no longer in it. Everybody from the C.O. down wanted out.

As the weeks rolled by the camp began to run down like an unwound watch. Training all but ceased. The men were being discharged at a painfully slow rate, and we officers were assigned to help with the demobilization process. People simply vanished, sometimes without a word. You never knew who would be next; every morning at breakfast a familiar face would be missing. Few bothered even to say goodbye; it was over, finished — the comradeship, the carousing, the intensity of training, the fever to get into action. One day Harold Bell vanished; I have not seen him since.

I told the adjutant that I wanted to go home; my old job was waiting for me. He looked embarrassed and explained that the army had somehow lost my documents and that I would have to stay in Brandon until they were found. That was an old story. Every time I had moved the army had mislaid my papers. But now this carelessness was keeping me a prisoner. We had little to do: we played cribbage, listened to the World Series on the radio, cashed in our war bonds, drank heavily in the bar.

Then a telegram arrived from my mother. My father was back in the hospital and not expected to live. I was given compassionate leave and took the next train to Vancouver.

I learned of his death when I picked up a copy of the *News-Herald* at the CPR station. There it was, at the head of the obituary column: BERTON. It was a sudden jolt, to find his passing noted in a single, clipped paragraph in pica type. But my main emotion was one of relief that he was finally out of his misery.

It was his heart that had kept him alive when every other part of him had collapsed — that so-called weak heart that had stopped him from climbing the Yukon hills in a search for wildflowers or using his boat on the river, the heart that had forced him to crawl like a snail along the sidewalks of Dawson and Vancouver, the heart for which he carried nitro-glycerine pills, the heart that had gone out of him, casting over him the pall of imminent death, draining his curiosity, dulling his enthusiasms, forcing him into half a dozen sad farewells. If it hadn't been for his heart, the doctor said, he would have died weeks before.

There was an autopsy, of course; I couldn't understand all the Latin words. When I had to write down on a form the cause of my father's death I put "circulatory ailments." But sometimes I think he just gave up.

I did not want to see him in his coffin. I wanted to remember him as he had been in my youth, bursting with energy and curiosity, full of the enthusiasms of life, making every moment count, studying, probing, investigating everything — the stars in the heavens, Shakespeare, the Bible, plants and flowers both wild and cultivated, the texture of woven cloth, contract bridge, neon signs, Silexes; and building things: a catapult for us kids, a beautifully tooled lampstand for my mother, a new room on our Dawson home, a rose trellis, a lych-gate, a rock garden. I wanted to remember him as a man who worked out algebra problems at night, and who read everything from *Beowulf* and the *Scientific American* to "Bringing Up Father" and "Alley Oop." No, I did not want to see his carcass, shrivelled and rouged on the frilled satin of an undertaker's casket. My mother agreed; her instructions were to keep the lid firmly closed during the service.

They played his favourite hymn, "Unto the Hills Around

Do I Lift Up My Longing Eyes." How many times had he looked up at those blue Yukon hills, rolling northward, ridge upon misty ridge — hills he had climbed so often that he knew every freshwater spring and gurgling gully? I thought of him, crossing himself, High-Anglican fashion, in St. Paul's in Dawson on those early Sunday evenings when we'd come down from those very hills after a long day of picnicking. I thought of the day when I had become panic stricken, fearing that I was lost, when my father left me on the lip of Thomas Gulch to fetch some water, and how comforting his presence had been when he found me again. I thought of the long days on the river, with the herds of caribou swimming all around us, so close you could reach out and touch the velvet on their horns, and I wished I'd gone with him on that last boat trip down the Yukon. And as I remembered these moments, the undertaker came over to our pew, rubbed his hands, and in an oily voice whispered to my mother: "Would you like us to open the casket now, Mrs. Berton?"

I could have strangled him. He simply had to show off his handiwork. She managed to emit a hoarse and negative cry while I gave him the kind of look that, alas, can never kill. He retreated hastily.

Two days later I was back in Brandon, putting in time. How can anybody lose one hundred dollars playing cribbage at twenty-five cents a game? Somehow I managed it. There were, as well, less innocuous pursuits. One day the Medical Officer called all the officers together to deliver a dressing down and a warning. He told us that the men in our camp now had the second highest VD rate in the Canadian army.

He paused to let this sink in. Then he added: "The officers have the highest!"

There was one movie house showing second-run features. I'd already seen Cornel Wilde's version of Chopin in *A Song to Remember*, but, having nothing better to do and

283

little money left, I saw it twice more, watching him cough blood on the keys as he rattled through the polonaise. Hearing again the Hit Parade songs of those days — "Prisoner of Love," "Sentimental Journey," "Till the End of Time" — brings back the memory of that lackadaisical, useless fall, with the sere leaves of the wolf willow and cottonwood drifting listlessly across the scrub prairie.

The C.O. was given his discharge and left abruptly. The story was that he simply climbed into the army station wagon and told his driver to take him to Regina. The driver thought he meant Regina Street.

"No, you idiot," said the Colonel. "Regina, *Saskatchewan*. I live there."

"What do I do then?" the driver asked.

"Any goddam thing you want," said the C.O. "I don't care. The war's over."

Then, at the end of October, with a light snow falling, my documents were located. Once again I went to Vancouver to get my discharge. When I returned to the house on Ninth Avenue I felt my father's loss even more keenly than before. It seemed so empty without him. My mother was trying to forget the events of the past year by returning to her typewriter, but she had, temporarily at least, lost much of her energy. She looked gaunt and tired but was obviously glad to see me, for she needed a man around the house. I moved back into my bedroom just off the kitchen, the walls still decorated with the leggy Petty girls that *Esquire* had printed in the thirties — much to the consternation of the bluenoses. Lucy was still on shift work with the weather bureau, but that job would be over by the end of the year; she was planning, she told me, to take a business course. She pressed my uniform for me and pulled a small package from a secret pocket that the army, in its practical wisdom, had designed especially for the purpose.

"Here," she said dryly, "you'd better hang on to this." It was a condom; I had the grace to blush.

I could scarcely wait to go to the depot at Little Mountain and be rid of the army forever. I was given another brief leave while they processed me out and lost no time getting down to the *News-Herald* to ask for my old job back.

Duncan Hamilton's old brokerage partner, C.B. "Slim" Delbridge, greeted me warmly enough but appeared a little disinclined to make me city editor. Maybe, he suggested, I should start a bit lower and try to work back into the job. I bridled. Dammit, I told him, we veterans had been promised our jobs back, and I wanted mine. Well, said Delbridge dubiously, they had a city editor, an old newsman named Bill Bell, and also an assistant named Ed Martin. Perhaps I could work on the desk with them and see what happened. It was not very comforting, but it was the best I could do.

I went back again to Little Mountain to see the adjutant about my discharge. This was a new adjutant; the old one was now a floorwalker at Woodward's. The new man looked at me with embarrassment, and I had an idea what was coming.

"Look," he said. "Just go away for a while. Get a job. Don't tell anybody you're still in the army. Don't worry; you'll continue to draw your pay. Call back in about three weeks and by then, I expect, we'll have it ironed out."

All this was fine with me. I didn't mind being paid by two employers, and I didn't have to ask the reason for the army's unexpected largess. I got the message and I was happy.

The war was over and they had lost my documents again.

Chapter Seven

The Name of the Game

October 1945–May 1947

1 My first act as a pseudo-civilian was to get rid of my uniform and buy a new suit. I purchased it off the rack at E.A. Lee's, a brown, single-breasted number with narrow chalk stripes. Brown was not a popular colour for a dischargee, being considered too close to khaki, but this was the only suit in the place that would fit me. I had joined the army weighing 165 pounds; now I was thirty pounds heavier. The returning horde had preceded me and picked up all the snappy gabardines in bright blues and greens. As for the shirt, I took what I could get: in tan, also uncomfortably close to the standard army hue. We all wanted white shirts in those days; there was something dazzling about them, especially when you splashed a yellow tie across the front, like an egg. But white shirts were at a premium, and again, nobody had my size.

That first suit was known as an austerity suit, without trouser pleats and pocket flaps and so skimpy it was almost Ivy League, a style that was at least a decade ahead. It had cost forty dollars. I immediately had myself measured for a sixty-five-dollar blue suit, double-breasted, of course, with enormous pointed lapels and a hefty amount of padding in the shoulders. There was a lot of space in that second suit. To quote a phrase of Jim Coleman's, you had to take two steps before the pants moved. I remember the tailor's instructions to his assistant: "Drop it from his shoulders like a plumb bob."

In those days I wore a long tie. We all wanted something broad and splashy, tied with a bold Windsor knot to match our Windsor collars. A really sharp tie at that time was a knit;

I bought one in rich raspberry rayon with a yellow embroidered border. Ties were a major topic of discussion among those of us who had been starved for colour during the wartime years; they were a symbol of our release from conformity. I had ties with nudes and palm trees painted on them and several abstract models with whirls of colour. Most of us wore tie-clips with several initials hanging from them, like earrings, as well as collar-pins shaped like Indian arrows.

With the rest of my clothing allowance I bought diamond socks in bright carmine, yellow, and chocolate and a second pair in green and orange to match one of my ties. These were not easy to get, but every mother, wife, and sweetheart was busy knitting them. Argyle socks, slightly more sophisticated, were even harder to come by. We all hitched up our trousers in those days to display ankles that fairly pulsated with colour. Some years went by before I got the army out of my system and toned down all this gaudiness.

But my mood did not match the brightness of my new outfit. In all my twenty-five years I had scarcely known a moment of true despair. But now, in the late fall of 1945, I suffered from my first — and indeed my last — real period of depression. My father was dead, my mother exhausted, and my sister about to lose her job and unsure of what to do with her life. I was experiencing the inevitable letdown that follows an army discharge. But these were contributing factors only. I had gone back at last to the *News-Herald*, the paper I loved, to find that it wasn't the same. *Nothing* was the same. In my innocence I had believed, against all evidence, that I could take up exactly where I'd left off, as if the world of 1941 had been frozen in time. It was at best wishful thinking.

It wasn't just that the newspaper itself had changed or that almost all of the men and women in the city room were strangers. The worst blow was my slow realization that I wasn't wanted. I looked around for a familiar face in the city room and found only two: H. Cromar Bruce, pink-cheeked and white-haired, was still tapping out his by-line on the latest report from city hall. He and Al Williamson, now a columnist, were all that remained from the old days. Ralph Daly, Evelyn Caldwell, and several others had defected to the *Sun*, which was going through a regeneration under its new managing editor, Hal Straight. "For God's sake, don't go back," Ralph Daly had warned me. "It's not the same." But I did go back, and it was like a douche of cold water. The men on the city desk wanted no part of me. Legally I was entitled to a job. In fact, the government had promised that every veteran would get his old job back and had set up machinery to ensure it. But I represented a threat, and they were determined to do everything they could to shoulder me out.

The paper itself, now returned to normal size, was like the ghost of the lively little tabloid that Elson had launched and Scott, Lewis, and I had so lovingly edited. The headlines were puerile, the writing flat, the columns unreadable. It lacked zest and personality. I suppose there are some who would say that, compared to our cocky little tabloid, it was a more responsible product. To me it was the least responsible paper I've ever known; it carried little news and much boilerplate (to use the newsman's argot for canned copy). And it didn't *care* about anything. The men who published and edited it went through the motions, nothing more.

There I sat on the city desk, marking copy and writing headlines, remembering how I'd waited for four years to get back in harness and asking myself how I could have been so naïve. The job I had once loved became drudgery, and it *wasn't* my old job. I was on trial, working only as a desk man, not a city editor. Bill Bell, who had the job, made no bones about his intention of hanging on. Once, while in his cups at a staff party, he took me aside and bluntly explained that he had to look out for himself. He was approaching the end of his career; I was at the start of mine. I'm afraid I didn't see it his way.

He skewered me neatly. One night he told me to edit all the copy and write headlines but to send nothing down to the composing room without his okay. He'd check it through when he and Ed Martin returned from their coffee break. I did as I was told. The print shop began to ask for more copy, but I couldn't release it. The coffee break dragged on — an hour, two hours. Finally Bell and Martin returned and the copy was sent down, late, to the composing room. Of course the paper was late, but Bell wasn't blamed for that. I was.

I'd had no experience with this kind of infighting. In the old days we'd been a team of close friends and drinking buddies. Now it was open warfare, but not the kind of warfare for which I'd been trained.

Bell told me he would have to take me off the desk; he acted as if it was the most reluctant decision he'd ever had to make. I'd go back on the street as a reporter, with a salary cut. I didn't propose to take this demotion without a struggle. In my guilelessness, I believed that as soon as my story was told matters would be set right. I went to see Slim Delbridge to explain again that, under the law, I was entitled to my old job back.

"But the paper was late," Delbridge said. "And you were on the desk at the time. We simply can't afford to have the paper late again, you know."

He talked to me indulgently, as if I was a small, errant child. When I tried to explain the circumstances, my reasons for not sending the copy down sounded weak and unconvincing. Delbridge indicated that I must have been mistaken; why would Bill Bell give such instructions? I wasn't mistaken and I knew it, but there wasn't anything I could do.

I decided to make a legal issue out of my demotion. The government arbitrator assigned to resolve such cases — for there were thousands — didn't understand the newspaper business. The editor, Ken Drury (known to one and all as Ken Dreary), whom I had secretly met, argued that the paper itself was quite different from the one I'd worked on. That, of course, was true. Moreover, my pay as a reporter was actually greater than it had been when I was city editor of the tabloid. This, too, was true. During the war the scarcity of good men had caused an inflation in newspaper salaries. The arbitrator threw up his hands; there was nothing, he said, that he could do. And so I had to make the best of it.

I was scarcely back on the street, covering the activities of returning soldiers, when Bill Bell gave me a macabre assignment. "Ever cover a hanging?" he asked. I shook my head. "There's one tomorrow at Oakalla," he told me. "It's something you ought to see." I didn't understand *why* I "ought to see" a man go to his death, but I was in no position to argue. The assignment only increased my darkening mood.

The execution was set for six in the morning, the traditional hour of dawn. The prison was in New Westminster. I set an alarm clock, but as it turned out, I needed no alarm because I couldn't sleep. Every movement of the clock made me think of that human life ticking out its final moments. An hour's drive away, I knew, another man was tossing on his cot waiting for an alarm to ring. In a few hours he and I were to meet briefly in a small, hushed room for a short, precise ceremony.

I rose at four and breakfasted on bacon and eggs, thinking all the while of another man who would also be eating his breakfast — his last. Then, with the fog rising from the Fraser River, I drove out to the prison with two other reporters.

They were both drinking. It was the custom of witnesses at hangings to take a stiff drink, just as it was the custom to give the condemned man a shot or two or at least a barbiturate. That was supposed to make things easier, but I'm not certain it didn't make things harder. At any rate, I refused a drink.

It was the last day of November. The morning was grey, the scenery desolate, my own mood melancholy. In a cheerless cell not far away a man was waiting to die, but at the prison the guards who would participate in the ceremony were grumbling about the weather. One said that driving conditions were terrible. Another complained about getting up so early. A third remarked that they'd had powdered eggs again for breakfast. The talk continued in an offhand, desultory fashion, and I was reminded, in an odd way, of the stilted conversation among the first guests who arrive at a cocktail party before the bar is opened.

The warden called in the press. He was a pleasant, almost genial man who called us "boys." He said he'd read our stuff, made a few remarks about the weather, and added that he'd answer any questions we had. Yes, he said, the condemned man had eaten a good breakfast: bacon, two eggs, toast, and coffee. No, he had been offered a drink but had refused it.

Outside, contrasting oddly with the khaki-clad provincial policemen, were two extremely well scrubbed young men in dark, impeccable suits, wearing grey gloves. I looked at this pair curiously. Who were they? What were they doing here? Then it came to me slowly but forcefully: of course! They were undertakers.

Suddenly there came a brisk and businesslike shuffling, and we found ourselves moving smartly off through the cell blocks and into a small, high-ceilinged, brightly lit room. We were actually beside the top of a disused elevator shaft, which by virtue of its shape and construction was admirably suited for the purpose at hand.

Except for a wooden railing surrounding the trap, around which we were grouped, the room was utterly bare. The noose hung from the ceiling, and because of the narrowness of the quarters it seemed to dominate the scene. In the Boy Scouts I had learned to tie a hangman's knot in order to win a proficiency badge, but that had always been done with thin cord. Here, in stout manila, it looked enormous.

I became aware of the presence of a small, round, faceless man. He was wearing a dinner jacket, which at an early hour gave him the appearance of a reveller returned from an all-night party. I say he was faceless because I can remember every detail of the condemned man's features, but I cannot recall the hangman's. It sounds contrived, I know, but it's true. He might have been anyone. He could pass me on the street and I wouldn't know him. Perhaps he has.

Now the door opened and a small procession entered: the prison chaplain reading aloud from his Bible, the condemned man, dwarfed between two guards, and the warden. As he entered, the little man looked up at one of the guards and gave a twisted grin. It was a self-conscious grin and there was no cheer in it. Yet it was somehow familiar and not wholly unexpected. I had seen that grin before on the face of an unwilling performer thrust alone onto the stage in amateur theatricals.

The condemned man looked up and saw the noose, and he too seemed surprised at its size. Indeed, it dwarfed and dominated him, and when they set it on his neck it seemed as if he might slip right through it.

Now things moved with efficiency and dispatch: with such precision, indeed, that it was difficult to feel any emotion. We stood on three sides of the railing, staring at the little man as the hangman placed the noose over his head. The policemen and guards had all sprung to attention, so that the entire incident had the air of a flag-lowering ceremony, or a service club investiture, or any number of formal rituals that help give society its structure.

The *Province* reporter stood next to me, fairly vibrating with enthusiasm. "This is it!" he said, in a hoarse whisper that carried halfway across the death chamber. I looked the other way, pretending we were strangers.

The padre continued reading from the Bible. The hangman stepped off the trap and pulled the lever. Suddenly the little man was no longer with us. Only the rope was there, stretching tautly into the dark pit and swinging ever so slightly. I looked at my watch; it was exactly six o'clock.

With the other members of the press I sat on the coroner's jury to establish the cause of death. I had heard that one previous execution had been bungled — a man had strangled slowly at the end of the rope. Nobody had ever reported that

292

incident, but if this one was bungled too, I was determined to write about it. But the little man had died almost instantly — within ten minutes — and so I went back to the office to write the story and to try, unsuccessfully, to wipe the spectacle from my mind and my future dreams.

But I did not write the story as I have told it here. I wrote a typically objective four-paragraph news story, following the mandatory five "W's" in the lead — Who, What, Where, Why, and When. An Indian named Prince had gone to his death with a twisted grin at dawn in Oakalla Prison to pay for the murder of two trappers in Finlay Forks a couple of years before. There followed a one-sentence description of the elevator shaft and a couple more giving the name of the doctor who pronounced him dead and the time of death; nothing more.

"Always describe the places; always describe the people," Jack Scott had once advised me. Why didn't I do it in this instance? Perhaps I might have, if this had been the old *News-Harold* and Scott and Lewis had been in charge. Perhaps not. I am not sure that I was yet capable of that kind of reportage; nor did newspapers welcome subjective pieces in which reporters described their own feelings. Like most newspapermen I was a prisoner of the cult of objectivity and conformity. Since you assumed that most readers would never get past the first paragraph, you told everything at the outset: who, what, when, where, why. Just the bald facts, nothing else. You kept your own personality, your own feelings, your own assessment out of the story. A man had been hanged on the dot at six and pronounced dead at six-ten. That was the story. If I had tried to write that this grisly spectacle was all the more chilling because of its resemblance to the other public rituals, I doubt that the copy desk would have passed it. But, to be fair, it didn't at the time occur to me to write it that way.

Then, a week before Christmas, I got a front page scoop. A pretty nineteen-year-old nurse had gone missing the week before. Her mother was frantic. The reported consensus was that she had been kidnapped. Suddenly, after a week of headlines, she turned up at home. If there is a secret to daily journalism it is that a reporter must move quickly. As soon as the news came in, I moved. I didn't wait for coffee. I didn't phone for an appointment. I took a taxi straight to her front door, an hour ahead of the two opposition papers, and interviewed her until we were both exhausted. By the time she had given me the story in detail, she was too tired to talk to anymore newspapermen. While they were knocking vainly on her door I was typing out my piece for the morning edition.

She hadn't been kidnapped; she'd run away from home. It seems a small matter today, but the build-up then had turned it into a sensation. My story got the top headline on the front page, and I milked it for everything. I was elated and waited for congratulations. But all Bill Bell told me was the front office had thought the story was too long. Then why hadn't *he* cut it, if he thought so?

I felt deflated. The fun had gone out of the business. My mother sensed my desperation, even though I tried to cover it up with a show of nonchalance. I didn't want to add another burden to her painful period of readjustment. "There's something wrong," she'd say. "You're not happy at the paper, are you?" I'd shrug and say it was nothing, and then, sometimes, she'd sigh heavily and look at me with those big brown Thompson eyes, so sad now and so despairing, and she'd say, "We never should have let him go back, should we? It was a mistake, wasn't it? A terrible mistake." And I'd put my hand on hers and say, no, it wasn't a mistake; he had his pride and he had to do what he thought was right for all of us.

"It wasn't the same, you know," she said to me once. "When he came back, it wasn't the same. It was that heart business." It was like an echo, that phrase. I thought back to the night of the blackout in the old *News-Herald* office, with Burton Lewis writing his editorial about nothing ever being the same again.

You can't go back, I thought (I had just finished reading Thomas Wolfe); *it never is the same.* I had to make a change.

2 For some time, Hal Straight, the managing editor of the *Vancouver Sun,* had been throwing out hints that if I applied for a job he might condescend to give me one. Straight wasn't about to invite me to join the paper; that would have been unnecessarily expensive. He was canny enough to know that sooner or later I'd come to him. After all, he'd taken on several former *News-Herald* employees, and he was well aware of my situation there. He was a close friend of Harry Filion, whom he'd already hired as a photographer-reporter, and when we all caroused together at Filion's basement apartment in Shaughnessy Heights he'd say to me gruffly, "You ought to be thinking about coming over to us." The time had arrived at last when I would have to swallow my pride and ask him for a job. He offered me the same reduced salary that I'd been getting at the morning paper, forty-five dollars a week, and put me on the city desk as assistant to Himie Koshevoy, the puckish city editor, who was also my close friend. I took the job eagerly — *any* salary would have been acceptable at the time — and on January 2, 1946, with an enormous sense of relief, entered the Sun Tower as the paper's newest employee.

Hal Straight was already becoming a legend in Vancouver as a hard-driving, hard-drinking, colourful, and sometimes eccentric journalist of the old Chicago school. I had once hated him because, as a sports columnist, he invariably referred to the tabloid *News-Herald* as "that little paper," a bit of purposeful patronizing that had driven Scott and me to a fury — which, of course, was Straight's intention.

Hal Straight was cast in the *Sun* mould, the perfect managing editor for what was then one of the most colourful newspapers in Canada. It had been founded by Robert Cromie, a brilliant if erratic journalist. With the founder dead, the family had decided to sell out. Straight, who was sports editor, convinced young Donald Cromie, the founder's son, to talk his family into hanging on. Now Donald Cromie was publisher, his younger brother, Sam, was vice-president in charge of production, and Hal Straight, a one-time left-handed baseball pitcher, was managing editor. The town was still buzzing with the story of his triumph over a recalcitrant city editor, Pat Terry. Terry had bridled at finding himself subordinate to a former sportswriter. When he refused one of Straight's orders, Straight simply picked him up and stuffed him into one of the big wire wastebaskets behind the city desk. Terry fell quickly into line.

I was anxious to work for Straight because he was known to pay a premium for imagination and daring. One day an angry woman shouted over the phone that one of his reporters was a thief — he'd crept into her home, pried open a dresser drawer, and filched all available photographs of her murdered husband. "Are you going to fire him?" the caller demanded. "No," said Straight, "I'm going to promote him."

It was Straight who put apple-blossom perfume in the printer's ink one day to accompany a photograph of apple blossoms. It was Straight again who encouraged an itinerant evangelist to walk through the composing room during a typographers' slowdown carrying a placard reading: "IT'S LATER THAN YOU THINK."

He always claimed that he hired me because of my size rather than my ability. Filion, his favourite photographer, tipped the scales at well over two hundred pounds. Straight himself stood six feet and must have weighed close to two hundred and fifty. At six foot three I was a slender one-ninety-five. Straight's wistful ambition was to have a staff that consisted entirely of giants and musclemen who would overawe all interview subjects and terrify them into spilling their most carefully hoarded secrets. He was frustrated in this by the fact that several of his best reporters weren't much taller than five feet.

He believed that all newspapermen should exude an air of supreme confidence, and he tended to judge his own staff by the way they stood up to him. I sometimes think Straight bullied his people in the hope that one or two might bully him back. Certainly he only favoured those who refused to knuckle under. I remember when Wally Gillespie, who had been the *Sun's* campus correspondent with me at UBC, finally got up the nerve to beard Straight in his den and to ask, in a quavering voice, for a five dollar raise.

"That's no way to come in here!" Straight thundered. "Is that the way you interview people? Well, it won't do."

Some weeks later Straight was working away in his office when the door was flung open and a wild figure seized him by the lapels, hammered on his desk, and demanded a fifteen-dollar-a-week pay hike. It was Gillespie. Straight immediately upped him five dollars and delighted in telling the story on himself.

And so I became part of the *Vancouver Sun* stable, now under the aegis of Hal Straight and the two young Cromies, whose father had set the pattern for journalistic enterprise by secretly slipping his favourite columnist, the late Bob Bouchette, an occasional five-dollar bill to attack the paper's editorials. (The whole enterprise was too much for poor Bouchette, who in the end walked quietly out into the waters of English Bay to his death.) The Cromie scions were cut from their father's cloth. They had the effervescence of youth, and they did not look like newspaper tycoons. They wore loud jackets and even louder ties. They played with Yo-Yos during business meetings. They partied with members of their own staff, all of whom called them by their first names, and they gave Hal Straight his head.

Not everyone liked Hal Straight. Some despised him; some of his staff were terrified of him; his rivals hated him. But most admired him, and he was, in my opinion, not only the best managing editor in Vancouver but also the best in Canada for the kind of newspaper the *Vancouver Sun* was.

For the *Sun* ran second to the good, grey *Province*, whose circulation was at least twenty thousand greater. The second paper in any town must always try harder. It cannot afford to rest on its laurels and it can never be conservative in its coverage. It is forced into stunts, eccentricities, wild, imaginative schemes, and a colourful style. Or at least that was the theory then, and that was the *Vancouver Sun* in the mid-1940s under Straight and the Cromies. It was the perfect place for a young man of twenty-five, fresh out of the army, disillusioned with his old job, bursting with energy and ambition, and loving every moment of what we called, with stunning accuracy, "the newspaper game."

It could scarcely be called a profession. In those days there were no professional associations, no watchdogs or journalistic ombudsmen, no codes of ethics, and no standards. It occurs to me now that the paper was run more for the pleasure of the staff than for the edification of the reader. That staff was a mixed bag. There were several old-timers who seemed to me to be in a state of perpetual intoxication. I would come into the office after a late assignment and there would be Jack King or Bill Short, both seated at their desks, pecking out stories. It was unnerving to discover that both men were so drunk they literally couldn't speak. Yet they continued to type coherent copy that would, on the following afternoon, be read by thousands.

Most of the newer and younger men and women had come over from the *News-Herald*. When Jack Scott finally returned from overseas, I gave him the same warning that Ralph Daly had given me. "Don't go back; it's not the same." But, as I had, Scott ignored the warning to discover, also as I had, that it wasn't like the old days. Straight reached out for him and Scott was soon writing his popular "Our Town" column for the *Sun*.

One day on the golf course, Straight ran into Slim Delbridge, who congratulated him on the *Sun's* brilliant coverage of a civic election.

"You did a great job, Hal," said Delbridge in his booming voice. "A great job."

"Yes, we did," said Straight, adding wickedly, "and we did it with your cast-offs."

Straight had stolen the best city editor in town from the *Province* to replace Pat Terry, who went back to reporting. Himie Koshevoy was widely known as the town's leading student of the pun. It was a joy to work on the city desk with him, for he was a master of the fast quip. Almost every news story brought a play on words. Francisco Franco, the director of Spain, was "the cynosure of all ayes." A newly formed Marital League was, according to Koshevoy, "compiling spatting averages." Kindergarten teachers planning a convention were "girding themselves for prattle." "Give a thief enough rope and he'll smoke," Koshevoy once remarked as his eyes swept across a news story about a captured burglar. The papers were already printing stories about the future of jet aircraft travel, when planes would leap oceans in a few hours or, as Koshevoy put it, "Eire today and Guam tomorrow."

From the city desk I was moved to the rim of the news desk, where I wrote headlines and edited copy under the gimlet eye of the man in the slot of the horseshoe desk, a morose character named Hickey. Hickey was known as a slasher. No matter how good a story was, no matter how compactly written, no matter how compelling the prose, Hickey would find a way to cut it. One afternoon, when the city edition had been put to bed and Straight, Koshevoy, and I were lounging behind the city desk, a group of midgets entered the editorial office, accompanied by a press agent from the Clyde Beatty circus. Straight watched as the little people headed off to one of the reporter's desks to be interviewed, then turned to Koshevoy and me. "Do you realize," he said, "that they were normal size until they passed Hickey?"

Hickey dealt out news stories like cards, his face never changing expression. He rarely if ever spoke. If he wanted to communicate with one of us, he would scribble a note on a piece of copy paper. If he was angry or the note was urgent, he'd scribble it in red pencil. Only at night, after the paper was put to bed, did Hickey's character undergo a remarkable metamorphosis.

For Hickey, in his off hours, was proprietor of the Newspaper Club, one of several so-called private clubs that had a licence to sell liquor to its members in an otherwise bone-dry city where draft beer was the only legal devil's brew. Of course, you didn't have to be in the newspaper game to be a member of Hickey's club. Anybody could join and anybody did, even some newspapermen. In these environs Hickey took on a radically different persona, greeting copy readers like me with genuine enthusiasm, slapping me on the back, propelling me to the bar, and talking volubly all the time: "Great to see you, boys! Come on in! Make yourselves at home! The first drink's on me, fellas," and so on. Hickey the taciturn slot man had become Hickey the genial boniface — a transformation as startling in its own way as Jekyll to Hyde.

This was the era of the headline shorthand and the all-purpose newspaper cliché. Cadis, solons, thugs, and yeggs romped through the paper, rapping, hitting, scoring, and otherwise making news. The reason Bill Short and Jack King and others could peck out acceptable news stories under the influence of cheap rye was that most stories were written to a formula. The cliché is the shorthand of communication, and we all made the most of it. People never fell out of windows or off cliffs; they hurtled or plummeted. They didn't jump; they plunged. They didn't flee *from* a burning building. They simply fled it. And they always fled in night attire.

Prices didn't just go up: they spiralled or soared. When they dropped, they tumbled. Restaurant proprietors were always genial; lifeguards were always bronzed; anybody over fifty was aged, and if he lived alone he was "an aged recluse." Anybody in skirts under the age of forty was automatically pretty. Pretty blonde cashiers foil holdups; pretty divorcees were held as material witnesses; pretty mothers of three awaited word about lost aircraft. Any aircraft, lost or otherwise, that carried a sick person aboard was automatically making a "mercy flight."

Tycoons, moguls, and titans were known as mystery men but never as mysterious men. Fires were mystery blazes, explosions were freak explosions (never freakish), and most mystery blazes were discovered in the nick of time by faithful dogs. Thugs and yeggs never hit people; they slugged or bludgeoned. "Hit" was a headline word, like "rap" reserved for politicians, whose hits, mercifully, were all verbal. Bandits staged daring daylight holdups before 5 p.m., daring night raids after supper. Criminals never escaped; they smashed their way to freedom. When police pursued them; it was invariably a "wild chase."

Police witnesses survived courtroom dramas, stolid and unshaken. Other witnesses testified nervously, confidently, or in a voice that was barely audible. Prisoners, after sentencing, were either visibly shaken or betrayed no emotion.

I soaked up all this verbal lore under Hickey's tutelage and felt proud that I was able to write the language so skilfully. I learned that local politicians always turned thumbs down on a proposal unless they gave it the green light. When they had nothing to say to the press, which was most of the time, they were MUM in headlines, "tightlipped" in the copy. They attended parleys, slashed estimates, scrapped prospective plans — all "behind closed doors." Local boys always made good. Dogs invariably saved small children in mystery blazes. Veteran newsmen, when they died, "wrote thirty to a varied career." *Would they write that about me when I went?* I gave it a little thought.

I looked upon these well-worn catch-phrases with wry amusement and some understanding. After all, when you have ten minutes to write a fifteen-paragraph news story and perhaps two minutes to edit it on the desk, there is little time for elegant variation. Often enough we rattled off these stories without realizing how remarkably similar some of them were; those who did come to realize it after several years of reporting the same kind of thing became too jaded to care. We went through seasonal cycles in which the same stories and the same pat phrases popped up again and again — like the Community Chest drives that always "went over the top as Vancouverites opened their hearts" or the winter fog that never covered the city but always shrouded, mantled, curtained, or cloaked it. Accidents, drownings, hold-ups, murders, and hangings each had their own set of bromides, which could be hauled out when required: victims who "cheated death" or "fought for their lives"; cancer victims who "lost a long battle" with the disease. Nobody in newspaper parlance expired gracefully. Life on the news pages was a constant struggle in which human beings were pitted against each other or against the implacable forces of nature.

There was a sense of *déjà vu* in all this that was, on occasion, justified. When I was on the desk we carried a non-interview with Tallulah Bankhead — a clever enough piece in which the reporter explained why he had been unable to meet the star personally. Only after it was printed did another reporter point out that *he* had written the same story about Miss Bankhead almost word for word, a few years before.

No one was more amused by all this than Harry Filion, who took a sardonic joy in newspaper clichés in general and those of Jack Nilan in particular. Filion had been assigned to the *Sun's* New Westminster bureau, where Nilan was chief. Each year Harry waited for Nilan's description of autumn coming to the Fraser Valley, and he was never disappointed because Nilan never changed the story's wording.

He called me once from New Westminster, positively chortling with delight.

"He's done it again," cried Filion. "It's in today's paper." I reached over for the New Westminster edition and there it was: "The Fraser Valley was a riot of colour today as Mother

Nature dipped her brush in Jack Frost's colours . . ." Word for word from the previous year and no one, apparently, except for Harry Filion, any the wiser.

Filion and I set out to invent the perfect *Vancouver Sun* headline — one that would incorporate all the elements that we deskmen were encouraged to use to sell a story.

We came up, at last with this one:

TALKING DOG SAVES
CRIPPLED CHILD ACTRESS
IN MYSTERY BLAZE

A worthy attempt, certainly, but not really on a par with an actual streamer line that had appeared some years before in a New York tabloid:

NAILED FATHER'S HEAD TO FRONT DOOR

That was still talked about in the office with both awe and envy.

The best headline I wrote for the *Sun* in those days was never used. Hickey had handed me the lead story for that day — one calculated to create a sensation in the city. It revealed that the daughter of a Vancouver florist had married Father Devine, the black cult leader who himself made regular headlines. I took one look at the lead and scribbled the perfect line on a piece of copy paper.

LOCAL GAL MAKES GOD

I passed it on to Hickey; at the very least I expected a half-smile on that impassive face. But he did not change expression. Not by the flicker of an eyelid or the quiver of a lower lip did he acknowledge my genius. He took his red pencil, scratched out my words, and replaced them with a more prosaic and, doubtless, more acceptable line, something like:

CITY WOMAN WEDS NEGRO "DEITY"

I didn't want to see my brainchild confined to limbo, and

so I wrote the line again and passed it across to Himie Koshevoy, my mentor in the art of punning. I knew he would appreciate it and he did. Himie made no attempt to steal my pun, but he was so well known in the field that when the story of the headline got around it was attributed to him. It's time I set the record straight.

I suffered one other disappointment while working on the rim of the horseshoe desk. For months I had been waiting for safecrackers to revisit the town of Hammond, British Columbia; I had the headline already written:

HAMMOND YEGGS
STRIKE AGAIN!

Weeks went by. Yeggs struck at other B.C. towns, vanishing with the swag after the usual wild police chase, in which innocent bystanders cheated death. But Hammond remained undefiled. Yeggs hit at Richmond. Yeggs struck at Langly. Yeggs blew up safes in New Westminster. But there was no Hammond Yeggs.

Then, at last, it happened. A safe in a Hammond store was splintered and looted. Alas, it all took place on my day off. The dolt who took my place on the desk had no poetry in his soul:

He wrote:

CRACKSMEN HIT
HAMMOND STORE

Shortly after that Straight gave me a raise and put me on the hotel and waterfront beat. I was happy for a change. My talents as a headline writer, I felt, were not really appreciated.

3 Janet Walker came from the Hammond area. Her parents ran a general store in nearby Haney, a community remarkably free of yeggs. She was by this time my closest woman companion. We had known each other for seven

years since that day when she first smiled on me so sunnily in the offices of the *Ubyssey*. We were, in the popular Hollywood phrase of the day, "just good friends," never lovers. I played the field, to use another current phrase.

I was still living at home with my mother and sister. Young men did not move out of the family nest then as early as they do now. Apart from any moral considerations, there was a desperate post-war housing shortage. You couldn't get an apartment in all of Vancouver.

Sometimes I brought girls home for a cup of coffee after a movie. My mother did not always approve, though she was too shrewd to voice her opinions. She was coming to terms with her widowhood and had not lost her dry sense of humour. "I'll be in bed by the time you get home tonight with whoever it is you're seeing," she said to me once. "But I'll *hear* you. So I want you to whistle a lot. Just keep whistling and I'll know you're not getting into trouble."

And so, to the bafflement of various young women seated awkwardly beside me on the chesterfield, I whistled for the fun of it so my mother would appreciate the joke. We became very close, she and I. (I scarcely saw Lucy, who was taking a business course and was involved with her own social life.) She would show me rough drafts of manuscripts, eager for my opinion. I wasn't as harsh with her as I'd been in my teens. It wasn't really important that she be published, but it was important that she keep busy.

With the exception of Janet, I rarely dated the same girl more than twice. I took one pretty teacher out on a Friday night and before I could invite her for the following evening she'd decamped for the B.C. interior, where she met another man and married him within a week. Perhaps I should have felt jilted, but, in fact, I viewed her departure with relief. In contrast to Janet, they all paled. Janet was the one girl I felt right with and the only one for whom my mother didn't require me to whistle. We saw a lot of each other, for we travelled with the same university and newspaper crowd. More and more I found myself taking her out — and not always at the last moment.

What a wonderful politician's wife she'd make, I thought. She loved kissing babies. She loved talking to people I considered boring, and she was genuinely interested in their wives, spouses, children, jobs, interests. *Any man running for office would be a shoo-in,* I thought, *if he had her on the platform with him.* I found myself secretly hoping that no budding politician — there were several in the offing — would be smart enough to carry her off.

Of course I was in love with her, but I wouldn't admit it to myself and certainly not to her. I was, in fact, stubbornly resisting the increasing pressure from family and friends to make the obvious move. At the same time I began to feel that the handsome young men who danced attendance on her weren't good enough for her. Indeed, I came to the conclusion that they were all slightly moronic, which suggests the depth of my feeling. On several occasions I got up the nerve to propose — but only after fortifying myself heavily with drink. She refused to take these maudlin expressions of affection seriously. "Ask me when you're sober," she'd say, "and then we'll see."

She put me to her famous Grouse Mountain test, which I failed miserably. In the company of a horde of athletic young men, she lured me up the mountain to a ski chalet. The athletic young men bustled about doing all the right things: chopping wood, building fires, cooking meals, and skiing. I didn't ski — didn't want to, didn't know how. I refused to do chores. While the others were proving themselves fit husbands, I lay on a couch, guzzling gin. I had clearly blotted my copy-book. Or had I? When the others went off for a wholesome afternoon on the slopes, Janet lingered behind. My memory is that she even had some of my gin. The famous Grouse Mountain test was supposed to separate the eligibles from the ineligibles — to finger and eliminate the layabouts and wastrels. I had failed the test, no doubt about it; but in the end it was the test itself that was a failure. She married me.

By February we had an understanding, to use an old-fashioned word. When I told my mother that I intended to marry Janet, she was immensely pleased: at long last one of her children was settled! It was not until I had children of my own that I finally understood the strain she was under. Would I never settle down? What if I married an impossible person? Or what if I married and simply continued drinking and tom-catting (my father's favourite word), sinking deeper and deeper into what she thought of as debauchery? In short, was I going to make something of myself or wasn't I?

She had always been ambitious for me — more ambitious, perhaps, than I was for myself. But I don't think she believed I could make it alone, hanging around Greasy Alex's or the White Spot, where Lord knew what temptations lurked. No; I needed an anchor, a helpmate, somebody sensible enough to curb my natural tendency to waywardness; and that person was Janet. I could see the look of relief that crossed her face when I broke the news. Down we went together to O.B. Allan's jewellery store to pick out a diamond ring in a fancy setting — not too big but not too small, either. It cost me five weeks' pay, which was about all I had.

I still hadn't formalized the offer. Janet, I knew, was a stickler for ritual. She would insist on ceremony, and she would want me to ask her father for her hand, and she would want a white wedding.

As a mark of my esteem, I decided to take her to the finals of the Golden Gloves out at Hastings Park. Something told me I shouldn't hand her the ring while two brawny young men were pounding at each other's faces, and so I held off. When the bouts were over I took her down to Stanley Park, found a suitably romantic bench, and there, in the moonlight, we plighted our troth, as Filion insisted on saying. "Few troths," he said with satisfaction, "have ever been plighted to greater applause."

Weddings made news in those days, and the newspapers always looked after their own. We might be poorly paid, but when we married, gave birth, won an award, or died, we could be sure that a few paragraphs would be reserved for the occasion. Both papers greeted the coming nuptuals in typical fashion. The *Province's* compositors actually lost the first line of the lead of its story, thus confusing all its readers. The *Sun's* headline was misspelled: "WIDLY KNOWN NEWSPA-PER COUPLE TO WED." Years later, when I moved into the Famous Celebrity class, Filion still insisted on referring to me as "widly known."

Janet, of course, had to quit the *Province.* (It occurred to nobody in those pre-feminist days that I might quit the *Sun.*) Straight was delighted, for she was a first-rate reporter who often single-handedly beat out the *Sun's* platoon coverage. It was a newspaper wedding. Harry was best man. Himie Koshevoy and Ralph Daly were ushers (Jack Scott was still overseas), and Bill Forst, the *Province's* managing editor, was engaged, to his personal delight, to sing "O Promise Me." We spent a brief honeymoon in Seattle and returned to Janet's small apartment in Stanley Park Manor in Vancouver's West End. She had shared it with a girl friend who had been her bridesmaid at the wedding and who now gracefully retired. Apartments were still almost impossible to come by in the spring of 1946, and there were those who claimed I married Janet because she was the only girl I knew that occupied one. The rent was forty-five dollars a month; my weekly salary then was no more than fifty.

These were carefree, romantic times. Our bachelor apart-ment was so small that when the Murphy bed was pulled down from the wall it filled the room. The kitchen wasn't much bigger than a broom closet. None of this mattered, of course. We were married and in love; I kicked myself for having waited so long. Stanley Park, with its thousand acres of natural rain forest, was only a block and a half away. In the late afternoon and early evenings we'd stroll hand in hand along the seawall, or visit the zoo, or take in the Theatre Under the Stars, or rent bicycles or horses or even a boat, to enjoy the water, the sand, and the brooding mysterious forest. This was our backyard, and we made the most of it.

I was still soaking up culture. We went to concerts of the Vancouver Symphony on press passes — Bernstein, Klemperer, Barbirolli had all been engaged as guest conductors in those days. We'd been given a twenty-five-dollar record player as a wedding gift, and, using cactus needles, we listened to Mozart, Bach, Haydn, and even William Walton. I squandered a week's salary on a vast collection of prints brought back from Europe by an army veteran who needed ready cash: these included everything from a book on Nazi architecture to *Seize Peintures*, a volume of Matisse's newest work published by Skira in Switzerland. I had never heard of Matisse, but we framed several of these prints, which some of my friends deplored as the daubings of a madman. I did not know then that half a century earlier Matisse had been called a wild beast by his contemporaries. We were a little behind the times in Vancouver.

My job at this period was to interview Famous Celebrities in various stages of undress. I interviewed Basil Rathbone in his bathrobe, Richard Greene in his underwear, Jack Teagarden while he pulled on his pants, and the entire Philadelphia Symphony Orchestra in their nightshirts (aboard a Pullman car). The reason for this *déshabillé* was that the deadline for the noon edition of the *Sun* was 10 a.m. That meant I had to grab an interview and write the story, all by nine-thirty. To do that I was forced to invade the hotel rooms of the stars while they were still half asleep. I walked into Oscar Peterson's room and shook him by the shoulder to get him out of bed. Eugenie Leontovich, the European stage actress, tried to stop me when I telephoned her from the lobby. "I jost voke opp!" she gasped. I thought she'd said "just walk up," and so I did. She had cream on her face, curlers in her hair, and a scared look on her face.

Yet none of these people seemed to mind. After all, they had spent much of their careers being interviewed by newspapermen while half asleep. They answered my questions amiably between yawns as if it was the most natural thing in the world, which, I suppose, it was, to them. They needed me as much as I needed them, for each was in town for a purpose, and so it was an even trade. I got my story, they got publicity. I asked stock questions, they gave me stock answers. It wasn't really news, for they had said the same things in Los Angeles, Las Vegas, New York, and Chicago. In most cases when I tackled them, they had already said it all the very day before in Seattle. But by the peculiar standards under which we operated, what was news in Seattle on a Wednesday wasn't news in Vancouver until they arrived in the city and said it all over again on Thursday.

I loved the work. I interviewed everybody from Yvette Dare and her Sarong-Stealing Parrot to Evelyn West, the Hubba Hubba Girl, whose hubbas had been insured for an astronomical sum by Lloyd's of London and was happy to pose for a gag photo wearing a tiny towel while I, blindfolded, sat on the edge of her bathtub and scribbled in my notebook. All these various Well-Known Personalities made believe that I was the first person to interview them, and all of them asked me to look them up when I came to Hollywood. We treated their profundities as gospel. Edgar Bergen explained that all future television programs would be shorter than radio programs because nobody would be able to stand looking at one show for more than ten minutes. Ziggy Elman, Goodman's great trumpeter, forecast that the kids would go back to listening to the classics because Tin Pan Alley had made the classics popular. Donald Mills of the Mills Brothers predicted the jukebox would kill radio music. Blackstone the magician dismissed the great Harry Houdini as "that lockpicker."

It wasn't enough to get the story. We reporters tried our damnedest to become part of it, because that would ensure a first-person account and a by-line in eight-point bold caps. One man actually tore off his clothes and got into the shower to sing a damp duet with a visiting tenor. I tried my best to get into the cage with the world's most famous lion tamer, Clyde Beatty. He put me off with a single chilling sentence. "They'd gobble you alive," he said. But when the first one-day shirt service opened in Vancouver I was there at the head of the line to have my shirt washed in a day and write about it. It's hard to believe that the novelty was so great then that my story made an eight-column headline on the *Sun's* section page.

Once I got myself hired as a spear carrier in a production of *Aida* by the itinerant San Carlo Opera Company, which took on locals as extras. A small, squat man with a fedora on his head and a half-chewed cigar in his mouth rehearsed us in the triumphal march between acts. Because I was tall I was chosen to lead the way. I paid careful attention, remembering the dreadful hash I'd made of my last attempt leading the choir the wrong way in St. Paul's Cathedral in Dawson. It went off without a hitch. There I stood in Egyptian costume complete with wig, hammering my spear in time to Verdi's music as the Welsh tenor, Mostwyn Thomas, was dragged on stage in his captive's cage. As I headed out the stage door following that scene (composing the lead for my feature story in my head), a gaunt figure emerged from the crowd and humbly asked for my autograph. Flattered, I searched for a pencil and looked into a familiar face. It was the mad Professor Francis, eyes expectant, hand outreached, and muttering a humble thank you.

There were no tape recorders in those days, and I'm not sure I would have used one anyway; there was scarcely time to transcribe an entire interview or even listen to it on a machine. I scribbled my notes, not on scattered sheets of old copy paper or the backs of cigarette boxes, as some of my colleagues did, but in a specially designed notebook that fitted snugly into my jacket pocket. I had the *Sun* make up copies of this invention, but as far as I know, I was the only one who used it. I had to work quickly. I'd figure out the lead paragraph of my story — the one that incorporated what we then called "the angle" — on the Number 1 streetcar that took me back to the Sun Tower from the Georgia or the Hotel Vancouver. If a famous celebrity had anything nice to say about the city, that, of course, *was* the story. Vancouverites ate it up, and the visitors made life easy for us scribblers by playing the game. *"Christopher Morley, novelist and book club judge, came to Vancouver today and described the city as 'Elysian' because it has so many secondhand bookstores."* I'd lope into the *Sun* office with a piece like that and start to type as soon as I hit my desk.

In the afternoons, I covered the waterfront, a coveted assignment for me. When friends asked me what I did on the paper I always replied: "I cover the waterfront." They were duly impressed. The phrase had entered the language thanks to a best-selling book, a movie, and a popular song, all with that title.

My own approach to the waterfront was equally romantic. Other reporters may have seen it more prosaically as a rather grubby collection of fish docks, grain elevators, and battered wharves, but to me it was the crossroads of the world, full of strange craft from exotic climes. This view of the Vancouver harbour undoubtedly helped my coverage. I was convinced that there was a story in every ship anchored there and that every captain and crew member had something in his background worth recounting. I was often right. There were former Liberty ships with adventurous wartime backgrounds, old sea dogs who had been shipwrecked several times, stowaways pleading to be given a new home, pet rats and canine mascots who had never known terra firma, stateless people living on the ocean, refugees fleeing from foreign oppression — all fuel for my typewriter.

I decided the best way to cover the waterfront was to hire a boat. Janet and I would pick up a tiny put-put for a dollar an hour at Stanley Park entrance and cruise the harbour. I'd climb aboard ship after ship, nosing out the news. Technically, my job came under the marine editor, with whom I had a running feud. Each day he would tell me there was nothing doing on the waterfront; each day I'd set out to prove him wrong. On one such newsless afternoon I came back to the office at five with seven waterfront stories. It occurs to me now that if he hadn't got my dander up I mightn't have come back with any. Perhaps he did it on purpose, but I rather doubt it. He left the *Sun* shortly after that and went back to teaching school.

We were locked in an absurd struggle with the *Province*, in which the most minor scoop was hailed as a victory. A story lost, no matter how inconsequential, was an occasion for mass mourning. Since only a handful of Vancouverites took both papers, these journalistic tussels had little meaning to our readers, who didn't really care whether we beat the *Province* by a few hours or not. But, as Straight used to say, it was good for office morale, and it added a certain zest to life. We may not have been advancing the cause of journalism in Vancouver in the late forties, but we were all having a wonderful time.

Straight used to infuriate the *Province's* editors by shameless acts of thievery. He stole the climax of one hugely successful campaign right from under their noses by an artful but ancient device. A little girl had had her nose bitten off by a dog, and the rival paper had exploited the story to the full, launching a front page campaign to have her sent to a Boston clinic to repair the damage; "Little Miss No Nose," I believe they called her, employing the high standards of good taste that were a hallmark of Vancouver journalism in those days. When the child emerged with her new nose, the *Province* was permitted to snap an exclusive photgraph, which it ran on the front page in its first edition. That was a mistake; the first edition was a street edition seen by a few thousand people only. Straight had the photograph copied from the *Province's* front page and ordered the staff artist to paint a doll in the child's arms to forestall any charges of plagiarism. It ran, even bigger, in the *Sun's* Home Edition.

When the *Province* at considerable expense purchased exclusive rights to a rare interview with Joseph Stalin by one of the young Roosevelts, Straight was ready. On this occasion the rival paper kept the story out of the early edition, knowing that Straight would try to steal it. Straight outwitted them. He had learned that the Toronto *Star* had also bought the rights to the story and because of the time differenc would be running it three hours ahead of the Vancouver release time. So he simply called Robert Taylor, a *Star* reporter who was also a *Vancouver Sun* stringer, to wire him the Roosevelt interview as soon as it appeared in Toronto. The story was published in the *Sun* under Taylor's by-line as follows:

By ROBERT TAYLOR

TORONTO — The *Star* in its early edition today reports that Elliott Roosevelt has interviewed Joseph Stalin, the Soviet dictator. Here is the text of the Roosevelt interview:

The entire interview followed, word for word — in the *Sun's* Noon Edition, two hours before it appeared "exclusively" in the *Province.* These triumphs were, of course, immensely satisfying, but with Straight it was the fray that counted. He enjoyed entering the lists even when there was no reward. One weekend, Ray Munro, the most flamboyant of the *Sun's* photographers, hired at considerable expense a steamroller to block the highway leading into Vancouver from the Fraser canyon, where a disaster of some sort had occurred. The *Province* photographer was held up for several hours, but since all this happened on a Sunday when no paper was published, it really didn't matter. Nonetheless Straight gave Munro an immediate raise. It was a signal to all of us that such enterprise would not go unrewarded in the future.

I still remember the afternoon when the final edition had gone to bed and a telephone call to the city desk reported a minor fire at the Terminal Dock in the city's East End.

"Doesn't sound like much," Himie Koshevoy said to me, "but maybe you'd better get down there and check into it."

At that moment, Hal Straight entered the city room.

"What the hell," he said, "there's not much doing here. Let's send a couple of carloads of reporters and photographers to the waterfront and scare the hell out of the *Province!*"

Off we all went, tumbling out of the *Sun* cars, notebooks and copypaper in view, pencils scribbling, flashbulbs popping. The *Province's* sole waterfront man looked panic-stricken, rushed to the phone, and pleaded for reinforcements. I returned to the office and typed out a single-paragraph story: the fire, such as it was, had been swiftly extinguished.

But the following day the *Province* came out with banner headlines and pictures on the front page.

Straight gazed at it ruefully. "Goddam it," he said. "We've been scooped on our own story."

By the summer of 1946 I had become one of the paper's leading reporters, covering stories of passion and revenge, murder and suicide, fire, flood and accident. Straight also invented the Stanley Park beat for me. It had never occurred to any paper that there might be news stories lurking in those dark, mysterious glades. But, like so many other Vancouverites, Straight was a devotee of the great park with its ring of white beaches, its famous Lost Lagoon, and its gigantic red cedars. It became a kind of ritual for the two of us to visit the park just after the Noon Edition went to press. We'd order grilled cheese sandwhiches from the stand at Prospect Point, gulp a few mouthfuls of rye, and enjoy the cries of the seagulls, the slap of the waves on the breakwater, and the moan of the wind rustling the Douglas firs above our heads.

One day as we swilled away at Straight's bottle of Canadian Club, a policeman trotted by on a magnificent black horse. I panicked. Drinking in Stanley Park was illegal;

drinking in the open in a car — and in front of a mounted policeman — was simple insanity. But Straight took it all calmly.

"Have a drink, officer," he said, thrusting the open bottle out the window.

"Well, thank you, Mr. Straight," said the policeman. "Don't mind if I do." And he downed a big slug.

This encounter produced a feature story for the *Sun* when the policeman revealed that he and his colleagues were about to lose their horses. Straight was scandalized: how could anybody patrol those sinister glades on foot? He vowed it would never happen and, thanks to the *Sun's* clout and my exposé, it didn't.

But we were still the second paper. "Goddam it, Hal," Scott said one Saturday night as we drank rye whisky in Straight's kitchen, "we're putting out the liveliest paper in Canada and we still can't get to first base against the *Province*. What do we need for God's sake?"

To which Straight replied, "What we need is an act of God and when it comes, we'll be ready."

He was right, of course. Eventually it did come, in the form of a disastrous printers' strike at the *Province* that reversed forever the position of the two leading papers in town.

I think we were all slightly demented in that first post-war summer. Five of us — Straight, Koshevoy, Scott, Filion, and myself — would sit in the office after the paper had been put to bed, sucking on bottles of rye and talking about how to improve the *Sun*. Sometimes we would roam all over town, like small boys out of school. We happened upon a street carnival, leaped upon the painted horses of a carousel, and whirled about, firing make-believe pistols at each other like Wild West bandits. We rolled up our trousers, removed our shoes and socks, and waded across the shallow Capilano River in North Vancouver. We hired an elderly black banjo player and marched behind him down Pender Street in the heart of Chinatown, searching for chow mein. We pranced

316

out onto the dizzy Capilano Suspension Bridge on which was posted a warning sign: "NO SWINGING ON THE BRIDGE." And there, in the late afternoon sunlight, we ignored the order and swung like crazy — five men charged with the awesome responsibility of guiding the destinies of one of Canada's largest newspapers.

In spite of all this excitement and tomfoolery, in spite of the fact that I had been accepted as a key member of the club, a tiny ember of discontent was smouldering somewhere within me — not yet an ember, really, not much more than a spark; but it was there. On the one hand, I was enjoying myself; on the other, I felt a vague sense of dissatisfaction. I was working hard and successfully, getting by-lines, enjoying the respect of my peers and superiors. But where was it all leading? What was my future? I had no plan and, in a sense, no purpose except to do my job as well as I could. I wanted something more, but what? Scott, Filion, and I were forever conjuring up vast enterprises that would make us all rich. We would launch a public relations firm or a new magazine or write a big-time radio comedy program. On Sunday afternoons we lay on the beach in front of Scott's West Vancouver home with our wives, dreaming impossible dreams. But the sun was always too warm, the sand too soft, the sea too enticing, the rye whisky too inviting.

"It's probably just as well we're poor," Filion said to me one night as we sat in his kitchen in the rented basement of a Shaughnessy mansion.

"We'd be drunk all the time," I said.

"You got it."

We turned the bottle upside down, trying to coax a few more drops from it. In the tiny living room Janet was helping Veryl change the diapers of the Filions' new daughter, Vicki. Filion cocked an eye at me.

"How could we be so incredibly clever," Filion asked, "to have married those two? I must say it took a certain genius on our part."

I nodded. "Incredibly clever of us," I said.

"We could have made a terrible error," said Filion.

"Or a series of errors," I added.

"They'll be the making of us," he said; and, of course, he was right.

This was Vancouver's Jubilee summer. The city was about to turn sixty — a fortunate anniversary for me because it got me into the radio business. Scott had been commissioned by the CBC to write and read four fifteen-minute broadcasts about Vancouver, past and present. But Scott had a horror of any kind of public appearance. He was himself a public figure because of his column, by far the best read and admired piece of journalism in the province. The words seemed to flow effortlessly from him, but the composition of that daily pillar of type actually caused him excruciating mental anguish. A lively and often raucous presence when among his drinking cronies, he was otherwise an intensely private man. He couldn't bear to make a speech in public. The idea of appearing on radio appalled him. So he turned the job over to me, and I grabbed it.

These four talks in the summer of 1946 led later to a weekly series called *City Desk* (complete with ringing telephone and shouted calls for "Copy!") in which I spun yarns about everything from the newspaper business to drug addiction. It was the beginning of a radio career that would continue for forty years, almost without a break.

My early broadcasts were a tiny part of Vancouver's ambitious celebrations to mark its Golden Jubilee. The city was planning a gigantic outdoor historical pageant in Stanley Park, and before many weeks went by I became very much a part of these plans. Thus began my brief involvement with an extraordinary man named John Harkrider.

Harkrider had been plucked out of Hollywood to produce and direct the Stanley Park pageant. A health faddist, he arrived at the Hotel Vancouver with a couple of crates of grapefruit and raw cabbage as well as two physical young men whom, it was said, he had hired to wrestle with him daily. It is a measure of my naïveté in those days that I did not question the presence of the wrestlers or cotton on to the fact that Harkrider, the health nut and food faddist, was also gay.

Harkrider commissioned a script for the great pageant from two of the city's best-known broadcasters, Dorwin Baird and Dick Diespecker of radio station CJOR. One was assigned to write the prehistory of Vancouver, the other the post-CPR period. They threw everything they had into it — several hundred pages, in fact. Both were exhausted, but Part 3, which was to deal with post-war Vancouver, hadn't yet been written. At this point, I received a telegram from Harkrider summoning me to his suite in the Hotel Vancouver.

When I arrived, one of the tame wrestlers met me at the door, balancing a tray heaped high with celery and carrots.

"Take some!" he said, and it sounded like an order.

Within the suite were show-business people, all munching on raw vegetables and saying things like, "Oh, that's very visual, John!" or "I'm beginning to get the full concept now, John!"

"Send a wire to Lucio Agostini," Harkrider was saying. "I want to talk music."

Somebody pointed out that Agostini, then the best-known musical director in radio, was actually *living* in the hotel, having come in from Toronto, and was only one floor down from Harkrider.

"*Send him a wire!*" said Harkrider. Somebody went to the phone, called the telegraph company, and dictated a wire that was eventually phoned back to a bewildered Agostini in his hotel room.

For one hundred dollars I was engaged to complete Part 3 of the script.

One of my problems was to figure out a way to work two

fading American Name Stars, Eddie Cantor, the comedian, and John Charles Thomas, the baritone, into the local scenery. The difficulty was complicated by the fact that Thomas had been given three fat roles — Captain Vancouver, Sir William Van Horne, builder of the CPR, and finally "Mr. Vancouver," or what Harkrider kept calling the Symbolic Figure.

In order to save Thomas from the impossible task of memorizing several thousand words of script in just twenty-four hours, Harkrider had come up with another device — a sort of alter ego — a second Symbolic Figure. He engaged a local actor to learn all of Thomas's lines and then to walk a foot or so behind him — the Man of Action supporting the Man of Vision — and speak all the words while Thomas warbled "Open Road," "Shortnin' Bread," and other favourites from his repertoire, which, though they had nothing to do with Vancouver, were the only kind he knew.

I worked Cantor into the script more simply. My section of the pageant revolved around the conceit that the modern symbolic figures, Mr. and Mrs. Vancouver and all the little Vancouvers, were throwing a big party at which Eddie Cantor would make a guest appearance. He would come on in blackface to tell American jokes, sing some old favourites from Tin Pan Alley, and then encourage young Bert Vancouver to do his Carmen Miranda act. *Carmen Miranda?* The Latin American singer who wore bananas in her hair? The very same. It so happened that that was the chief stock-in-trade of the one local performer whom Harkrider had hired as a concession to local pride.

And so I churned out my section of the great pageant under Harkrider's direction after endless story conferences. Story conferences! A Hollywood director! I was seduced by the glamour of it all. Harkrider said my stuff was wonderful and told me I ought to go at once to Hollywood. Was this to be my future? Alas, in the end he used scarcely a word of mine.

It poured with rain right up until the night of the show, making dress rehearsals impossible on the vast stage that had been specially constructed in Stanley Park. Opening night was a disaster. The show ran on and on past one o'clock. To shorten it, Harkrider threw out the entire script and replaced our dialogue with voice-over narration. That cut the pageant down to size but baffled the audience. Why were there *two* Captain Vancouvers wandering around out there along with the Indians, the Boy Scouts, the army cadets, and the PTA?

The situation was so confused that I bet a friend that I could go on the stage in civilian clothes and mill about unnoticed with all the Vancouverites who were appearing free of charge dressed as Indians, railway workers, and Cariboo prospectors. No one spotted me. I won the bet easily and wrote a front page feature story about my escapade, thus biting one of the hands that were feeding me.

At one point I stumbled upon John Charles Thomas, playing William Van Horne, the Man of Vision, talking to the local actor playing William Van Horne, the Man of Action.

"What's going on here, anyway?" asked the Symbolic Figure in a kind of panic. "What happens next?" But his alter ego, standing a pace behind him, wasn't able to tell him.

And so the great Vancouver pageant lurched to its conclusion. The stars returned to Hollywood. Harkrider left in triumph. The production company that had been paid a flat fee by the city to mount the big show teetered on the lip of bankruptcy. Fortunately, somebody tipped me off and I rushed down and picked up my cheque for a hundred dollars just before the final collapse. It helped pay for a much-needed holiday that Janet and I took at a dude ranch in the Cariboo.

There I had an unexpected encounter. A pretty blonde

chambermaid arrived to clean up our cabin just as we headed out for a horseback ride in the woods. Something about her seemed vaguely familiar, and all during that morning I racked my brain. Where had I seen her before? At last it came back to me. This was the same girl who, in a WRCNS uniform, had sat for so long on a bench at the Regent's Park Zoo in London, while I struggled with my conscience. This was the girl that I had contemplated asking out to dinner. It turned out she was the rancher's daughter. Perhaps it was just as well, I thought, that I had forsaken her for the more cerebral pleasures of Gielgud's *Hamlet*.

4 In common with most papers — especially most second-place papers — the *Vancouver Sun* fed on misfortune. Disaster was our business, bloodshed our stock in trade. Certainly the *Sun* gave full coverage to national and international politics: the great Bruce Hutchison was one of its ornaments. But when a child went missing or a policeman was shot, when bodies were mangled in auto accidents or private citizens were bludgeoned to death, the front page was torn apart and the great international events of the day given short shrift.

In these daily chronicles of human misery I was an active participant. I interviewed my share of distraught parents, bereaved husbands, and new widows. I cannot in honesty say that I was in any way affected by their plight. I did not weep for the victims or feel sympathetic elation for those who, in the newspaper phrase, "cheated death."

Why? I wonder. Was it because we reporters, like physicians and nurses, deliberately remained aloof from human suffering to save our sanity? Was it because we had read too many stories and seen too many movies about "hard-boiled" newsmen of the Chicago school and were playing out a role? Perhaps. But I think the main reason was that none of these tragedies were real. These weren't people I was dealing with;

they were "stories." On top of Burnaby Mountain one grim morning, a doctor's wife was found dead in her car (but with her small baby still miraculously alive) — a victim of post-natal depression. It was a stunning tragedy and a hot story, since the hunt for the missing pair had occupied the best part of a week. But even after I had squeezed the details from the young husband and put them into print, the story seemed remote. It was as if I were watching it on a movie screen and the participants were actors, following a script.

Hard-boiled journalism is a game for young men, preferably single and not too sensitive. I remember in my *News-Herald* days Jack Scott, then a new father, returning haggard from interviewing a young mother who had lost her child in a car accident.

"I can't do any more of these assignments," Scott said. "They're too much for me."

I know now what he meant. I didn't know it then.

I remember once, when I was on the *Sun's* city desk, sending a new woman reporter out to cover a Legion breakfast. I needed a story by ten o'clock for the Noon Edition and was more than annoyed when I didn't hear from her. Nor was I able to contact her in time to make the deadline. Finally she phoned.

"Where the hell's your story?" I asked her.

"There's no story," she said.

"Whaddya mean, no story?"

"They're all sick from some kind of food poisoning."

I put my head in my hands. The oldest chestnut in journalism ("There's no story here, Chief. The church burned down before they could hold the wedding"), and I was its victim!

"Why in God's name didn't you phone?"

"There wasn't time. I was helping out."

Helping out! I could scarcely speak. This was the biggest story in town; she had it in her mitt; and she was helping out! Where were her priorities? The answer is that she had her priorities exactly right; it was my priorities that were wrong. But it was some time before I realized that some things are more important than journalistic scoops.

Janet understood this. She was a good newspaperwoman — calm and unflustered and always accurate, but never so obsessed by the business that she forgot the importance of human relations. Once, a couple of months before our marriage, she had caught on to a scoop by accident sitting in the *Sun* office, waiting for me to finish up. I was working on a story about a "mystery philanthropist" named Ranji McWalker, a man of immense wealth (so it was said) who was announcing legacies of enviable proportions. The *Province* was working on the story to discover something about the background of the mysterious McWalker. But what they didn't know and I had discovered was that McWalker didn't exist: the press and the public had been objects of a mammoth hoax by an experienced hoaxer.

It was this fact that Janet overheard as she waited for me in the *Sun* newsroom. She had a brief struggle with her conscience and, as always, her conscience won. When the story broke — top line, page 1 — she told me about it.

"If it had been me," I told her, "I'd have been on to my city desk in about thirty seconds." I was, after all, one of Hal Straight's boys.

"I know you would," she said. "But I just couldn't."

"Why not?"

"It wouldn't have been right," she said. And then she added: "Besides, it wouldn't have done our friendship much good."

Years later when we were reminiscing about old times, I told her I agreed with her.

"I wouldn't do it now," I said.

"No," she said, "I don't believe you would. You're growing up."

But in those days, to Harry Filion and me the story was everything. More and more we found ourselves working on major news; we made a good team, and Straight and Koshevoy exploited it. More and more we found ourselves hoping for something big, which to us meant something violent. But the big stories were few that season. It was a quiet fall in which buildings refused to collapse, flood waters neither ebbed nor flowed, and domestic relations continued at such an even tenor that no embittered lover or battered wife was to be found brandishing a bloody carving knife or a suspiciously lethal hammer.

We were bored — tired of covering rallies and conventions where men were shown shaking hands with one another or handing out cheques for charity while grinning at the camera. I will not say we hoped for a murder; we weren't that callous. But if a murder should happen, in the orderly statistical course of events, we wanted to be in on it from the beginning, foiling the other papers, bringing exclusive pictures and exclusive stories back to the office.

Then one grey morning, wet and chill, it happened. I was awakened early and told to get over to Deep Cove, a gloomy bay on the north shore of Burrard Inlet, to cover a slaying. Filion picked me up, and the two of us drove across the Lions Gate Bridge in the early dawn and out along the rutted roads of the north shore, through a dark corridor of firs and cedars, soggy with new snow.

The murder had taken place the previous afternoon in the woods overlooking an arm of the sea, but the word had only just got out. A man named Teeporten had been building a woodshed near his cottage, helped by his eighteen-year-old house guest, a lifelong friend. For reasons unknown, the youth had emptied a shotgun into his host's body and then rained blows so furiously upon it that he had broken the butt of the weapon. Following this grisly encounter he had dashed into the house, apparently in a panic, and beaten Teeporten's wife into insensibility while her baby slept in a nearby cot. After that he had fled.

It had taken some time for the news to filter back to the

city, but it was generally believed that the young killer was still lurking in the vicinity and might return at any time, as killers were said to do, to the scene of the crime. It was clearly a big story. Teeporten was well known. The isolated nature of the murder and the apparent lack of motive added the kind of spice that newspaper readers (and newspaper reporters) gobble up.

The scene of the crime was uncannily silent when we arrived. No cordon of police surrounded the house of death. Apart from Filion and myself there wasn't a soul to be seen. The police had been and gone, leaving the door unlatched and a bloody piece of firewood just where the widow's attacker had dropped it. To our enormous satisfaction there was no sign of anybody else from the Vancouver press. We were alone on the very spot that is usually marked with a great X in newspaper photographs — alone in a eerie silence broken only by the steady drip of the snow melting from the evergreens and the moan of a foghorn far out in the Strait of Georgia.

"I bet he's still here," Filion whispered. "In the attic. Climb up and see."

"*You* climb up. Take his picture."

"I'm too big," said Filion quickly, boosting me through the trapdoor in the ceiling.

I peered briefly into the gloom, satisfied myself that the attic was empty, and dropped down again. Filion was standing by to slug the killer. He almost slugged me.

We crept out of the house. En route to the car I noticed a collie crouched beneath the steps. A headline flashed through my mind: "FAITHFUL DOG WAITS VAINLY FOR DEAD MASTER." A good follow-up story. I filed it away for future reference.

We learned from local residents in that small isolated settlement that the murdered man's widow was being cared for by neighbours. Filion said that she'd never talk to us, bereaved and stunned as she was; it would be an invasion of her privacy. I had a feeling she would. During a previous

Vancouver murder, I recalled, the victim's relatives had actually held press conferences.

We knocked on the door of the house where she was sequestered. The owner greeted us enthusiastically. He was a *Sun* subscriber and a "Li'l Abner" fan. "That fella sure does get into some crazy scrapes," he said, chuckling and slapping his thigh. It was to his home that the blood-drenched woman had stumbled the previous day, carrying her baby. As I had suspected, she seemed quite willing, even eager, to tell her story.

As she talked, Harry raised his Speed Graphic to take her picture. She stopped, automatically brushed back a strand of hair, and then broke into a reflex smile, a Pavlovian response from years of candid shots. This invariable reaction was always a problem to photographers taking pictures of people in trouble. As Filion well knew, the paper couldn't use a cut of a murdered man's battered wife smiling cheerfully at the camera.

"Er . . . perhaps something a little more serious, Mrs. Teeporten?" Filion grunted. "Just for contrast?" And that, of course, was the picture we printed.

"What's coming up in 'Li'l Abner'?" our host asked as we left. I told him I was sworn to silence but promised to send along some glossy prints of the pictures we'd taken. We sent the smiling ones.

Did I shed a tear for Mrs. Teeporten? She had gone through a horrifying experience that involved her husband, her baby, and a close friend. Did I put myself in her place and ache for her sorrow? To be honest, I didn't give it a thought. I saw her as a story, not as a person of flesh and blood. I saw her as a picture on page 1, the bandage on her head and the serious expression graphic evidence of her woe. As we drove back to the Sun Tower, I was concerned only with the leads of two stories I intended to write: the main front page story about the murder and a second story (we called it a sidebar) about her fears that the killer might return to wreak vengeance.

Mrs. Teeporten's life had been desolated; I wince when I recall that I came close to revelling in her misery.

Over the next several days, the rewrite desk was compiling reports from people who had spotted the killer, usually in their own back yards. They came in a steady stream. The police announced first that he was hiding in the woods and later that he'd taken a canoe and reached New Westminster, a bulletin that caused people in New Westminster to see him in *their* back yards. After that people began seeing him farther and farther east until some believed he had escaped to the prairies. The newspapers published maps showing his route leading out of the province.

The day after the murder, Himie asked me to brief a cub reporter who had been assigned to interview the suspect's mother. I was to counsel him on the technique of handling the afflicted, now that I'd shown it could be done.

"She'll never talk to me," said the new man nervously. "Not with her boy a killer."

"Yes, she will," I told him. "She'll tell you that he was always a good boy and that she just can't believe he did anything wrong. She'll say she has faith in him."

That is almost exactly what she did say. The cub's story was badly garbled and had to be rewritten, but he got a by-line and asked for a raise on the strength of his scoop. The *Province,* which had missed two stories because they hadn't believed that either Mrs. Teeporten or the killer's mother would talk, spotted the story and thought they'd discovered a new Richard Harding Davis. They promptly stole him from the *Sun* for an extra five dollars a week. On such flimsy underpinnings are careers born.

Meanwhile, I was interviewing the chief of the North Vancouver police, who pronounced himself stymied by what he called the Murder Without a Motive. The simplest explanation was that the youth was the victim — or perhaps thought he was the victim — of a homosexual proposition and simply panicked, but nobody ventured to suggest that. Instead we grilled everybody from rookie cops to second cousins. Then Harry and I returned to the scene of the crime to interview to collie, still crouching below the steps of the cottage (FAITHFUL DOG VAINLY AWAITS DEAD MASTER'S RETURN). The killer was still missing — probably in Winnipeg by now.

He wasn't, of course. He was found sometime during the night of the annual *Vancouver Sun* staff party, an uproarious wassail in which, I believe, Miss Evelyn Caldwell, late of the *News-Herald* and now author of the *Sun's* shopping column, broke her leg. She was carried off in high style on a stretcher, preceded by three Highland pipers hired on the spot by Sam Cromie, munching on a gardenia garnished with French dressing. Not the best possible night on which to track down a wanted man.

I had not recovered from the party — indeed, I had scarcely tumbled into bed — when the night desk called me. The hunted man had been found in a second-class hotel no more than three blocks from the *Sun's* office. He'd been there since the night of the murder and had never attempted to hide. He gave himself up without a struggle to about sixteen policemen — a nice quiet boy, to paraphrase the landlady, whom I managed to interview and exhaust before the rest of the press descended upon her.

The Teeporten murder case had scarcely faded from the front pages before another sensation took its place. The civic election campaign was in full swing and the most colourful mayoralty candidate of all, the Honourable Gerald Grattan McGeer, was suddenly struck down by acute appendicitis.

McGeer, who had not only been mayor of Vancouver ten years before but was also a former member of Parliament and senator, had been on the comeback trail — a newsman's dream candidate whose florid prose rolled off the North Shore mountains like distant thunder. He had promised just about everything, from the beautification of False Creek to a shake-up of the local police force, a perennial plank in the campaign platform of mayoralty candidates. Now suddenly he was flat on his back in St. Paul's Hospital, denied all visitors, and held incommunicado from the reporters and photographers who were swarming in the corridors outside his room.

In the ephemeral world of journalism, the tiniest eddies in the mainstream of history are whipped into whirlpools. It now seems ludicrous that in late November 1946, Harry and I were convinced that the most important thing in the world was to shoot, sneak, or steal a photograph of G.G. McGeer, KC, groaning on his sickbed.

Everyone in that crowded corridor had similar instructions, but it quickly became apparent that no one was going to be allowed within fifty feet of the ailing candidate. We discussed various improbable schemes — the impersonation of hospital attendants, the sneaking in of a woman friend disguised as a nurse, the jimmying of windows reached by outside ladders. But these highly romantic pipe dreams were just that. This was real life, not *The Front Page*.

That reflection triggered my memory of an old front page photograph. The previous January, Constable Bobby Hooper, having chased a thug or a yegg down Burrard Street, had been shot in the chest, and the newspapers had photographed him in bed in this same hospital. I saw the picture in my mind and mentally read the line: ROOKIE COP FIGHTS FOR LIFE.

We slipped away, repaired to the *Sun's* photo morgue, and sure enough, there was the picture we sought — a large, clear photo of P.C. Hooper smiling gamely from his St. Paul's Hospital cot.

Out came the McGeer file — twenty pictures of the candidate. We spread them all out on the floor. Here was the flamboyant former mayor in a variety of poses: McGeer flaying, attacking, rapping, hitting, and pointing with pride: McGeer in Indian headdress, miners' helmets, cowboy hats, and robes of office; McGeer shaking hands, turning sods, laying cornerstones, handing out cheques.

But the best picture for our purpose was a ten-year-old photo of Gerry McGeer in action. His head, clipped from his body and pasted over Hooper's face, fitted exactly. Some clever airbrush work by Fraser Wilson, the paper's staff artist, followed. Filion then rephotographed the result, printed it, and laid it wet on Hal Straight's desk with no comment but a look of triumph.

Straight picked up the picture and looked at it. Then he turned it about and looked at it again. Then he laid it on the desk and gave it a bit more scrutiny. Finally he turned to Filion.

"It's a fake," he said. Filion looked crestfallen. "But it's a damn good fake," Straight added. He called a copy boy. "Page 1. Four columns!" he said. Shades of Little Miss No Nose, thought I.

I should like to have been an eyewitness to the scene that took place in the *Province's* city room when the *Sun's* Home Edition appeared with McGeer's picture and a slightly ambiguous caption that suggested but didn't quite say that it had been taken that day. The *Province's* leading photographer, Claude Detloff, had just returned from the hospital to report that an armoured car couldn't get past McGeer's door. Spies told me the following day how Reg Moir had lined up his men in front of the city desk and delivered a tongue-lashing that befouled the air.

Even as this was happening, some of us were harbouring second thoughts. Into the city room walked an old McGeer crony, former alderman Harry de Graves, who invariably made the rounds of the newspaper offices every afternoon.

"That's a wonderful, wonderful picture of Gerry, Hal," de Graves said. "Why, you know, I'd swear he looks ten years younger."

Straight modestly accepted the accolade. Filion gave me one of his deadpan, raised-eyebrow looks.

"I don't figure it," said Harry de Graves. "I've just come

from the hospital and the news isn't good. They say he's fadin' fast, Hal — *fadin' fast!*"

Even before de Graves had finished Straight was on the intercom to the newsroom, ordering them to pull the picture out of the final edition.

Such uncharacteristic prudence was unnecessary. McGeer survived the operation, which helped his campaign more than it hindered it. He was swept into office by a landslide, and though he was never able to clean up False Creek he did shake up the police department unmercifully. Heads rolled right and left. The chief, his deputies, his squad leaders, all tainted with corruption, were supplanted. One committed suicide. I covered the inquiry that followed, which saw the installation of a new chief of police who reigned for a decade before he was ousted in yet another of Vancouver's periodic crime probes. Giants toppled before the McGeer storm, but one man remained untouched by scandal. Fortunately, Constable Bobby Hooper, the rookie cop, emerged unscathed.

5 The excitement over the McGeer election had scarcely subsided before a new sensation began to occupy the Vancouver press. Somewhere beyond the mists of the North, so it was said, lay a mysterious tropical valley complete with a lost gold mine, headhunting Indian cave dwellers, and perhaps even prehistoric beasts. At one point a "white queen" was tentatively introduced but quickly discarded.

I have written so much in the past about Headless Valley and my own part in that story that I blush to return to it; but, since it was a turning point in my life, I can't ignore it. For years, Headless Valley was a kind of minor industry with me. I recycled the tale in every form — as a series of broadcasts, as a radio play, as a magazine article, as newspaper features, and finally, as a chapter in a book that actually won an award. Although at long last I gave up exploiting Headless Valley as a literary property, that did not stop the Headless Valley industry for others. For years afterward I would read accounts of the mysterious valley in the North, where thirteen men had met their death (it was always thirteen), and of expeditions that were being fitted out to explore the region. Since the valley of the South Nahanni River, to give it its proper name, was made a national park the stories have become less bizarre; but even today one occasionally finds a cheap men's magazine or a sensational tabloid resurrecting the old chestnut.

In the winter of 1946-47, thirteen men were already said to have perished in Headless Valley. To an old northern hand, this was not remarkable. The name "Headless Valley" was a vague one, used to cover most of the watershed of the South Nahanni River. The deaths had occurred over a forty-year period. One could take any similar area — my own Klondike, for example (or the Bermuda Triangle) — and make the same assessment. Still, the first men to die in the valley, in 1905, had apparently been murdered. Their skeletons had been found three years later — allegedly headless. This, plus the fact that these men had earlier found some gold on one of the river's tributaries, was enough to start the legend. The valley where they died was, and is, known as Deadman's Valley on the map. The newspapers preferred Headless Valley, a colourful and convenient term that soon came to be applied to the entire region. It was decapitated skeletons and the absence of the mysterious third partner that caught the imagination of the northerners. Grizzly bears, famished after a winter's hibernation, have a habit of tearing the heads off corpses, but nobody suggested that prosaic solution to the mystery.

There are hot springs all through the Northwest, including some in the South Nahanni country; thus the tropical valley legend was already a perennial favourite with the pulp magazines. But it took a seasoned newspaper stringer named George Murray to put Headless Valley onto the front pages in those early post-war years when the public was thirsting for a new kind of adventure.

Murray lived in Fort St. John, where he and his wife, the soon-to-be-famous "Ma" Murray, published the *Alaska Highway News.* George's tales about Headless Valley were made to order for the *Chicago Tribune* and the Toronto *Star.* The *Sun* in Vancouver picked them up and ran with them; within a few days, Headless Valley tales from other sources began to spring up in print.

Newpapermen are supposed to be the most sceptical of humans. My own observation from those days is that the opposite was true. At least, our scepticism was never allowed to intrude upon a good story. To print almost anything about Headless Valley required a willing suspension of disbelief, something from which we all suffered. As long as you quoted your source you could publish the most outrageous hokum. News was not truth; it was what somebody *claimed* was truth, even though the phrases that somebody uttered were clearly balderdash. If it made a good story it went into print without qualification.

I can remember interviewing a young man named Walter Tully, in a run-down Hastings Street hotel, who said he'd been to Headless Valley and talked of walking down paths of ice where weird carvings stood out like guardian angels. He claimed that the valley was shrouded in low-lying mists which screened it from the outside world, that the temperature within this mysterious vale was thirty to forty degrees above that of the surrounding countryside, and that the vegetation was immense as a result. He talked of seeing a three-thousand-foot-high waterfall and of finding a headless skeleton in the underbrush. Filion took his picture and I wrote up the interview which began: "The true story of the South Nahanni River's bizarre 'Headless Valley' was told today by a man who has actually explored its 200-mile length and lived to tell the tale . . ."

Here was I, born and raised in the Yukon, knowing for certain that there couldn't be a tropical valley anywhere north of fifty-five. Yet it never occurred to me to make that point to the *Sun's* readers. One Sunday supplement writer had called the valley "a poisonous Shangri-la, deep in the heart of the North." Who was I to dispute that? After all, hadn't another prospector reported that his partner had gone missing in the valley, failing to keep a rendezvous at the foot of a gigantic waterfall? "There is no denying the sinister atmosphere of the whole valley," this man had told the press. "The weird continual wailing of the wind is something I won't soon forget." This was the flimsiest kind of evidence to hang any kind of story on, but I swallowed it and so did the public. Overdosed on years of wartime realism, the world that winter was hungry for escape.

Everybody, it seemed, wanted to go to Headless Valley, including me. Various expeditions were being fitted out to become "the first into Headless Valley," so that the story took on the aspect of an international race. A group of American Marines announced they'd head for the valley that summer. Not to be outdone, a group of Canadians announced that, in the interests of patriotism, they'd head for the valley in March. One prospector, advertising for a partner to help find a lost gold mine in the Nahanni country, got 154 replies within a week. A motion picture cameraman who wanted help in making a Headless Valley movie got five hundred responses in just three days. The *Sun* printed Headless Valley maps with the words "Unknown Territory" plastered all over them. It was said that the country had never been mapped and that "even the exact position of the valley has never been properly located." The last was true enough, since Headless Valley was an invention of the press and not the cartographers.

Harry Filion and I were dying to go to Headless Valley and break the story before anybody else. So, it turned out, was my mother. "Oh, if I could only go!" she said to me. "Oh, how I would love to go to Headless Valley!" It was at this point that I realized the full power of the story. If she, who had spent twenty winters in the North, could still get fired up over the mystery of Headless Valley, then it had to be hot stuff. She was, of course, a romantic at heart, otherwise she would never have set off for the distant Klondike forty years before. Now she lived vicariously in the short stories she was trying to write — stories about handsome detectives falling in love with pretty young women. She could not sell them, but that didn't stop her writing; it had become her form of therapy after those months of nursing my father. Headless Valley caught her imagination — perhaps because it had all the elements of pulp magazine fiction — as it caught almost everybody's. Only Jack Scott was immune. In his *Sun* column he spoofed the whole enterprise mercilessly, inventing a Bodyless Valley," which he claimed had captured the imagination of the world.

At this point, *Maclean's* in Toronto asked Clyde Gilmour, who'd done several pieces for the magazine, to develop a story about Headless Valley. Gilmour, then a reporter for the *Province*, was busy with another assignment; he turned it over to me. Something told me that *Maclean's* wouldn't swallow the usual hokum. I plunged into some serious research and discovered that the area, just north of British Columbia and east of the Yukon, had been thoroughly explored, mapped, and photographed. There were also plausible explanations for the thirteen so-called mysterious deaths. The South Nahanni had been visited intermittently by trappers and prospectors since the days of the Klondike rush. R.M. Patterson had written a good book about it; Harry Snyder, a big game hunter who knew it well, had left a memoir. A prospector named Jack Stanier had visited it nine times on a fruitless search for gold.

Indeed, the facts about the South Nahanni seemed to me to be more interesting than the legends. There were certainly hot springs into which people could plunge during the iciest winter, great canyons hollowed out of limestone, numberless caves carved by erosion in the towering cliffs, and a magnificent waterfall on the upper river, not three thousand feet high but impressive enough at more than three hundred.

I tracked down the stories of each of the thirteen missing men, most of whom had drowned or been attacked by wild animals, and had no difficulty writing a lively but factual article about the South Nahanni and its history. I mailed it off with a greater sense of satisfaction than I'd got from any of the slapdash features I'd done for the *Sun*.

This made me the paper's resident expert on the South Nahanni country. Now I knew from my researches that it was just possible to land a plane with skis in Deadman's Valley, where the apparently headless corpses had been found. The race for the valley was hotting up; all sorts of expeditions were being planned by foot, by dog team, and later by canoe. But Hal Straight had no intention of letting anybody else beat the *Sun* to the valley of mystery. He told me to find a pilot and make plans to leave at once.

I had said it was possible to land in Deadman's Valley. I did not tell Straight that no one had ever done it. Nor did I bother to dispel all the myths I'd punctured for *Maclean's*. Adventure lay ahead and, more important, a by-line series with the resultant notoriety — everything a young reporter craves. I had no intention of missing out on any of it.

By sheer chance, Russ Baker, a bush pilot of long experience and now president of a then fledgling charter firm, Pacific Western Airlines, happened to be in town from his home in Fort St. James. I went over to the Georgia Hotel where he was staying to sound him out on landing me in the South Nahanni. To my astonishment and delight, he was bending over a large map of the Northwest Territories, which he'd spread out on the floor — and he had already pencilled a circle around the Nahanni country! We hit it off immediately. It turned out that Baker, a thick thong of a man, tanned almost black by the sun, was an even greater romantic than Straight or I. He too desperately wanted to go to the Nahanni. In fact, he claimed he'd been there — a bald lie, but an understandable one.

That was mid-week. Baker proposed that we take the

regular Canadian Pacific flight to Prince George that Saturday. One of his crew would fly down from Fort St. James with his low-winged Junkers monoplane. Then we'd take off for Nahanni.

Filion, by rights, should have gone with us. He'd actually broken the first Headless Valley stories in the *Sun*. But Veryl wasn't keen on the idea, and Straight ruled that a married man shouldn't be exposed to so much danger. I was just as married as Filion, but Straight conveniently ignored that fact and Janet knew better than to protest. And so Art Jones, a former *Ubyssey* photographer, was chosen.

Before we left, Straight took me aside and urged me to stake a gold claim in his name and another for Don Cromie when we reached the valley. I was flabbergasted. I knew there was no gold where we were going. But Straight had apparently fallen hook, line, and sinker for the stories in his own paper.

Our first attempt was aborted. We flew off to Prince George in a storm so blinding that the CPA plane had to turn back. My morale was not helped by watching Baker, a man with ten thousand flying hours in the mountains of B.C., break out in a cold sweat as he watched the ice forming on the wings. Back in Vancouver that night, Janet cried in my arms. She was certain I would be killed — the fourteenth victim of the poisonous valley.

Her peace of mind was not helped when she heard from my insurance company. The previous week — before I knew I would be going on the adventure — a smart salesman had signed me up for an annuity. At the age of fifty-five (I did not then believe that I would last beyond sixty) I was to receive the munificent sum of fifty dollars a month. The company found it hard to believe that I had taken the policy out in all innocence. Having read about Headless Valley they were convinced I was about to commit suicide at their expense. They announced that they would double my premium and only rescinded the order after the agent convinced them that my intentions were honourable.

The two weeks that followed were the most exciting and sometimes the most uncomfortable I'd known. It was January. The weather was dreadful — the coldest in recorded history. The thermometer dropped to minus 80° F at Snag in the Yukon — a new record. At Finlay Forks, where we were trapped for four days, it nudged seventy below. The telegrapher's cabin in which we bunked had no indoor plumbing; the outhouse was a hundred yards away through high snowdrifts, the door frozen open. My typewriter froze. Jones's camera froze. The plane's engine froze and had to be thawed with a plumber's blowtorch. When we were able to get into the air an oil line broke, masking the windshield and forcing Russ Baker to land blind on the river. The following day we finally got away only to find that at Fort Nelson the airport runway had been ploughed. We couldn't land on it on skis. So down we came, to bump our way along the snow-covered grass at the side.

Yet there was one bright spot in all these misfortunes; they added fuel to the series that I was wiring daily to the newspaper. I did not know then that Straight had held all my copy for a week while he negotiated a sale to International News Service in New York. The resulting stories got worldwide attention in hundreds of INS outlets (Straight claimed two thousand) and "Headless Valley" became a kind of catchphrase, the subject of an editorial in the New York *Daily News*, and even a joke on the Jack Benny program.

I knew nothing of this. "GREAT SERIES" Straight wired me at Finlay Forks. "GIVE US MORE HEADLESS STUFF." I knew what he meant, and so when Baker made a side trip from Fort Nelson to the Deer River to pick up a pregnant Indian woman, Art Jones and I eagerly went along. A mercy flight! Who could ask for more? We landed in snow so deep that Jones and I, up to our waists in it, had to pull on the wings to shake the plane free, then flounder alongside as it gathered speed, until we were hauled in through the back door. Back at Fort Nelson, with our patient safely in hospital, we tried to

339

take off, only to be refused permission by the tower because the weather was so bad. Baker ignored the order and off we flew, heading for the Liard and another mercy flight — an Indian woman with a broken collarbone who had to be taken to hospital at Fort Simpson on the Mackenzie.

All these fits and starts increased the tension I was building into my series. Would we never get to Headless Valley? What would we find if we did? I knew from my researches that we would find very little, but I wasn't about to let out *that* secret yet. Instead, I concentrated on the colourful adventures of Russ Baker, the quintessential bush pilot, who had cheated death on various occasions and wasn't shy about retelling old tales.

After our second mercy flight we found ourselves at Nahanni Butte, where the South Nahanni River empties into the Liard. I had brought along a young Mounted Policeman, Jim Reid, from Fort Liard. The Nahanni country was his patrolling area, and the flight would save him weeks of travel by dog-team. My ulterior purpose was to have an independent witness aboard in case some rival paper challenged the truth about our exploits.

In the shadow of the five-thousand-foot butte, a single cabin crouched. We spent the night there, with Jack LeFlair, a trapper, and his Indian wife. The following morning, after more than a week of setbacks and side trips, we were ready to fly into the valley.

Off we flew over the frozen skein of water known as the Splits and past the sulphurous pools, steaming in the snows below, which had helped give the region its tropical reputation. On we went, through a canyon half a mile deep, its limestone walls pocked with eroded caves, and into a labyrinthine world of canyons wriggling off the main gorge in all directions. The Junkers tossed in the turbulence, banked around a curve, and burst out into an oval bowl in the mountains. This was Deadman's Valley, where the two McLeod brothers, Willie and Frank, had been murdered forty-one years before. Below us, the river wound lazily along its floor to vanish again into the mountain wall at the far end.

I felt a sense of growing elation. There, at last, was the valley that I had written so much about and read so much about. The setting was exquisite — the sawtooth pinnacles of the Mackenzie Mountains stood out, stark white against the sunless wash of the sky. I thought of Robert Conrad in James Hilton's novel, pushing his way back to Shangri-la — and looking exactly like Ronald Colman. But how on earth were we going to set down on that frozen waste below? I should have been scared, but having interviewed Russ Baker exhaustively I had perfect confidence in his abilities as a pilot. Hadn't he gone through the ice on Pinchi Lake and hauled himself out unscratched? Hadn't he come down on lakes ringed with fire to pluck forest crews from a fiery doom? Hadn't he saved three planeloads of U.S. airmen from freezing to death after their Martin Marauders were forced down on the Yukon border? Besides, he'd been here before; he'd know where to land.

It became clear, however, that he *hadn't* been here before as he circled the ten-mile length of the valley seeking a suitable spot on which to settle. Below us, I could see the ice of the river rent by an ugly black scar; clearly, it was rotten. A mile farther on it looked firmer, and down we went. I actually thought we'd landed, but at the last minute Baker gunned the motor and rocketed skyward. I felt a vague sense of disquiet. What had happened? Only later did Baker tell me quietly that he'd seen what he thought was the shadow of the plane on the ice below — and then it hit him that the sun wasn't shining. The movement below wasn't a shadow; it was running water, just a few inches below the surface.

We circled the valley again until Baker spotted the overflow from a little creek that ran down from the mountains into the river. On this washboard of ice and snow hillocks we landed with a bang and a bounce. In that shadowless land it was not possible from the air to check the surface of the ground. We bounced, hit a second time, bounced again, and headed directly for a six-foot hillock of snow. I was convinced now, as Baker was, that we'd break our skis and be imprisoned here in this valley of death to add to the roster of victims claimed by Headless Valley. But our luck held. At the last moment a tiny gust of wind lifted the plane up and over the barrier, and we shuddered to a stop.

"By God," said Baker, "we showed her who's boss!" That was the way he talked — a big, barrel-chested man who approached life with zest and treated every encounter with nature as if it were a challenge, like a boxing match in which he and the elements sparred with one another, trading hard blows, bobbing and weaving, sometimes drawing blood, but never achieving a knockout.

We stood with him beside the plane on the ice of the creek — Art Jones, Jim Reid, Ed Hanratty (Baker's engineer), and I. Once again I felt, almost *heard*, the silence of the North. No wolf called in the distance. No bird sang. No other human voice broke the stillness. We were the only living things in this dead land.

Now that we'd arrived at our goal there wasn't a great deal we could do. On the far bank, across the valley, we could see some broken log buildings half hidden in the snow. We floundered, knee-deep, in the dry powder, testing the river ice with an axe, and explored the two crumbling cabins and three log caches. The promotion department had given us a banner to photograph: "THE VANCOUVER SUN — FIRST INTO HEADLESS VALLEY." Jones photographed Baker and me holding it against a background of conifers. Here, where the dead hand of decay lay so heavily, it seemed grossly out of place. And men had actually been here sometime in the past decade: someone had pinned a yellowing photograph of Rita Hayworth to the log wall of one of the cabins.

What was it about this valley that puzzled me? What caused these great sculptured drifts and hummocks that had almost brought us to disaster? Why were there so many fallen trees, some thirty feet high and ten inches thick, strewn about — almost as if uprooted by a giant's paw? What force had wrought this devastation?

And then, in that ghostly hush, I got my answer. A low, moaning whine intruded upon the stillness, increasing in pitch until it became an eerie drone, echoing across the valley. It was some moments before we realized that this banshee wail was the wind funnelling down the tunnels of the canyons and bursting into the valley's bowl, rather like air pumped through a pipe organ. I remembered the remark I'd once quoted in the *Sun* about "the weird, continual wailing of the wind" and the Indian tales of a devil who howled in the mountains. If the Nahanni had a secret, this was it — the sound that chilled men's souls and helped build up the folk-lore of the valley.

Russ Baker spoke: "We'd better get out of here or we'll never get out." Already little whirlpools of white were pillaring into the air. We wasted no time as we floundered back to the aircraft. Baker stuck small broken spruce trees into the rough surface of the overflow to mark a crude take-off strip. Then, with the wind rising and the snow whirling about us, we rose again into the grey skies.

We flew north for a hundred miles through wild country, plunging into a second canyon — a mile deep at one point — twisting for twenty miles through the mountains. Here we burst upon that curious limestone formation known as the Gate, where an immense sentinel of rock rises from the heart of a box canyon. On we went to the Virginia Falls, almost twice Niagara's height, locked now in their mantle of ice, the supreme spectacle and the climax of our day.

There was one final vision, bizarre and symbolic, to cap our adventure. As we left the sinuous river behind, Baker nudged me and pointed off to the southeast. There, on the horizon, rose a magnificent range of rose-coloured mountains, the highest I had yet seen, as jagged and as ruthless as

343

the Nahanni's peaks but painted in Disneyesque hues of pink and coral, lavender and purple. Strangest of all, this mountain barrier appeared on no map of the land. Even as I gazed out at these ice cream peaks, they began to ripple in the sunset as if I were examining them through a sheet of moving water. The rippling increased. Great, wavy shadows began to dash across those roseate slopes at express train speed. I blinked, and the ghostly mountains vanished — a northern mirage as ephemeral and as haunting as the legend of Headless Valley itself.

We made our way back through the heart of British Columbia in the leisurely fashion of the North, and I continued to churn out stories about lost airplanes, eccentric trappers, and wild Indians. When we reached Vancouver at last both Jones and I had a fortnight's growth of beard and were photographed looking suitably grizzled. My mother approved. "It's the first time you've looked like a gentleman," she remarked, for she had married a man with a beard who truly *was* a gentleman.

Janet, who had spent a very bad fortnight worrying, was so glad to see me safe and in one piece she didn't complain about the whiskers. She told me she'd painted the kitchen, in the interval, to help calm her nerves.

My series was still running, and Straight went to great pains to keep us from public view, maintaining the fiction that we were still in the North. Janet and I flew off to Seattle at the *Sun's* expense and enjoyed a few days' holiday until the series wound up. There we were wined and dined by the local INS representative, who had only one quibble with what he said was the best "Man Against Nature" story of the year. "You should have gone missing for a few days," he said. "Lost in the North always makes a good story." I remembered Christy McDevitt's advice, "Always lose the elephant," but I felt that we'd done quite enough without the entire air force conducting a search for us. I had at last debunked the myth of a tropical vale — or thought I had. Of course, I could more easily have done it without moving out of the *Sun* office, but that wasn't the way the game was played in those days.

When the series ended, Straight got on the phone to Seymour Berkson of the International News Service. Berkson was enthusiastic about my copy.

"How about an award?" Straight asked him.

"What kind of an award?" Berkson asked.

"Oh, some kind of scroll saying this was the greatest newspaper adventure story since the war."

"Sure," said Berkson amiably. "I'll have our scroll maker knock one out immediately."

A few days later a suitably handsome scroll arrived, the fulsome phrases beautifully hand-lettered and illuminated. Straight hung it in his office, and as far as I know it still graces a wall at the *Vancouver Sun*.

Maclean's had already bought my magazine piece, which didn't need a syllable changed because of our expedition. Now the magazine's editors asked me to suggest others. And I had become, briefly, a reasonably Well-Known Personality. When I returned, I actually heard two people whispering to each other as I took the Point Grey streetcar out to visit my mother and Lucy: "That's Pierre Berton. He went to Headless Valley."

There was one snag. Art Jones had shipped all but half a dozen of his pictures immediately to the *Sun* to arrive with my copy, wired from Fort Liard. Somehow Canadian Pacific Airlines managed to lose them, somewhere between Whitehorse and Watson Lake, giving rise to rumours that we had faked the story. Nobody, however, said it out loud, which was just as well, for I had Constable Jim Reid's witness that we were there. Fortunately, the rest of the pictures turned up a fortnight later and the *Sun* splashed them over two pages, not only dispelling the rumours but also keeping the story alive.

It had been marvellously exhilarating, flying about the North in a plane designed in 1918, typing my colourful copy in trappers' cabins, wiring it to the paper from obscure points, seeing my by-line on the front pages of newspapers from eastern Canada and the States, and beating the opposition hollow.

Yet I was already feeling a sense of letdown. Back I went to the daily routine, covering everything from the McGeer police hearings — front page news every day — to the court case against Lois DeFee, a six-foot stripper known as the Eiffel Eyeful, charged with giving an obscene performance in the State Theatre on Hastings Street. The judge had publicly singled me out for a dressing down for treating the DeFee case like a circus, which it was. But even that notoriety — every newsman's dream — failed to raise my spirits.

It seemed to me that I had already done just about everything there was to do on a newspaper except to cover sports, which didn't interest me. Murders and fires, scandals and stunts had begun to lose their excitement. Surely, I thought, there must be something more than this in my future. Harkrider had said I should go to Hollywood. I hadn't believed him, but he had planted a seed. *Maclean's* had liked my piece on the Nahanni, and that had given me more satisfaction than half a dozen front page scoops. I suggested two more subjects to the magazine and to my surprise got the go-ahead on both.

I felt a growing discontent, in spite of the fast pace of the newspaper game in Vancouver. What did it all mean? Where was I going? What was my future — more fires and murders, more police hearings and court cases? More interviews with Hollywood celebrities? More searching for the "angle" to brighten up an otherwise mediocre interview? There had been a time when I thought I would have been content to work on a newspaper for the rest of my life. In those university and army days the future had stretched ahead of me, all sunshine and promise. Now, in March of 1947, as I approached my first wedding anniversary, my future looked less inviting. My total professional career as a newsman before and after the war had lasted no more than twenty-seven months, and already I was growing restless.

6 I sat at my typewriter in the *Sun* office and nodded at Jack McDonald, whose desk faced mine. He was a small, neat man with a complexion made ruddy by a network of bright little veins that contrasted sharply with his white hair and his white moustache.

Jack winked at me, opened his desk drawer, and revealed a mickey of rye.

"Care for a shot?" he asked. I shook my head.

"I just think I'll have a small one," said Jack, and off he shambled to the men's room, as he did periodically every morning, to take a pull on the bottle. I did not know his age but knew he had been officially retired some years before and given a gold watch by a grateful newspaper for which he'd worked all his life. Knowing no other trade or profession and bored with retirement, he had wandered back to the city room, where he was put on a small stipend and given two minor tasks: to write up the weather forecast and produce the "Twenty-Five Years Ago Today" column. There he was now, back from the men's room, with a glint in his eye, typing away.

A short time later Himie quietly called me over to the city desk and handed me Jack McDonald's copy.

"You'll have to fix this up," he said. "Jack's not up to it any longer. But for God's sake, don't let him know you're rewriting his stuff."

I read Jack's story and decided I'd better do a little research before I rewrote it. I got down the old files in the morgue, found the edition of twenty-five years before, and began to read it. There was a big story splashed all over the front page. I cannot now recall the details, only that it was a scoop for the reporter who singlehandedly uncovered a local scandal.

His by-line ran triumphantly above the lead; there it was in bold print: "BY JACK MCDONALD."

Oh God, I thought, and today he can't even rewrite his own scoop! Is this my future? To hang on here, writing the same stories over and over again until somebody gives me a gold watch and I don't even have the wit to rewrite my scoops of twenty-five years before? Surely there must be something more.

I decided to use Jack McDonald's story as the basis for a radio play for the CBC. It was accepted and produced for Vancouver Theatre under my title: *By Line Story*. I even had a small acting role in the production. I was moonlighting now as much as possible, knocking out pieces for the *Sun's* magazine section, for the Montreal *Standard*, and, of course, *Maclean's*.

I was still a key player in the crazy Vancouver newspaper game, which seemed to me to reach the heights of lunacy in what I call the Great Vancouver Pig Derby. The inspiration for this piece of goofiness came from Ray Munro, the wildest man on the paper. He and Art Jones had worked their way into the good graces of the local ambulance company, which alerted them to tales of accident and mayhem. So well entrenched were they that they spent many an evening actually driving an ambulance, a feat that produced several spectacular photographs. These joyrides came to an end when they appropriated the body of a very ancient and very dead Chinese, which they wheeled around town, photographing it in various situations — holding a bottle, seated on a couch, even (if I remember rightly) gazing blankly at a copy of the *Sun*. At that point the ambulance company put its foot down.

Munro was still riding high. He'd been a flyer in the war and drove his car as if it were an aircraft. He sometimes flew on photographic assignments. On one memorable story involving that erratic Doukhobor sect known as the Sons of Freedom, he had made a forced landing and claimed that certain of the Sons had shot him down. Certainly he had the bullet holes in the fuselage to prove it.

With the help of Ray Gardner, Munro that winter concocted what he thought would be a sure-fire scoop. Gardner, a first-rate all-round newspaperman who had been sports editor of the *News-Herald* in my day, was noted especially for whimsical stories on bizarre subjects. He had a captive eccentric who had built himself a set of wings and who was continually threatening to leap off the Burrard Street Bridge and fly across English Bay. On a dull news day, Gardner would bring him out for another try. The birdman never actually carried out his promise; there were always extenuating circumstances that prevented him from flying. But that made Gardner's witty stories all the more hilarious.

Now Munro had invented a feat made to order for Gardner. A young and active pig would be smuggled into the Hotel Vancouver and released into the lobby at high noon. He would photograph the resulting chase and Gardner would write the story. They had worked out a complicated cover plan by faking a plausible assignment in the hotel.

Straight, of course, was enthusiastic. Only at the last moment did he have second thoughts. What if the pig's mad, erratic dash through the crowded lobby resulted in a broken leg? If the scheme was discovered the paper could be sued for a fortune. Straight quashed the plan, to the huge disappointment of Munro and Gardner and of Jack Scott and me, who had been let in on the secret. Scott especially brooded. It was, he kept saying, too good a plan to be aborted.

Gardner, meanwhile, had been awarded a Kemsley scholarship, which would give him a free year in England working for Lord Kemsley's newspaper chain. That was a blow for me. I had applied for the same scholarship. Straight, as managing editor, was supposed to write assessments for both of us, but only after Gardner was proclaimed the winner did I learn that Straight had allowed him to write his own assessment, which, of course, was positive enough to win him the laurel.

349

This angered me. I was certain that if I had ghostwritten my own assessment for Straight, I might easily have beaten out Gardner, for I had even less humility than he. Why, I asked Straight, didn't he tell me Gardner was writing his own and let me write mine, too?

To which Straight bluntly replied: "Because I didn't want to lose you."

It was, perhaps, just as well. I got the Headless Valley assignment about the same time that Ray went to England, where he quickly became a thorn in Lord Kemsley's side by trying to start a union on one of his newspapers. Had I spent a year on Fleet Street my life might easily have taken a different course but not necessarily a more satisfying one.

Meanwhile Munro, Scott, and I continued to brood about the pig. In late spring one of us had a brilliant idea. The Fourth Estate Frolic, the annual ball given by the Women's Press Club in the Hotel Vancouver, seemed to us the perfect place to release a young and energetic animal.

We borrowed a pig from a farmer in the Fraser Valley by promising him unbelievable publicity. It was the most active pig I've ever seen. We kept it in a truck tied up in a sack, from which it somehow made a miraculous escape. We chased it all over the *Sun* parking lot and finally locked it in a hut, where it spent the afternoon flinging itself at the walls. We booked it into a room at the hotel, locked it this time in the bathroom, and listened, awestruck, as it hurled itself about.

The rest is anti-climax. At ten that night, Munro released the pig, offering a bottle of whisky to whoever was able to catch it. Alas, the pig was exhausted from the day's exertions. It simply stood there until its knees buckled. Then it lay down on the floor at Munro's feet and went to sleep. George Young, The *Sun's* chief photographer, picked up the snoring animal and demanded his prize. Munro snatched it away and gave it another shove. It was no use.

"The poor little thing's played out," said a sentimental girl reporter and began to cuddle it. A buzz, half amused, half

350

angry, rose from the assembly as Munro, with the practised movements of a man who has filched many a murder victim's photograph from under the noses of his rivals, looked about for the nearest exit. I never did find out what happened to the pig.

This unsatisfying schoolboy prank gnawed at my subconscious. It was akin to the chemical shows that I had once produced in our garage in Oak Bay — all smoke and flash with no substance. We tended to produce the paper in the same way, talking often in terms of the *look* of the front page — the size of its headlines, the play of the stories, the shape of the pictures — and not the content. We were more fascinated by stunts than we were by solid reporting, by putting something over on the opposition than by putting something across to the reader. And it was beginning to pall.

I had sold two more pieces to *Maclean's*, one a long article on Stanley Park. I had, in fact, just returned from the park one day in April when I received a message saying that a Mr. Scott Young of *Maclean's* was staying at the Hotel Vancouver and would like me to drop around. I sat down and wrote my front page scoop. I had discovered (thanks to a tip from one of the mounted policemen) a hermit living in a hollow tree deep inside the park, wearing discarded clothing and living off picnic scraps, a typically bizarre *Sun* story.

Then over I went on that beautiful spring afternoon, shook hands with Young, and exchanged a few pleasantries.

"You've got a magnificent city here," Young said.

"You bet we have," I said, gazing out across the sparkling harbour toward the blue North Shore mountains where the twin peaks of the Lions stood etched against a cloudless sky.

"You're lucky to live here," said Young.

"I'd be crazy to live anywhere else," I told him. "Only a fool would want to leave Vancouver."

"Gee, that's too bad," said Scott Young in his slow way, "because I was about to offer you a job on *Maclean's*."

I turned back from the window and without missing a beat said, "I'll take it," Young gave me a slow smile.

This sudden offer, coming out of the blue, both elated and puzzled me. Why me? What had caused these eastern journalists to reach out and pluck a hack reporter from Vancouver to work on the most distinguished periodical in the country?

Young said it was my piece on Nahanni that had helped them to make up their minds.

"We thought it was an adult piece of work," he said. "None of the usual hokum. That impressed us."

Arthur Irwin, the taciturn, blunt-spoken editor, had read the piece, liked it, and decided to check up on me. He had known F.H. Soward, my old history professor at UBC — the one who had done his best to fail me — so he phoned him.

"What's your opinion of this man Berton?" Irwin had asked.

To which Soward had replied, "He could have been a brilliant student if he hadn't wasted so much time on the college paper."

"Sounds like just the man we want," said Irwin and sent Scott Young out to hire me. "Try to get him for four thousand," he told Young. "If you have to you can go to forty-five hundred."

Now Young turned to me and said, "I am empowered to offer you either four thousand a year or forty-five hundred a year."

I paused. Then, "I'll take the forty-five hundred," I told him.

It was almost exactly what I was making in Vancouver. Straight was paying me sixty-five dollars a week, and I was picking up an extra twenty-five doing a weekly newsboys interview show the paper sponsored on CJOR. Straight had a knack of keeping his budget balanced by handing out such patronage jobs.

But between *Maclean's* and the *Sun* there was no contest. I figured I'd stay two years in Toronto at the most — who could stand Hogtown for any longer? Then, with that experience under my belt, I'd try to get a job on a big American magazine like *Life* or the *Saturday Evening Post*. I did not realize the seductive powers of Canada's National Magazine. William Van Horne, the Yankee who built the CPR and became a Canadian in the process, once remarked that the enterprise would have made a Canadian out of the German Kaiser. *Maclean's* was to make a nationalist of me.

I broke the news next day to Hal Straight. His eyes widened. "Why didn't you come to me?" he said. "I'd have raised the ante."

"But," I pointed out, "you never offered to. Now it's too late."

Straight didn't reply. He simply put on his coat, picked up a bottle of rye, beckoned to me, took me to his car, and drove to Stanley Park.

It was another of those perfect Vancouver days. He drove very slowly. We rounded the park and stopped to talk to a cop on the beat, seated on the horse I'd helped save for him; it was he who had given me the tip about the hermit. We fed Trotsky, the Russian bear, at the zoo. We bought a hamburger at Prospect Point and then walked down to the beach, not far from the shallow pool where the *Sun* gave free swimming lessons each summer. Straight, the old hunter, gave his duck call and several mallards arrived to inspect us. Little pinpoints of light danced across the waters and a slight salt smell swept over the inlet. A freighter passed under the Lions Gate Bridge — one that I had been aboard not long before in my search for news. We sat with our backs against an old log, warmed by the sun, talking as always about the newspaper business and drinking rye out of paper cups. After a while we stopped talking and just sat, tossing pebbles into the water.

Straight broke the silence.

"Still want to go?" he said, cannily.

I nodded.

"You won't get any of this in Toronto, you know," he told me.

"I know," I said. "But it's something I have to do."

"Well," he said, "I figured it had to end. You can always come back, you know."

But he knew and I knew that it wasn't so. One part of me desperately wanted to stay, to continue on forever as I had been — that easy, lazy life in that beautiful, eccentric city on that wonderful, wacky newspaper. It would have been nice to stay on, but something told me that only hermits in hollow trees can live exactly as they want to.

The days that followed remain murky in my memory; all I know is that they were hectic. Janet was packing; I was still working. We had to break the news to our parents and friends that we were leaving for a foreign land — for that's how Toronto was viewed in British Columbia. The Mysterious East was three thousand miles away — four days by train in a time when only a privileged few travelled by air. "We'll never see you again!" Veryl Filion cried plaintively. My mother accepted the move with quiet satisfaction; indeed, I think she'd expected it. The boy she'd nurtured through essay contests and public-speaking exercises was on his way at last — as an assistant editor on a national magazine! Her only regret was that my father wasn't alive to see it.

"How proud he'd be," said Lucy. "He'd want to tell everyone!" Lucy had finished her business course and landed a good job in the office of Norman MacKenzie, president of the university. I felt that I'd be leaving my mother in capable hands.

I had a week's holidays coming. We accepted an invitation to spend the time with Russ Baker and his wife in his rambling home on a cliff overlooking Stuart Lake at Fort St. James. I had the idea of writing a book about Baker, to be called, naturally, "Snowball in Hell." And so I interviewed him at length, making copious notes. Later I actually produced a manuscript but, like "Marching As to War," it was never published. I was not distressed. I knew there would be other books to come after I had learned my craft.

The *Sun* gave us one of the wildest farewell parties in Vancouver's history — a Saturday afternoon bacchanal on the editorial floor that bewildered those citizens who made the mistake of turning up with reports of club meetings and tennis matches. The climax came when Munro and Jones called on their friends from the ambulance company, strapped us into strait-jackets, carried us downstairs, and, with the sirens blowing, trundled us around the block. "They're both having epileptic seizures," I heard Evelyn Caldwell tell members of the gathering crowd.

We returned that night, slightly worse for wear, to our little apartment near the park, stark and empty now except for the Murphy bed. Everything else had been crated and shipped to Toronto at *Maclean's* expense. Here in these bare quarters, we both felt a sense of letdown after the party — a sense of finality mingled with no little apprehension about our future in the big city.

What would Toronto be like? At the party, George Young, who had once worked for the *Star* and who always sported a straw boater and a celluloid collar, had taken me aside to warn me that in Toronto one *never* wore a summer suit before May 24 or after Labour Day. My God, I thought, are they that hidebound? My wartime memories of the city had given me no enthusiasm for it. I had never had a duller time in my life than when on leave in Toronto. There was nothing to compare with Stanley Park or English Bay or the North Shore slopes or the UBC campus. What did people *do* in Toronto, I wondered, besides work? Probably very little. Well, I had made my decision; now I was stuck with it. Perhaps I *could* come back, as Straight had said. But I had tried once before to come back — to the *News-Herald* — and it hadn't worked. No; I was through with that.

The following evening we took our bags down to the CPR station to say goodbye to those friends and blood relatives who had been part of our lives. There was Lucy, looking more like Hedy Lamarr than ever, though to me she would always be a solemn, round-eyed little girl in a fairy costume. There was my mother, both sad and proud, her shoulders thrown defiantly back in that familiar posture; was it only a decade ago she'd baked that birthday cake for me — the one I hadn't had time to eat? There was Jack Scott and his wife, Grace, whom he called Brown Eyes in his column — the same column that had been launched on that hectic day six years before when the *News-Herald* went tabloid and I began my newspaper career. There were Janet's former roommates from UBC days, the ones who had giggled behind the door when I tried to kiss her in the rain. There was Muriel Whimster, who had cheerfully vacated her share of the apartment (and of the Murphy bed) when we were married. And there were Harry, Veryl, and little Vicki, bringing back memories of another, less cheerful, goodbye ceremony in wartime Calgary.

Now here I was again, standing on the CPR platform in Vancouver as of old, performing a familiar rite. I thought of all the embarkation leaves I'd had and all the goodbyes I'd said, and how, on each of those occasions, even when most people grew tired of it all, Janet had come down to the station, usually with a box of cookies. This time, thankfully, she was going with me.

The train pulled slowly out and once again everybody waved goodbye. But this time it really was goodbye for us — goodbye to the evergreen mountains and the sky blue sea; goodbye to our honeymoon flat and our long walks in Lord Stanley's park; goodbye to the newspaper game and all its players; goodbye to the mystery blazes and the Hammond yeggs, to endless bottles of rye drunk in half a dozen kitchens, and endless glasses of beer guzzled in the Georgia tavern — goodbye to family, goodbye to friendships, goodbye to fantasy — and goodbye forever to the sweet summer of my youth.

Index

357

361

365

Printed in Canada